Dolls
and Doll-makers

*Decamps catalogue
pages. Paris, 1911.*

Mexican toy of a girl on a swing with holes for cords running through the outstretched arms and beneath the seat; 1st century AD; *8½ inches*

MARY HILLIER

Dolls
and Doll-makers

WEIDENFELD AND NICOLSON

5 Winsley Street London WI

© by Mary Hillier 1968

Designed by Jane Mackay for Weidenfeld and Nicolson

SBN 297 17667 6
Printed in Germany
by K. G. Lohse Graphischer Großbetrieb OHG, Frankfurt am Main

CONTENTS

ACKNOWLEDGEMENTS A book of this sort, with such a wide scope, could never be attempted without the friendly cooperation of a great many people all over the world and I have a special sense of indebtedness to all who have offered advice, helped with information and in some cases allowed me to use facts from their own published research, or photographs from their collections. Especially I would like to thank:

Mrs Lesley Bannister; Miss Blair-Hickman; Miss Pamela Clabburn of Norwich Museum; Mr Robert Culff; Mr Peter Earnshaw (son of Mabel Lucie Attwell); Miss Faith Eaton; Miss Jane Evans of Worthing Museum; Mr Geoffrey Godden; Mr Cedric Hamley; Mrs Housa; Miss Christine Hughes and Mrs Hughes; Mrs Cicely Hutchinson of Washington, Sussex; Mr Arnold Mountford of Stoke-on-Trent Museum; Mr J. Ogden of Keighley Museum; Mrs Jean Ogilvie; Mr Philpott of Fulham Library; Miss Ruth Robertson; Mr G. W. S. Sherratt of Hanley; Mrs Mary Speaight of the London Museum.

In Paris, M. Gaston Decamps; Mlle Nelly Delay; M. and Mme Ostier; Mrs Estrid Faurholt in Denmark; Mr Heinz Kaempfer of The Hague and Mr Cornelius Ouwerhand of Leyden Museum in Holland.

Frau Emmy Lehmann of the Sonneberg Toy Museum; Dr Leonie von Wilckens of the Germanisches National Museum, Nuremberg; Professor Franz Winzinger of Regensburg, Bavaria; Dr Helena Johnova, National Museum, Prague; Mr H. Bartlett Wells, American Embassy, Athens; the Rev. M. V. Mandeville of Clonmel, Eire; Mr Patrick Murray, Museum of Childhood in Edinburgh; Mr Raymond Bushell, Dr Richard Lane and Mr Charles Mitchell, all of Tokyo, Japan. Help from the USA has been generous and positive and thanks are especially due to Mrs Thelma Bateman of Washington; Mrs Dewees Cochran, Felton, California; Miss Ann Coleman, Newark, NJ; Mrs Jo Clay Gerken, Lincoln, Nebraska; Mrs Jane Heimerdinger, University Museum, Philadelphia; Miss Marian Howard, Miami, Florida; Mrs Grace Kelagher, Fond du Lac, Wisconsin; Mr and Mrs R. C. Mathes, California; Mrs Richard Merrill, Saugus, Mass.; (and The Doll Collectors of America inc.); Mr Benjamin Michtom, President of Ideal Toy Corporation; Mrs Estes Pickup, Winter Park, Florida; Mrs Rowena Godding Ruggles, Oakland, California (for kind permission to use material from her book on Rose O'Neill *The One Rose*) Mrs Pat Schoonmaker, North Hollywood, California and Mrs Joan Severa of the Wisconsin State Historical Society, Madison, Wisconsin Husbands are inevitably involved in the exploits of their wives. I must thank Jack Hillier for being such a willing ally in addition to his professional help with proof-reading and producing line illustrations to order.

The collector of dolls in speaking of or explaining
her hobby to the uninitiated is sometimes horrified
when a chance remark reveals that she has arrived
too late on the scene to rescue what may well have been
a treasure.

'We found some old dolls when we cleared out the attic,
but they wouldn't have interested *you:* they were
dirty old things and we burnt them. One was a big
wooden doll with eyes that followed you round . . .'
So an elderly lady told me and she agreed when
I showed her a photograph of a Queen Anne doll
that, yes, it was just like that!

This, by way of introduction, is a special plea to those
who read or look at this book that they may
spread to others the need to 'Spare that doll',
however worthless or ugly it may seem to them,
and at least show it to an expert, a museum curator or
collector of antique toys before they consign it to
the rubbish heap.

Sometimes such a doll may give the clue to some vital
piece of information in doll research because of rare
mechanism or mould number, patent label or merely a point
of construction or pattern. Occasionally, even a smashed head
has yielded up some scrap of printed paper that reveals
a date of making, and old materials of dress in an
early fashion are interesting to a collector who is
delving back into the past for information.
The whole history of dolls has been built up
bit by bit by careful research and almost every survivor
has some detail to add to the record.

A Plea for Old Dolls

PHOTOGRAPHIC CREDITS: The Publishers are grateful to the following for help in assembling illustrative material and for permission to reproduce photographs.

The names of photographers and photographic agencies are given in *italics*.

American School of Classical Studies, Athens 11; Bayerisches National Museum, Munich 36, 37, 58, 59, 60, 61, 62, 63, 64, 65, 66, 154

Bethnal Green Museum 94, 182; Bibliothèque Nationale, Paris 210, 211; British Museum 1, 16, 43, 81, 215

Chester County Historical Society, Penn. 49; Cliffe Castle Museum, Keighley *C. H. Jones* 85

Costume Museum, The Hague 70; Daily Mail *Walter Brown* 264; Deutsches Spielzeugmuseum, Sonneberg 155

Dresden Art Gallery 45; M. Gaston Decamps 131; Essex Institute, Salem, Mass. 48, 207

Focke Museum, Bremen 71, 160, 161; Germanisches National Museum, Nuremberg 39, 72, 73, 124, 137, 138, 159

Ghana National Museum, Accra 22; Gulbenkian Museum, University of Durham, on loan from Royal Scottish Museum given by Sir John Home Bt 4

Historical Association of Pennsylvania 212; Imperial College, London 15

Institut National de la Propriété Industrielle, Paris 133, 163, 200, 201; Kestner Museum, Hanover 7

Kunsthistorisches Museum, Vienna 38; Landesmuseum Joanneum, Graz 77, 83; Leeds City Museum *John Armitage* 86

London Library *John Freeman* 197; London Museum 69, 76, 97, 98, 114, 136, 145, *Derrick Witty* 198, 202

Metropolitan Museum of Art, New York 3, 9, 10, 12 (Rogers Fund 1911), 13 (Rogers Fund 1923)

Museo Capitolini, Rome 14; Museum of Childhood, Edinburgh *Derrick Witty* 17, 18, 19, 20, 24, 25, 26, 30, 34, 53, 68, 74, 80, 104, 147, 152, 170, 171, 175, 177, 185, 186, 189, 196, 209, 218, 233, 242, 244, 251, 262

Musée de l'Homme, Paris 23; National Archaeological Museum, Athens 5, 6

National Museum of Prague 99, 100, 101, 102, 103, 105, 106; National Museum, Tokyo 227, 228, 229

National Trust *Edwin Smith* 42; Neuchâtel Museum 119

Norwich Museum (on loan from Captain William H. Bulwer-Long) *A. E. Coe* 113

Rijksmuseum voor Volkenkunde, Leiden frontispiece, 240; Rijksmuseum, Amsterdam 33, 111, 112

State Historical Society of Wisconsin *Justin M. Schmeideke* 158, 164 (E. B. Trimpey Collection), 169, 199, 214, 217, 219, 221, 254, 256, 263

Stoke-on-Trent Museum 176; Tiroler Volkskunstmuseum 78; Toy Cupboard Museum, Lancaster, Mass. 54

Toy Museum, Rottingdean, *Derrick Witty* 148; University Museum, Philadelphia 2, 8, 27, 28, 31, 32

Victoria and Albert Museum *Derrick Witty* 52, 54, 55, 56, 91, 172, 208, 252

Worthing Museum *Derrick Witty* 21, 35, 50, 67, 82, 84, 88, 92, 109, 110, 115 (Guermonprez Collection), 123, 125, 126, 129, 132, 134, 143, 151, 162, 166, 173, 180, 188, 203, 243, 245, 259

Lucie Attwell Ltd (courtesy Peter Earnshaw) 247, 248, 249; Barway Display Services Ltd 261

Century 21 Productions, Slough 261a; Hook & Franks Ltd, London 250; Ideal Toy Corporation 255

Mattel Inc, California 257; Peggy Nisbet Ltd 260; Wendy Boston Play-Safe Toys Ltd 258

Collection of: Raymond Bushell (courtesy Charles E. Tuttle and Co., Tokyo) 230, 231

Cavailles Collection *Hachette* (by permission of Eliane Maingot) 121; Robert Culff 220; Mrs Dewees Cochran 253

M. Damiot 130; Mrs Alice Early (courtesy of Chelsea Antiques Fair) *Susan Macfarlane* 150

By Gracious Permission of Her Majesty the Queen 144, 167; 168

Prince Ernst Heinrich, Herzog zu Sachsen-Moritzburg 40, 41; Mrs Grace Kelagher 224, 225; Mrs Jean Latham 93

Marshall McClintock 205; Mrs Richard Merrill *Richard Merrill* 216; Mrs Rowena Godding Ruggles 222

Mrs John Scripture (courtesy Doll Collectors of America Inc.) *Richard Merrill* 213; Mrs Caryl Smith 223

Mrs Helen Winter and Mrs Yvonne Winter Harless 195; Mrs J. D. Yates 153

Photos by Windsor Spice Collections of: Author 29, 44, 96; Miss Blair-Hickman 122, 181, 206 *(A. C. Cooper)*

Mrs Goodinge 135; Geoffrey Godden 184; Mrs Hughes 183; Mrs Jennings 140; Soame Jenyns 226; George Speaight 120

Photos by Derrick Witty Collections of: Author 149, 157, 174, 190, 191, 192, 194 *(Mr Ames,)* 204, 232

Miss Bourne 47; Miss L. Coules, 127, 128; Mrs Terence Doyle 193; Jack Hillier 234, 235, 236, 237, 238, 239

Mrs Hutchinson 46, 57, 75, 79, 89, 90, 95, 141, 142, 146, 156, 165, 178

Mrs Keene 179; Mrs Jean Ogilvie 87, 116, 139, 187, 246, Mrs Rouse 241, Mrs Trew 117. 118

1

....

The Earliest Dolls

It is a pity that some of the picturesque and curious old terms for describing a child's doll have disappeared or have narrowed down to some specialist meaning. The Latin *pupa*, meaning a young or new-born child and used also to describe a doll, became *poupée* in French and *puppe* in German in the Middle Ages and in English 'poppet' or 'puppet', 'pup' or the Frenchified 'puppy'.

Shakespeare, with a double reference to the rag doll of childhood and the adult 'dolls' of dalliance, wrote:

> *...This is no world*
> *To play with mammets, and to tilt with lips.*

But the early names, like the playthings they stood for, have vanished. Dryden translated the Latin *pupae* as 'baby-toys' in 1670 and Richardson in a dictionary fifty years later explained that these were 'little Babies or Poppets as we call them'. 'Baby' or 'a child's baby' was the general term in England by the seventeenth century and was used also for a 'baby-house', meaning dolls' house. The term continued well into the eighteenth century and appears even in American advertisements, such as one of 1750 which proclaimed:

> *Sold by Wm. Price at the Corner Shop*
> *Next the Old Brick Meeting-house, Boston*
> *London Babies*
> *English and Dutch Toys.*

Various theories exist as to the emergence of the actual word 'doll', but by far the most plausible is that put forward in a little book published last century by Henry Morley on the history of Bartholomew Fair, one of the most famous of London public fairs, celebrated with hardly an interruption each year from the twelfth century:

Because to the fair sex belong pretty faces and gay dresses, and doubtless also for other reasons known to the toy-maker, dolls with a few ridiculous exceptions have at all times been feminine. Bartholomew Babies (the dolls sold at the Fair) were illustrious, but their name as the licence of the Fair increased was of equivocal suggestion. Therefore when some popular toyman, who might have called his babies 'pretty Sues' or 'Molls', or 'Polls', cried diligently to the ladies who sought fairings for their children 'Buy a pretty Doll' (it was at a time too, when the toy babies were coming more and more into demand) the conquest of a clumsiness was recognised. Mothers applied for dolls to the men at the stalls and ere long by all the stalls and toy-booths the new cry of 'Pretty Doll' was taken up. We have good reason to be tolerably certain that Bartholomew Fair gave its familiar cry to a plaything now cherished in every English nursery. A provincial toyman could not have enforced the change; and there were no tradesmen in London who could diffuse as private dealers a new name for the toy in which Bartholomew Fair dealt most especially and dealt also among throngs.

The one word 'doll' is now left to describe all manner of children's toys, and also early doll-like figurines or images from ancient times,

which have sometimes led people into associating the word with 'idol'. Even from the Neolithic period widespread finds have been made of curious feminine figures crudely shaped from clay or carved from bone or stone. But with such objects we are left in no doubt at all as to their meaning, however mysterious the rites which accompanied them. In the words of Professor E. O. James: 'Whether or not they were emblematic of the Mother Goddess as such they certainly suggest the veneration of maternity as a divine principle. Some are naturalistically modelled in the round, others are flat and hardly more than a stump with no attempt to fashion the face or head. But they all emphasise the breasts, the navel and the vulva region.' They symbolized the superstitious reverence with which very primitive peoples regarded fertility and fecundity and which reappears in the customs and images of native tribes even down to the present day.

'Those are always the chapters I skip,' a collector friend of mine confided when we were discussing the interest of early and primitive dolls. The truth is that they are in the sphere of the archaeologist and almost unobtainable for the average collector, whose interest tends to fade when confronted with an object out of reach. Not only are they materially out of reach but also figuratively. It needs considerable force of imagination to replace some of the relics from the museum shelf back under the hot sun of Greece where they were first played with or into the sticky clutch of a child lolling on the Egyptian sand three thousand years ago. The history is so remote and the sort of child to whom they belonged so unfamiliar as to be almost untranslatable into modern thought.

There is no positive link between such very ancient dolls (even when it is proved that they were in fact play dolls and not intended for some purpose of ritual or sacrifice) and later European ones, though it is evident that doll-making spread from the East to the West. But it is worth studying the workmanship of some of the examples which have survived. Every material seems to have been used: wax, wood, clay, ivory, marble, bone, leather and textiles. Surprisingly modern techniques of painting, jointing and modelling were capable of producing not only dolls, but, in some cases, their furniture and their clothes, their pots and pans and ornaments.

We tend to relate unknown things to our own experience, and it is not surprising that objects as playful looking as [1] the Egyptian paddle-shaped dolls, with their gay patterns, hair of clay pellets and almost modern stylized shape were originally associated with children and thought to be toys. Apart from their voluptuous curves and the emphasis on sexual detail there are usually scribblings of fertility emblems or designs of fertility gods on the reverse side which quite conclusively prove that they had ritual significance. They date from about 2000 BC and during this period and earlier very good and life-like models of little figures were made of painted wood to occupy the tombs of the dead and to impersonate servants and tradesmen who were ready to perform the tasks they represent – such as brewing, brickmaking, farming. Known as *shabti*, their tools and utensils throw an invaluable light on methods of the time and often they

*1 Egyptian paddle-shaped dolls
of 2000 BC; 7½–10 inches*

were accompanied by some such inscription as: 'If – [the dead man] is detailed for any tasks in the underworld, then say thou O Shabti "Here am I"'.

Figure 2 shows a wooden doll with arms jointed at the shoulder and made a hundred years or so later than the paddle dolls. The fact that

3 Egyptian wooden doll from Lisht;
12th Dynasty

2 left: Jointed wooden doll from
Egypt, 12th Dynasty; 7 inches

the arms are movable has led her to be identified as a child's doll but the shape of the body is that of a mature woman and she could equally well represent a slave in the long close-fitting robe with painted details.

Figure 3 shows a wooden doll, also of about 2000 BC, found at the cemetery of Lisht in the central Nile Valley. In style it is vastly superior to [2] and has been made with every attention to detail, beautifully proportioned and with inlaid eyes and nipples, and pegs which once attached its hair. The arms are missing, though a hole through the shoulder line shows that they were made to move, and the legs are rounded at the knee. Age has worn and disfigured the features, but it has a careful beauty as though it had been intended for a portrait statue or memorial rather than a doll. The Egyptians early perfected the art of inlaid eyes and a powerful fragment [4] shows a death mask in plaster from the Roman period (first century AD) with eyes of black and white inlay held in place by a spoon-shaped *cloison* with a little spur that 'tied' it into the modelling material.

Wooden dolls did perhaps exist in Greece, but they have not survived as successfully as they did in the dry heat of Egypt. Most of the examples from early periods are of baked clay or terracotta.

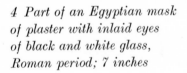

4 Part of an Egyptian mask of plaster with inlaid eyes of black and white glass, Roman period; 7 inches

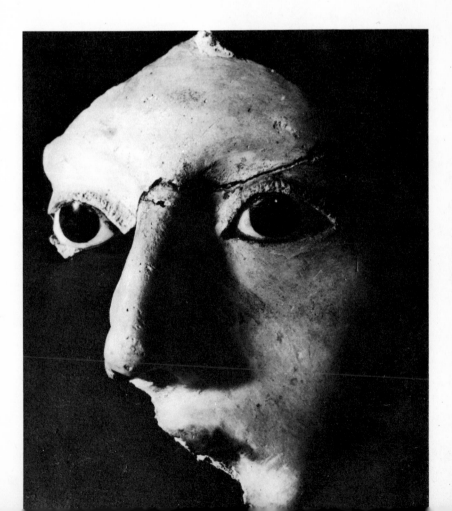

The Boeotian doll illustrated here [5] represents a type which has puzzled archaeologists and raised various conjectures. The body is always bell-shaped, the legs were made separately and swing easily from a thread or wire running from side to side, the neck is abnormally elongated and the head is birdlike, as here, or with a stylized face and sometimes a head loop by which the creature could be hung up or dangled. Sometimes lines painted on the legs and feet represent sandals and thongs. The arms or sleeves are held up and are sometimes simply indicated by a raised slip attached over the round of the body. The breasts are painted discs and the pattern drawn on the tunic is geometrical or decorated with symbols of swastikas, birds, palm leaves. They have the appearance of that game dear to the nursery 'Heads, Bodies and Legs' where figures are composed of unrelated drawn faces, torsos and limbs: they are amusing enough for toys, mysterious enough for charms or idols.

The Mycenaean dolls made from baked clay found at a tomb in Nauplion [6] come in the same category; decorative as they are, their purpose remains a mystery. They sufficiently resemble folk-toys of dancing figures for us to believe that they were children's playthings, but with some underlying meaning, ceremonial or ritualistic. There is no reason why they should not be both, for many folk-toys first emerged with a religious significance and were put into a child's hands both for instruction and as a memento.

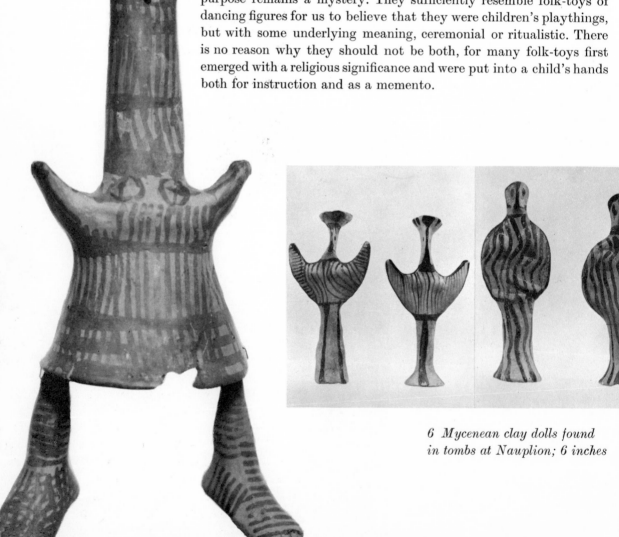

5 Boeotian doll found in tomb; 7 inches

6 Mycenean clay dolls found in tombs at Nauplion; 6 inches

7 Jointed terracotta doll from Greece; c. 5th century BC; 5 inches

Very many examples of the little jointed clay dolls have been discovered, usually in the temples dedicated to Demeter and Persephone, Aphrodite and Artemis [7 and 8]. The period in which they were made seems to have extended from the archaic period (900–400 BC) to the fifth or sixth century BC and they are still being found in excavations at Corinth. These two represent distinct, but often recurring types and sometimes painted details are added. The first has hair curling beneath the high headgear called *kalathos* and showing each side of the neck and she wears the short loose draped *chiton* or tunic to the hips, where a modelled spur insets the legs so that they can swing freely. The other is of a tall slim girl with hair loosely dressed in a topknot and sometimes wearing a wreath or ribbon. Here the leg joint is slightly different and seems to approximate to where the knee should be, as the crutch of the body is indicated under the tightly fitting tunic. Such figures usually hold clappers or cymbals in their hands.

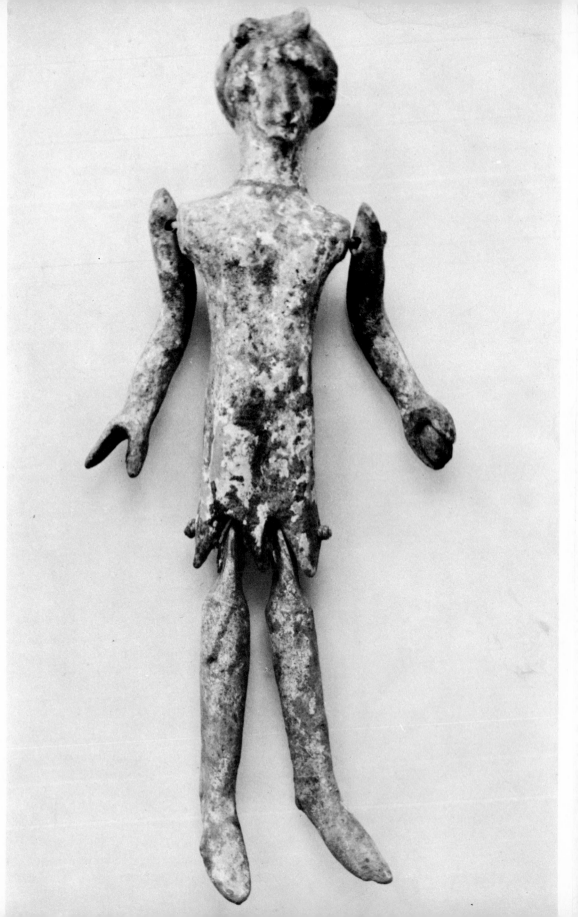

8 left: Jointed terracotta doll from Greece c. 5th century BC; 5 inches

9 and 10 Greek terracotta figures, seated, with jointed arms possibly for play-acting; 7 inches

An epigram in the Greek anthology in which a girl called Timarete dedicates her dolls to Artemis along with her cap, her tambourine and her favourite ball, gives a clue to the sort of feeling behind this ceremony and translated literally reads: 'The maid, to a maid, her maiden gives' – an allusion to the acceptance of maturity in marriage and the making over on the shrine of the virgin goddess both of the literal virginity of the doll and the abstract virginity of the girl. It may be assumed that boys sometimes took part in a similar act of dedication as their toys have also been found at shrines of Apollo and Hermes.

Persius, the young Roman poet of the first century AD who died before he was twenty-eight, left six short satires of which one excerpt translated into verse reads:

> But ye, ye priests (for sure you can) unfold
> In heavenly things what boots this pomp of gold
> No more indeed than dolls to Venus paid
> (The toys of childhood) by a riper maid.

This indicates a similar tradition in Roman times.

A pair of dolls said to have been found in Thebes and measuring about seven inches in height presents another problem. Though they have sockets for movable arms both are seated, and the missing arms might have been used to indicate which one was speaking in some form of miniature theatricals [9 and 10]. The modelling in this case is so fine that one might rather associate the work with ornamental figurines than consider them to be playthings. They are realistically nude and were never meant to be clothed.

17

11 left: Baby's clay rattle from Corinth; 1st century AD; 7 inches

12 centre: Roman bone doll from Tarentum; 3rd century BC

13 right: Roman terracotta doll bust; 7 inches

14 opposite: A jointed wooden doll discovered in the sarcophagus of a little girl of 1st-century-Rome, complete with gold bangle and ring

A baby's rattle discovered in Corinth and dating from the time of Nero, in the first century AD, shows what subtle modelling could be employed for a child's toy [11]. It depicts a little Negro slave boy fallen asleep beside his bundle and is quite beautiful and tender in sentiment. A few beads enclosed in the hollow body provide the rattle.

Bone was also used for early dolls, but it was never capable of such detailed treatment, though it was possibly more suitable for a plaything than brittle clay. Figure 12, dating conclusively from about the third century BC, was found at Tarentum in Italy. The figure wears a short fluted tunic very like some of the most modern slips of the present day. Its legs are socketed into holes which do not allow much free movement and are joined from outside with wire, as are the arms at the shoulder. Figure 13, a more childlike bust, is moulded of terracotta with holes through the shoulders for the arms. It is un-dated and is so narrow-waisted that one wonders whether it could originally have been supplied with a fitted body. Obviously the rough area of the crown was once covered with hair.

One of the finest examples of dolls which have survived from anti-quity dates from the time of Antoninus in the first century AD. This doll is cleverly fashioned out of oak with joints at shoulders and hips, whilst the limbs are also made to bend at elbows and knees [14]. The loose-jointed articulation of the early Greek dolls has been overcome by means of accurately adjusted tenons and mortises. The body is as carefully modelled and proportioned as the face and head. There are even finger and toe joints. This one doll survived in the sarcophagus of a little girl aged fourteen who died before marriage and it depicts beautifully the adolescent girl, the rounded shape of developing femininity.

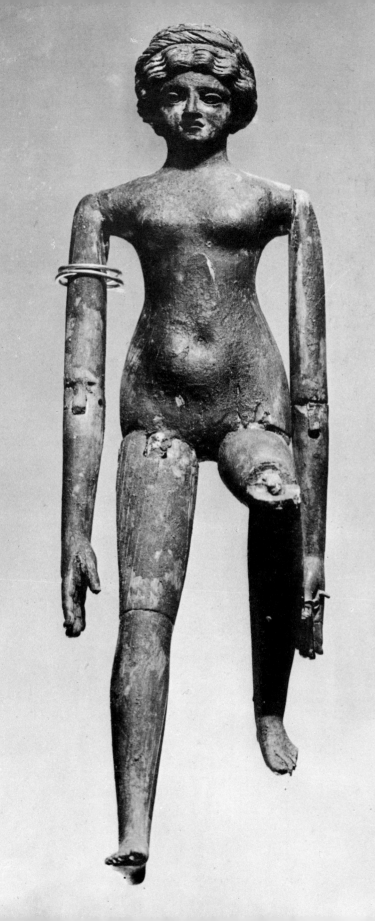

Finally, we have the nearest approach to our modern idea of a child's play doll, found in a child's tomb dating from the latter half of the third century AD. It is a pottery doll, painted white with traces of pink, with black hair and eyes, made by modelling and baking separate limbs and joining them together with plaster. This is particularly interesting since it could scarcely have been an isolated example, as the finely carved wooden doll was. It was accompanied by a positive treasury of little knicknacks a child would cherish: tiny glass jars, pottery jugs, wooden boxes with sliding lids, necklaces of glazed pottery beads, white, blue, buff, brown and black; taper holders and spindles; a model table and a model bed for the doll made out of split palm sticks; wooden combs and rush sandals; a model sphinx; the remains of a little oval box, painted with pink flowers and green birds on a yellow ground, and a small doll made of rushes and covered with linen and thread [15].

As far as excavation goes the story is never complete and new finds may yet throw fresh light on the toys of the past. It is interesting to find how dolls created in the ancient world in different countries and quite independently often corresponded in shapes and materials. With the dolls found in grave burials in Peru, however, a quite individual type has been discovered: they are amazingly like the sort of primitive shapes a child produces when asked to draw the human figure. The body is squarish, the arms and legs straight strips, the features marked in with a sort of geometric precision. Figures 31 and 32 show two dolls in the possession of the University Museum, Philadelphia. The top one [31], depicts a baby on a wooden cradle board and is made of bound cane with a pottery head and a stuffed body of woven patterned material; the bottom one [32], of woven material with embroidered features, is made of finely threaded canvas and stuffed, with arms and legs of wood bound with cords of straw. Other early pottery dolls have the features and body patterns painted on and some examples exist which are made of wood enlivened with metal eyes and teeth.

16 A simple rag doll from about 300 BC found in a Roman grave; 7 inches

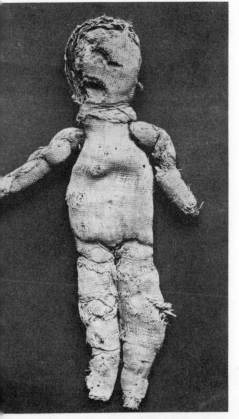

17 *Achewa spirit doll from Central Africa; 10 inches*

18 *French ghost doll with wax cross 'lost soul' token; 8 inches*

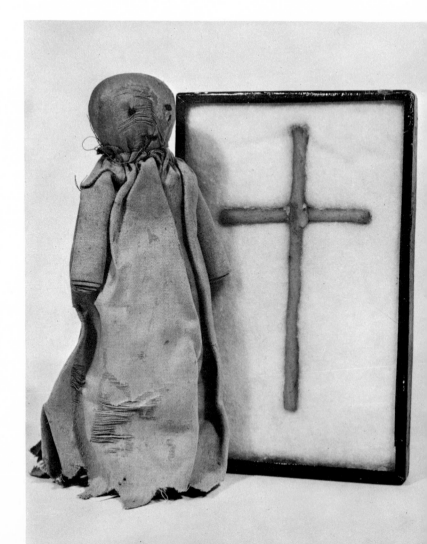

2

....

Primitive
and Ritual Dolls

Man, faced with forces he did not understand in a primitive society, made little figures to intercede for him. Sometimes it is not clear what their true purpose was, except that they connected with the fundamental needs of the human race. Birth and death, seed time and harvest were occasions for the propitiation of the gods, the unseen powers. Often an image was made to represent the victim in what had originally been an occasion for human sacrifice: dolls which might act out the ritual in place of men, women or children. The ancient clay figures found in Japanese tombs, *haniwa*, or the Egyptian servant tokens *shabti* (mentioned in chapter 1) are examples of such silent burial guardians. Sometimes dolls have been found in the foundations of ancient buildings: a substitute for the living child which it was once thought necessary to sacrifice to the gods. The people of the Nile threw a doll into the river when it did not rise high enough to fertilize their land and in a similar ceremony on the Tiber, dolls made of rushes were offered to the river god.

'The genesis of the doll is to be found in a quality shared by primitive races and children,' wrote Max von Boehn. In acting out their hopes and fears, as among children playing and identifying themselves with little home-made characters, it was not necessary for the personification of such magical figures to be other than simple and rudimentary. Branched twigs resembling the human form lent themselves readily to such symbolism, just as the curious shapes of the mandrake root became invested with magical significance. The materials which were readiest to hand would be used: clay or grass and straw, leaves, cones, nuts, tree-bark or skin, fur and feather.

As part of their religion, the Achewa tribe of Central Africa cherished home-made spirit dolls which were intended to house the spirits of departed ancestors [17]. The crude 'wishing-bone' shape is made of small sticks bound together with thongs of bark rope and wound round with a scrap of rag which hides a small box made out of the handle of a gourd cup. Shaped rather like a pill-box, this is meant to contain the departed spirit. Sacrifices and prayers offered to the spirit doll acted as a means of communication between the living and the dead. In the Congo a similar superstition was represented by rudimentary iron figures which look rather like 'pin-men' and which were also intended to offer a final resting-place to the spirit when a man was buried.

In Christian burial, the soul is believed to ascend to Heaven, but an interesting religious observance was discovered by Dr Lovett among simple sea-faring folk. When a sailor or fisherman was lost at sea, his relatives would use a little substitute coffin containing a tiny effigy for the church service and memorial. The custom has been traced in Scotland and in Germany and figure 18 shows a wax cross in a small casket used for a similar ceremony which was discovered in the Ile d'Oussant, Brittany, in 1912. The curious 'ghost-doll' shown in the same picture is also French and came from the Gironde district, where the natives could not exactly remember the local tradition, except that it represented some commemoration of a departed soul. It is about eight inches long and is made of little rolls of ashy grey material with faintly marked, indistinct features.

19 opposite: Sudanese fertility doll with pregnant shape hung around with charms and ornaments; 16 inches

20 Gourd head child's doll with coral-coloured rath seed decoration on head, Botswana; 8 inches

The fantastic figures marketed in the Sudan by 'witches' or medicine men [19] were thought to have magic powers for inducing fertility in women of the tribe. In Lesotho and Botswana the empty gourd shell, roughly decorated with paint and studded with beads, served as a useful head for similar fertility charms and the doll would be given a child's name. If the owner's prayer was granted and a baby was born, the child received this same name. Perhaps sometimes the child also inherited the doll as a plaything. The empty dried shell illustrated comes remarkably close to the little native dark-skinned baby in colour and texture [20].

The two chubby Lesotho girls (who look no more than children themselves) have babies of their own to carry; these have been cunningly contrived from cartridge cases bound round with strings of tiny coloured beads [21]. The dolls themselves are perhaps a Mission product, as their faces are moulded with inset eyes of coloured glass, and they must have proved a very saleable tourist attraction, since they turn up fairly frequently in doll collections.

Among the Ashanti tribe little girls were given flat carved wooden dolls to be worn tucked into the small of their backs, training them to be good mothers and produce beautiful daughters. The A'kua-ba dolls reproduce a style of beauty which at its finest is a work of art,

21 Lesotho dolls with 'cartridge-case' babies; 12 inches

22 *Wooden carved dolls carried by Ashanti children in Ghana — a tradition aimed at encouraging them to grow up to be good mothers*

23 *Wooden doll from the White Nile, serving as an amulet for gaining height; 15 inches*

with large flat discoid heads with small features and long slim necks marked with parallel rings [22]. Whereas such charms are intended to promote beauty, the members of another race living along the Valley of the Nile were famed for their great height and gave their children dolls to carry which might encourage long limbs and the stature of seven or eight feet which was most admired [23].

The set of wooden jointed dolls from Lesotho strung together on a leather thong has the superficial appearance of a plaything [24]. But when a man at either end set them in motion by shaking the string he was enacting a hunting or marauding expedition and encouraging those watching who were about to take part in the affray. The dolls are armed with native weapons and decorated with amulets and charms against evil spirits and in this way the team of men setting forth was praying for good fortune. Sports teams going out to play with a mascot dressed in the team colours represent a modern version of such sympathetic magic.

The great forests of Russia must have aroused the superstitious fears of those who lived and worked there, just as, in a very different climate, did the jungles of Africa. Figure 25 shows a group of curious 'moss men', traditional dolls made from cones, sticks and straw with

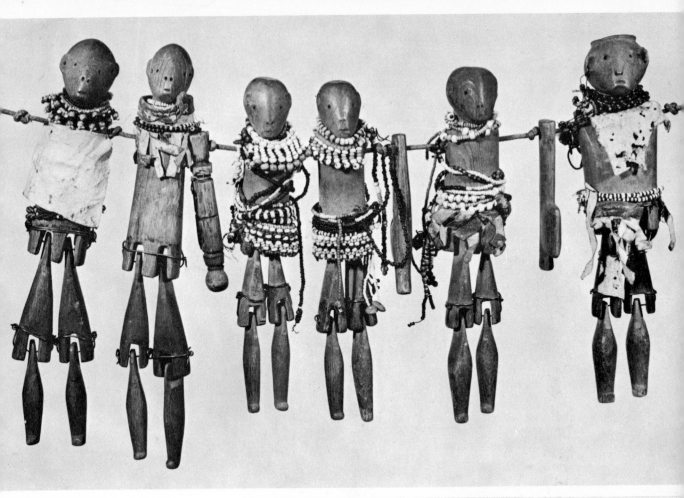

24 Six African wooden dolls
strung together and armed with
native weapons.
A 'Good Hunting' charm

25 Russian 'moss men' said
to represent the Demons
of the Forest; 10 inches

painted faces. Even further north, the Eskimos of the Arctic placed their faith in little dolls made of drift wood or roughly carved from walrus ivory; clothed in scraps of skin and fur, these good-luck tokens were lashed to the kayak in which they set out to fish the forbidding waters. The primitive dolls with block wooden feet and painted or covered with skin and decorated with a few crude beads are more likely to be children's toys [26]. Eskimo children were sometimes taught the art of curing skins and sewing them together with leather thongs for dolls' clothes, just as a European child might learn needlework and knitting for dressing up her doll.

26 Primitive Eskimo dolls of wood and skin; 3–6 inches

There are still many people half-inclined to believe in 'what the stars foretell' or willing to carry a good-luck charm round their neck or as a mascot on their car. Perhaps they are a relic of the votive images and talismen of the past, for there is an intrinsic superstition in man and it is on this that the strange rites of witchcraft have traded through the ages. The Egyptians record the use of waxen effigies for magical purposes and the Middle Ages were full of astounding accounts of trials in which witches were accused of harming people by incanting over wax and clay dolls made in their image and melting or defacing them. The rituals which attended such ceremonies were revolting and the susceptible person made aware of such evil-wishing could well become sick or even die of fright. A seventeenth-century witch in Scotland, Isobel Gowdie, gave an account of one such ill-wishing effigy which she made with the object of destroying the male-line of a local nobleman:

> John Taylor brought home the clay in his plaid; his wife broke it very small, like meal, and sifted it in a sieve and poured water among it in the Devil's name and wrought it very sore, like a rye-bowt [a pudding dough] and made of it a picture of the Laird's son. It had all the parts and marks of a child, such as head, eyes, nose, hands, feet, mouth and little lips. It wanted no mark of a child; and the hands of it folded by its sides...

This image was committed to roasting in order to bring on a fever in the child and make the spell fatal.

It might have been thought that in these days of sophistication and scientific knowledge the practice of witchcraft would have lapsed in civilized countries, but the Museum of Witchcraft at Bourton-on-the-Water in the Cotswolds, England, possesses examples of much more recent date made with the same intention. A television programme in 1965 was even able to show such a ceremony carried out in a remote country district of England by a witches' coven, the recognized company made up of thirteen members. One of the witches invoked the spirits of darkness and use was made of a waxen effigy to dispel ill-health. To bring the matter really up-to-date, an enterprising San Francisco dealer was recently marketing a voodoo set through the post: an outfit which Mr Patrick Murray has aptly called a 'Do-it-yourself-curse-kit'. The darker side of human nature reflected in the arts of black magic and voodoo remains repellent to most people and ritual dolls were certainly never meant to fall into the hands of young children.

A curious instance of dolls used in tribal customs and afterwards given to children as playthings is shown among those famous native-made dolls, the *kachina* of the Hopi Indians of Arizona. As they were an agricultural people, it was of paramount importance that their crops should be fertile, and at annual tribal feasts masked dancers portrayed the gods of storm and rain, sun and drought whose whims would influence the harvest. Coloured wooden dolls, dressed in leather and adorned with feathers, picturesque in a gay assortment of costumes and fantastic headgear, represented these dancers, and after the

27 *Hopi* kachina *dolls
representing Tiweni and Shalaho*

28 *right: Indian corn husk dolls*

ceremony were passed on to the children as a means of teaching them the tribal mythology. From the numbers of them now available in collections, it is clear that the interest shown in them by the outside world promoted an even greater production than all the tribal children concerned could ever play with [27].

The cornhusk dolls of America may also have originated with the native Indians. Figure 28 shows some amusing examples complete with feather headdress and fancy beadwork. The children of the pioneers in America found this a game very much to their liking and it is a child art that has survived down to the present day, even when more sophisticated dolls are available.

When a corn-dolly or corn-baby is spoken of in England, it refers to the ancient custom of celebrating the gathering in of the wheat harvest by making a symbol from the very last sheaf reaped. Sometimes this 'dolly' was no more than a bundle tied with ribbon and carried in honour to the harvest supper celebrated by all the reapers. More often it was made in a vaguely human shape and was decorated with ornamental braiding and weaving. In his *Everyday Book* (1826/7), Hone refers to a ceremony where the figure was not only made in the form of a baby but was dressed by the women and adorned with paper trimmings cut out to resemble a cap, ruffles and handkerchief of the finest lace. The doll was always kept in the farmhouse until the next year's harvest was reaped and a new corn-baby usurped its place.

How relished in those times were such old customs; they lit up the long hardworking days before any mechanical equipment had eased the tough manual methods. Each simple festival had its ritual, and its fun, merrymaking and feasting were looked forward to in the country-man's year. It did not matter if the original belief was quite forgotten, for the spirit was carried on, and the farmworkers shared the super-stition that the corn-baby would bring luck without knowing that it must have originated with the legend of the Greek corn-goddess Demeter. Yet another classical deity was celebrated in the May Day revels which still linger on in country villages in England. The young girls would bind together two hoops so that they crossed each other vertically and make garlands of flowers to cover them. This con-traption was fixed to a staff some five feet long and decorated with coloured ribbons and strings of blown birds' eggs, whilst the aperture between the hoops was filled with a beautifully dressed doll represent-ing the 'May Queen' or, as she was sometimes called, 'The Lady'. The whole standard had a Roman look and perhaps derived from the goddess Flora, whose annual Roman festival, the Floralia, was cele-brated from 28 April to 3 May. The village girls carrying this pretty garland from door to door would receive a trifle in tribute; the custom is now almost obsolete, and the May Queen is more often represented by a little girl or local beauty. Even 'dancing round the Maypole' has only been revived in a rather self-conscious way.

Finally, as the year neared its end, the Catholic countries of Europe celebrated St Nicholas, patron saint of little boys (just as St Catha-rine is the saint of little girls). The well-loved Christmas image of Santa Claus or Father Christmas with long hooded red cloak trimmed with white fur and long white beard is our modern version of the legendary character who has brought happiness each year to children. In the toy bazaar he has become a commercial asset and his religious significance is almost forgotten.

In a painting dating from the middle of the seventeenth century in the Rijksmuseum, Amsterdam, a delightful family scene by the painter Jan Steen shows the Eve of St Nicholas, which occurred on 6 December [33]. It was an occasion which was no doubt very familiar to the artist and was enacted in homes all over Holland. The children of the house have offered their shoes to be filled with gifts and sweet-meats; fruit and nuts, fancy breads and cakes are scattered on the chair and the basket stands ready for the feast day. The little daugh-ter of the house is made much of and carries her bag of gifts, which include a little toy on a stick made of moulded gum tragacanth. She proudly grasps her new doll, which is, at this period, a true St Nicholas doll with a halo and a long cross, mounted on a stand. The baby of the house also has a flat doll, which might be made of wood or of cakebread. An older boy holding her in his arms draws her attention to something, perhaps out of the window. But the really appealing character is the naughty brother on the left, smearing away his tears as he realizes that all he is being offered in his shoe is a birch of twigs! His family are enjoying the joke and the scene is far too amiable for us to believe that he will not be forgiven later and join in the fun.

In Germany, St Nicholas is depicted as accompanied by the devil or 'Krampus', who carries the birch for naughty children whilst his

29 The May day garland with 'lady' doll: an old English countryside custom

31

31 and 32 Child's play dolls
woven textile and in clay resti
a bed of sticks, from Peru; 1st
century AD

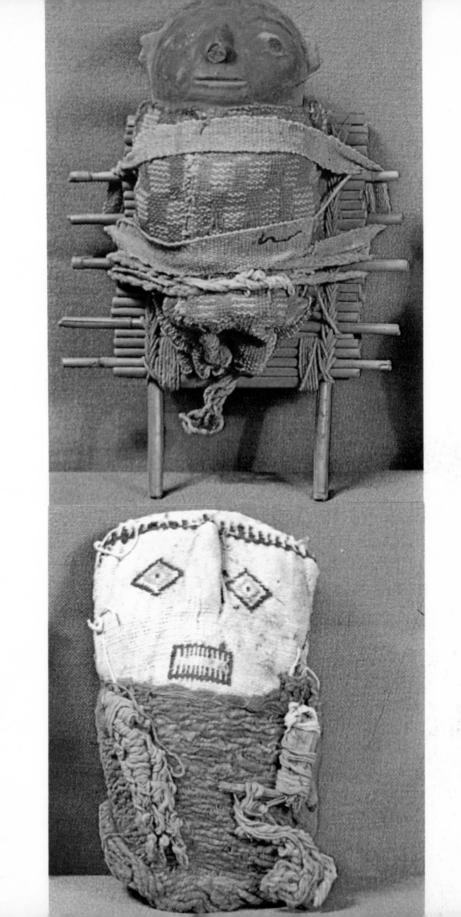

master is in charge of the sack of gifts for the good ones. Sometimes as part of the Christmas decorations, and as a reminder of the same ceremony with its moral of rewards and punishments, a large birch is hung up, decorated with ribbon, with a little wax doll representing the Christchild [30]. Or else, little model birches with a present of a packet of sweets are given to children to remind them of Christian forgiveness.

In Holland and Flanders, St Nicholas becomes Santa Klaus and rides on horseback through the streets with an attendant, this time called 'Rupprecht', who no doubt also represents the little devil figure but appears less forbidding dressed up in pretty white fur [34]. With wax face and 'Baby Bunting' look he seems ill-suited to his rôle of clambering down chimneys to deliver gifts. St Nicholas himself is a handmade doll thought to have come from Sweden [35]. He is made of hard-packed stockinet with jolly painted features and a stuck-on beard. His mitts are finely knitted in a traditional pattern and his loose-fitting jerkin is of a coarse plush material. A few little parcels are strung at his waist, having spilled over from the load in the sack on his back. Children always long to know what is in those parcels so that this little fellow intrigues them with the same anticipation as their own Christmas stockings!

34 Rupprecht doll clothed in fur
with a wax face and wooden limbs;
12 inches

35 St Nicholas doll made from
stockinet. Swedish? 12 inches

3

German Dolls from Medieval Times and Trade with England

37 *Figurine of pipeclay, German, c. 1525; 6 inches*

'*Nürnberger Tand geht durch alle Land*' sang the old couplet: 'The little playthings of Nuremberg are found in every land.' Old Nuremberg, as picturesque as a city in a fairy story, had an early history of toy-making. The names of famous doll-makers were listed in the city records as early as the fifteenth century. Guilds were organized which strictly limited the type of work carried out by each specialist trades-man, and the goods were distributed by pedlars.

Figure 36 shows two little figures from the fifteenth century, typical of many discovered over a wide area of Germany and not just in Nuremberg, though they are thought to have been made in that dis-trict as well as in Thuringia. They represent women in long close-fitting gowns, one with low-cut neckline and the other with decorative shoulder style and long trailing sleeves. Both wear the distinctive *kruseker* headgear of the period, a cap of stiff, folded linen. These are particularly fine unbroken examples, but figures are often broken off at the upper part or the head, as the skirt base is hollow and more delicate. The Nuremberg Museum possesses a large and representative collection of both complete dolls and fragments. They measure be-tween three and six inches in height and bear a certain resemblance to each other, though they differ in detail; sometimes the decorative *kruseker* is replaced by a married woman's coif or by the 'virgin crown' worn by young unmarried women. From their devout pose with hands clasped before them it is generally thought that they may have had religious significance and been produced for some other pur-pose than as mere playthings. Many of them show a hollow disc clearly moulded on the breast which could have held a token coin at a christening, and it seems very likely that they were baptismal dolls given as a present to a baby girl, or even that they represented St Catharine, patron saint of little girls.

There is nothing so controversial about a figurine in pipeclay which dates from early in the next century [37]. She is a typical woman of the period, beautifully posed as she sways forward with basket on one arm and wearing the fashionable clothes of her day, a flat, scarved head-dress, which is broken slightly, and a low-cut slashed gown with puffed sleeves and full skirt. It might be objected that this does not look like a child's doll, yet at approximately the same period, equally ornamental wooden dolls were also carved with details of clothing and in one piece. They are represented for instance in the paintings of Lucas Cranach (1472–1553), who was a native of Thuringia and work-ed in Nuremberg. A naked child in 'Charitas' by Cranach (1537) in the National Gallery, London, is clutching a stiff one-piece wooden 'stump' doll, with painted clothes. Even more detail is evident on a similar doll in a painting by an unknown artist in the Kunsthistori-sches Museum, Vienna [38]. This is a fine triptych painted on wood in 1503 portraying the three children of Philip the Fair of Burgundy. The youngest, Isabelle, aged only one year and three months, has just learnt to walk and wears a *fallhütchen* – a padded baby crash-helmet – to save her from hurting herself in tumbles. The wooden doll she clutches is dressed in grown-up fashion just like her five-year-old sister in the left-hand picture and according to the custom of the period.

38 *Triptych by an unknown artist (1503) showing the three children – Leonora, Charles and Isabelle – of Philip the Fair of Burgundy*

39 *An early Rhenish doll, c. 1530 found in 1966 hidden behind panelling in a Rhenish castle; 9 inches*

Until recently such dolls were known only by hearsay, in written tradition and in such fine portraits as those mentioned, but by a rare chance an actual example was discovered in 1966. This doll, measuring about nine inches, carved from limewood and coloured with paint, was found behind some old wooden panelling in a Rhenish castle, where she must have lain hidden for four hundred years or so [39]. In remarkably good condition, she has a tightly bodiced dress with long thin sleeves and a full-length narrow-pleated skirt reaching to the ground. The fine white folds of her linen shirt reach to the neck, where it is fastened with precious gold embroidery. A similarly embroidered wider stomacher is worn over the narrow girdle and hides the opening of her dress. The original, wide, wine-red cross-strings of her skirt give a good idea of the colour that has been lost. A net cap drawn down each side over her ears has rounded points and, covering her head, reveals the high domed forehead. Countless dolls of such a type must have been lost, but one fortunate accident has preserved this example of 1530.

Perhaps the complication, or refinement, of jointed dolls came later, when clothes of real material were substituted for painted detail, but carved one-piece dolls continued to be a speciality, particularly of the master carvers of the Bavarian towns of Berchtesgaden and Oberammergau.

The Cranach family seem to have had a weakness for dolls, and in a portrait of a child painted by the younger Cranach, Lucas the son, in 1564, it is interesting to see how the artist has made clever use of the deep colour of the doll dress to provide a foil for the beautiful plump little hands of the child [40 and 41]. The child was Princess Marie, sister of Christian I, and she is painted on a wooden panel about four foot by two foot which still belongs to the family for whom it was first painted. It shows a solemn little blue-eyed girl who wears a close-fitting white linen bonnet with white collar. Two gold necklaces hang over her quilted front, and she wears a splendid gown, patterned in lozenges of light and dark red, with full puff shoulders and tight-fitting sleeves showing a little frill of dainty lace at the wrist. The doll held tightly against the child's long white pinafore reflects the same fashion, but she has a neck ruff, besides gold necklaces and a rich underskirt of gold beneath her stiff red gown. It is clear from the detail that her hair is applied, not carved, as in the earlier one-piece dolls. She has dark eyes, which could be glass, and very delicately chiselled features. Like Marie's mother, who was painted the same year, she is dressed in the Elizabethan or 'Spanish' style of aristocratic fashion.

40 Portrait of Princess Marie von Sachsen by Lucas Cranach the Younger, 1546

41 Detail of the doll held by Princess Marie von Sachsen

42 *Arabella Stuart, 1577, portrait by an unknown hand, at Hardwick Hall, Chesterfield*

Even more Elizabethan is a little doll painted by an unknown artist [42]. This famous portrait of Arabella Stuart, which hangs at Hardwick Hall, Chesterfield, has often been reproduced, but I make no apology for using it again. It could scarcely be left out of a history of dolls. For one thing, it is a very beautiful picture, and, more important to this subject, it is absolutely accurately dated: Arabella was born in 1577 and this portrait states that she was only twenty-three months old. It is a sedate likeness of a child not yet two who has been dressed so elegantly for the occasion and even the doll's gown is decorated with drop pearls, perhaps a touch of artistic licence! About her neck a jewelled insignia on a chain bears the motto of the Lennox family: '*Pour Parvenir j'endure*'. Little Arabella had very much to endure, for she was close enough to the English throne to be continually the centre of intrigue. After a marriage forbidden by James I, her cousin, and an attempt to escape to the Continent, she was finally imprisoned in the Tower of London, where she died a hopeless lunatic at the age of forty. But in this moment of babyhood, she stands for ever with her precious doll before fate has caught up with her.

Arabella's doll is similar to that held by Marie von Sachsen and the same type of doll, with stiff ruffs and open gown over a conical farthingale, is represented in a little engraving [43] showing a market place in Holland in the sixteenth century, though the costumes, as may be expected, are not quite as luxurious. The open-air booth shows other toys: hobby horses and drums and trumpets for boys, besides warlike crossbows, wooden halberds and costumed soldiers.

The 1614 Bartholomew Fair, described in the play of that name by Ben Jonson, must have presented just such a scene, with the same sort of goods. As already mentioned, Bartholomew Fair, held at Smithfield in London, was one of the most famous and oldest established of open-air markets and it was attended by all sorts of showmen and pedlars who would gather there on 24 August. *Wit and Drollery* for 1682 shows that the Fair dolls were a byword in frippery:

43 Sixteenth-century Dutch market place doll and toy stall

> *Her petticoat of satin*
> *Her gown of crimson tabby,*
> *Laced up before and spangl'd o'er*
> *Just like a Bartholomew Baby.*

Some little woodcuts in Morley's *Memoirs of Bartholomew Fair* copied some remarkably informative scenes which had been made on the spot by a local artist about 1728 and were sold, reproduced on fans, at the Fair itself [44]. These scenes represent people indulging in all the fun of the fair: making free with mugs of gin, watching one of the licentious puppet shows, quizzing a peep-show, *The Siege of Gibraltar*, buying apples from the costermonger and even riding on the *Ups and Downs* – a primitive version of the Great Wheel with rotating carriages. At a little toy booth, a bonneted woman proffers a necklace to a gentleman, perhaps the children's father, while a small boy pickpocket slyly robs him. The children look very diminutive, out of proportion, almost like toys themselves. While the boy has acquired a wooden halberd, the girl is obviously taken up with the dressed dolls.

What was the connection between the dolls made in Nuremberg and those sold in London and Holland? In early times pedlars on foot and with packhorse must have taken cargoes to sell outside Germany and later consignments of toys may have travelled abroad with other sorts of goods. Although examples of dolls have not survived, it is interesting to find in customs' records that consignments were certainly arriving in England by the early sixteenth century. A small tax was levied on them and a study of early customs' indexes shows, besides an entertaining selection of goods which were handled on entry into London, an almost arbitrary method of taxation. A book of rates for 1550 mentions a set rate introduced for 'Babies and Puppets for Children the Groce, containing twelve dozen, thirteen shillings and fourpence and Babies Heads of Earth the dozen ten shillings'; it may be guessed that they came from Germany through the Low Countries, as later entries specified: 'Babies for children from

44 Bartholomew Fair stall about 1728. Note the child pickpocket

41

Germany brought with other toys such as wooden pipes, rattles and swords' (the very toys sold at the Dutch and London fairs).

There is no way of telling at what date such cargoes first began, but customs had been levied officially since the time of King John in the thirteenth century, and in 1671 Charles II created a customs board with fixed tables of rating and embargoes on certain goods. In 1725, Henry Crouch, one of his Majesty's Customs Officers, wrote a *Complete View of the British Customs containing Tables of Taxable Goods with the Rates of Duty*. It does not deal very fully with toys, which must have been a quite inconsiderable means of revenue, but in the few lines which do appear quite a lot is to be learnt. On 'Babies and Puppets for Children, the groce containing twelve dozen' now costing 17s 10d, the British payment on import was 3s 5d but for 'Strangers' (foreigners trading in England) it was 3s 7d, and more interesting still, there was a 'drawback' on such consignments if they were re-exported – a refund of tax of 3s. By this time there were outgoing cargoes to some of the British Colonies and it is possible that cheap wooden and clay dolls were brought here in bulk and sent out dressed. From the records, there appears to have been a continuous import of complete dolls and of dolls' earthenware heads from the sixteenth to the eighteenth century, though it is not known just what sort of dolls these were.

Over the next twenty years, the *Complete View* of Henry Crouch ran to five editions and it further stipulated certain taxes 'for all other Toys for Children, not anywhere particularly rated in the first column of Rates for every twenty shillings of their Value upon Oath' and added 'But *if painted, prohibited to be imported* as per painted Wares in the Index'. Under this category were listed 'Babies, jointed, the dozen (toys)' at two pounds on which the British tax was 11s 5d, the Strangers' tax 11s 11d and 10s 2d was drawback re-payable on re-export. The goods on the lengthy prohibited list were extraordinarily varied and included all sorts of things made in England which would have been adversely affected by foreign competition: garments made of wool, silk and ribbon; leather goods; metal tools such as scissors and razors, knives and needles; and even such oddments as 'tennis balls, chasing balls, dice and playing cards'. All such things, it was stated, 'MAY NOT BE IMPORTED by any persons to be uttered or sold in Great Britain upon forfeiture thereof except made or wrought in Ireland, or taken upon the seas without fraud or collusion or wreck'd'.

If we are to conclude from this that there was a well-established English industry producing painted, jointed wooden dolls which needed to be protected from foreign competition, it is a forceful argument in favour of the so-called 'Queen Anne' type of doll being quite genuinely of English workmanship (see chapter 6); this would also partly explain how these dolls vanished towards the end of the eighteenth century when the customs' laws were relaxed and under Pitt the Consolidation Act of 1787 codified a mass of previously scattered duties. By this time other types of foreign dolls were allowed to enter the country and supplant English dolls in popularity and in cheapness.

4

Fashion Dolls

With the possible exception of some of the early Japanese dolls, the most beautiful work in a technical sense is to be seen in the German lay-figures for the use of artists. These little models, usually of beech-wood, reproduced the proportions of the human figure in miniature and were made completely movable by the ball-and-socket joint which imitated the natural bone construction at shoulder, elbow, wrist, thigh, knee and ankle. The head swivelled at the neck and the waist was made to turn and bend, whilst at the same time the joints were put together stiffly enough to retain any position in which they were set. In some of the finest and largest even the fingers and toes were made with movable joints.

It is not known with whom the idea of such articulated dolls originated or where they first appeared, but they seem to have been in common use in Europe by the sixteenth century. Some of the finest were at one time actually ascribed to the master hand of the German artist Dürer, who is known to have used them, but it is now thought that they were produced by wood-carvers of the Regensburg-Salzburg school. A painting of about 1640 by the Dutch artist Adrien van Ostade in the Dresden Art Gallery shows the painter at work in his studio using one such figure, posed in a slightly running position, and supported on a wire stand [45]. The model could help the artist both in capturing a position of arrested action, like a slow-motion film halted at the dramatic moment, or, when it was dressed or draped, in demonstrating folds and shadows over the line of the limbs. It was essential that it should be accurate in size and proportion as it had to represent the lines of a human figure.

The two manikins, as they were called in Germany, seen in figure 46 are probably also of the eighteenth century and are perfectly articulated at shoulder, elbow, wrist, thigh, knee and ankle, though it is not possible to examine the wooden details as the clothes are in a very frail condition and are sewn on. Both dolls stand eleven inches high and have had lifelike features added in plaster. They must, when new, have presented a handsome appearance, but the remnants of flounced silk shirts and breeches fastened with a sash at the knee are sadly tattered, though obviously of fine quality material. One wears leather riding boots with spurs and the other has fancy bows on his shoes. They stand completely balanced and at one time both held swords in their hands. Perhaps they were originally posed for a duel, or they could have taken their place in one of those romantic pictures with landscapes peopled by characters in sumptuous dress which were influenced by stage sets of the period.

If the German wooden manikin was the lay-figure of the artist, in France the *mannequin* or *poupée modèle* was from very early times the servant of fashion and its ambassadress abroad. By the nineteenth century, the technical construction of the one and elegance of the other were to reach their culmination in combining to produce some of the most beautiful and expensive play-dolls ever made. As archivist to the Bibliothèque de l'Arsenal in Paris, Henry d'Allemagne was well placed to research into early records and he drew attention in his very beautiful book on toys, *Histoire des Jouets*, to some of the first

45 'The Artist at Work' by Adriaen van Ostade (about 1663) showing the use made of a wooden lay figure

46 Two eighteenth-century manikins with plaster features on ball-jointed bodies; 11 inches

references to the function of the doll in France. These made it clear that it was as couriers of fashion rather than as playthings that French dolls were first exported.

An early mention of such dolls in court records refers to those which were sent across to England from France by Queen Isabella of Bavaria in 1391 to show the court the new fashions which had been introduced when she married Charles VI. The dolls were made by the valet and embroiderer to the King, one Robert de Varennes, and he was paid 459 *livres* 16 *sous* 'for dolls and outfits of clothes for the English Queen so that she could wear them as well as see how they looked'.

A century later, in a eulogy written on the city of Paris by Antoine Asteran, there is a description of luxuries to be obtained in French shops, which included 'those presents so dear to the hearts of little girls: beautiful dolls, marvellously dressed'. This shows that play-dolls existed beside their elegant fashion sisters. Another shopkeeper, Raoulin de la Rue, recorded in 1455 the sale of 'a doll made in the fashion of a lady on horseback with a little footman', intended for Madeleine of France, the little daughter of Charles VII.

In 1497 Anne of Brittany had a large doll made for Queen Isabella of Spain; as its apparel was not at first thought to be splendid enough, it had to be reclothed in more beautiful clothes and the workman responsible was paid seven *livres* for making and remaking the doll. The secret papers of Henry II of France in 1550 mentioned a sum of nine *livres* four *sous* for six dolls to be sent from Paris to some 'ladies'. Our curiosity is immediately aroused: who were these ladies and for what reason were they sent the dolls, presumably portraying fashions? When the Duchess of Bavaria had a baby daughter in 1571, her friend Madame Claude de France, Duchess of Lorraine, wanted to send the little princess a gift which would also give the mother pleasure, and she chose to send a beautiful doll dressed in the latest Parisian style. The gift was so admired that an order was given from Munich for five or six more dolls 'not too large and as nicely dressed as can be found'.

Few of these early records ever give a description of the doll itself: they are concerned, naturally enough, only with the fashion and the magnificence of the clothes, or the cost of the work. But in his *Traité d'Architecture* (1567) Philibert Delorme gave at least some hint of their construction and described them as made of a kind of paper paste pressed into hollow moulds similar to the material used in eastern countries for making decorative things prettily, easily and cheaply.

By the eighteenth century there must have been considerable exchange of such fashion dolls between the capital cities of Europe and even of the United States of America. The *New England Journal* for 2 July 1773 carried the advertisement: 'To be seen at Mrs Hannah Teatts, Mantuamaker. At the head of Summer St Boston a baby dressed after the newest fashions of mantuas and nightgowns and everything belonging to a dress. Lately arrived on the *Captain White* from London.'

It seems that certain regulations were laid down for exporting fashion dolls from Paris; Furetière, in his *Roman Bourgeois*, explained that a bureau or registry was set up and various measures established for figures clothed in the latest fashions to be sent to the provinces, so that all might follow these models – just as workmen erecting a building are given a plan from which to work. Fashion dolls, it is clear, enjoyed special privileges, since Furetière wrote: 'By an act of gallantry which is worthy of being noted in the chronicles of history for the benefit of the ladies, the ministers of both courts granted a special pass to the *mannequin;* that pass was always respected and during times of greatest enmity experienced on both sides (between England and France notably) the *mannequin* was the one object which remained unmolested.'

A popular name for the fashion doll at this time, and typical of the affectation for neo-classical references in the arts, was 'Pandora'. The novelist Mlle de Scudéry (1607–1701) used to stand two dolls in her salon, the one a large pandora fully costumed and the other a small pandora in negligée. In Greek mythology Pandora was the woman made of clay by Vulcan on the order of Jupiter and endowed by the gods with every gift that might captivate the mind of man.

Later in the eighteenth century, Jean-Jacques Rousseau expostulated against the luxury and folly of expensive dolls and toys which were presented not to children but to adults. One example of such indulgence is given in a contemporary journal which relates that Louis xv made a present to the Infanta, who arrived from Spain to marry him, of a doll costing twenty thousand *livres*. This, it is true, was a royal present, but it is difficult to judge how a doll could be so expensive if she were not clad in clothes of gold thread and decorated with precious jewellery.

Apart from the vogue of the pandora or fashion doll, another craze which occupied eighteenth-century Paris for a time was the *pantin* doll. The *pantin* was an old toy with a new name which is thought to have derived from a little village on the outskirts of Paris which was famed for its dancing. The principle of the toy was originally German and was probably inspired by the wooden 'jumping jacks' which were strung and articulated in the same manner. In his journal for 1747, Barbier wrote the best account of these pasteboard dolls:

> At first the *Pantins* were designed for children's toys but after a time they were used to amuse the entire public. They were little figures made of pasteboard. All the parts of the body were separate and were attached by strings at the back of the figure. When these strings were pulled, the arms, legs and head were all joined together and the *Pantin* could be made to dance. Such little figures could represent Harlequin, Scaramouche, a simple pastrycook, a shepherd or shepherdess and so on and were consequently printed in all kinds of ways. Some of them indeed were painted by famous artists; among them Boucher, one of the most famous members of the Académie, and these sold for very large prices. The Duchesse de Chartres for instance paid 1500 livres for one of these *Pantins*.

The craze probably died out of its own accord, but it has been said that the law interfered and prohibited the use of *pantins* because

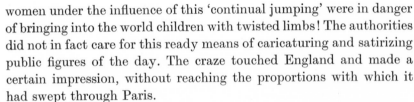

47 Harlequin 'pantin' made by a little midshipman, William Harvey West, in about 1802, and his portrait miniature as a child

women under the influence of this 'continual jumping' were in danger of bringing into the world children with twisted limbs! The authorities did not in fact care for this ready means of caricaturing and satirizing public figures of the day. The craze touched England and made a certain impression, without reaching the proportions with which it had swept through Paris.

One cardboard doll [47], showing a jointed Harlequin, has an interesting history as it has been passed down in the family of Miss Bourne of Redhill, England, since it was first made in 1802 by an ancestor of hers, a little midshipman called Richard West. It is an artless drawing, carefully made with the limbs attached by knotted thread and is perhaps a copy of some French *pantin*. The illustration includes a portrait of Richard West, who was only fifteen when he served at the Battle of Trafalgar in 1805 and was accidentally drowned two years later 'whilst in command of the Ship's boat'. Pastimes of this sort perhaps served to amuse these young sailors, hardly more than children, while on board ship.

The ballerina doll [48] in the collection of the Essex Institute, Mass., is not properly a *pantin* but is obviously meant to perform and has a cord passing through a central hole in her chest which could be used to make her skip and dance up and down and also move horizontally. She is said to have been made by Mrs Lucy W. Upton in about 1800 and is formed of two paper layers back and front, pasted to a central body of thicker paper or card. Her legs are jointed, the upper section hinged to the body with thread, with the lower section ending in the feet hinged to the upper one at the knee. Her arms are not jointed but permanently hold aloft a wreath made in one piece with them and decorated with flowers in blue, green and beige muslin. Over the card base, the doll's costume, which seems to be original, is made of pale blue muslin over a white satin petticoat. Her delicate features, with

48 Dancing ballerina marionette of paper with fabric costume, said to have been made about 1800 by Mrs Lucy W. Upton, Mass.

blue eyes and fair hair painted in water-colours, could be a child's work, but give more evidence of being a loving gift from a grown-up relative.

The custom of advertising current fashions by forwarding a little dressed doll was replaced to some extent in the last years of the eighteenth century by the use of hand-coloured fashion plates; there were very obvious advantages in a system by which a number of facsimiles could be distributed at one and the same time. Domestic or fashion magazines made their appearance both in England and on the Continent, such as *The Lady's Magazine or Entertaining Companion For the Fair Sex* (1770) or *The Lady's Monthly Museum, or Polite Repository of Amusement and Instruction, being an Assemblage of what can tend to please the Fancy, Instruct the Mind or Exalt the Character of the British Fair* (1798). Such magazines were a medley of town gossip and fashion notes and are a fascinating source of information on the period.

It is not known who first thought of cut-out paper sheets with changeable costumes, but they began about this time and indeed the earliest seem to have stepped straight from the pages of such magazines. They consist of an upright character in profile standing in a short shift with a selection of dresses which may be cut out and placed flat over the model. The German *Journal des Luxus und der Moden* referred in 1791 to such cut-outs as 'English Dolls'; German and French publishers were swift to pursue the novelty and reproduce sets of their own. If originally the cut-out paper doll sheets were a follow-on from more orthodox fashion sheets and were intended to give adults the opportunity of trying out different costumes, it is clear that the idea soon became incorporated in a plaything – just as juvenile drama and toy theatre evolved from early theatre characters issued as mementoes in the form of prints. It is true that, looking at a set such as *The Protean Figure* produced by S. and J. Fuller at the Temple of Fancy in Rathbone Place, London, we might suspect that such sets were published to catch an adult fancy. A complete set of

49 Protean Figure of Metamorphic Costumes *published by S. & J. Fuller, London 1810; 8¾ inches*

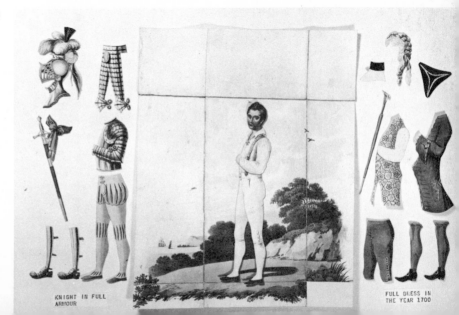

KNIGHT IN FULL ARMOUR

FULL DRESS IN THE YEAR 1700

the game originally sold at £1.1s. with ninety different parts of dress, comprising Walking Dress, Naval Uniform, Monk's Habit, Turkish Costume, Quaker's Habit, Mourning Suit, German Hussar, Full Dress in the year 1700, Knight in full armour, Officer's dress (Land Forces), Gentleman's Evening Costume, French Uniform (Imperial Guard); all these individual sets could be laid over the handsome male model, piece by piece, shoes overlapping stockings, coat overlapping waistcoat and hat over head. They did not actually attach in any way [49].

This seems almost to be a gift for a romantic young girl picturing her heart's delight, but S. and J. Fuller produced at about the same time a whole series of little books which were very popular and entirely for children. They included a moral story which was illustrated by some central character with additional dresses and changeable heads fitting into a slot in the body. One of the most popular, published in 1810, was *The History of Little Fanny* [50]. She has six different outfits which change according to the episode represented in the story. Other titles included *The History and Adventures of Little Henry, Ellen or the Naughty Girl Reclaimed, Phoebe the Cottage Maid, Hubert, the Cottage Boy*, most of which are comparatively rare and certainly not often found in the beautiful mint condition of the Worthing copy of *Fanny*. One of the rarest in the series commemorates the fame of 'Young Albert, the Roscius', a boy star of Drury Lane Theatre called William Betty, who is said to have earned a fortune of £34,000 or over $1000 in fifty-six consecutive nights of acting! Even down to the present day, 'doll-dressing' sets have remained popular, and current stars of television or film sometimes earn fame in just the same way as the popular hero of the 1800s.

The principle of the English toy-books was copied in the United

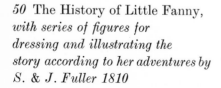

50 The History of Little Fanny, *with series of figures for dressing and illustrating the story according to her adventures by S. & J. Fuller 1810*

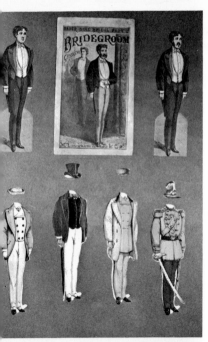

51 Bride and bridegroom and groomsman doll-dressing sets 7⁷/₈ inches; McLoughlin & Co., USA 1875

States of America. Herbert J. Hosmer Jr, of the John Greene Chandler Museum, South Lancaster, Mass., said that in Boston, Mass, in about 1812 J. Belcher published an edition of *The History and Adventures of Little Henry*, and a Boston edition of *Little Fanny* is recorded from the same period. The most famous *Little Fanny* was lithographed by John Greene Chandler and published by Crosby Nichols & Co. of Boston in 1854. Like the English version, it had a booklet with coloured figures to illustrate each episode, but these differed from the original and did not have quite the same moral flavour.

The firm of McLoughlin Brothers, who began issuing paper-dolls in about 1857, produced very popular sets at cheap rates. The subjects ranged from nursery-tale characters such as Red Riding Hood, Cinderella and Goody-Two-Shoes, to some of the celebrities of the day such as General Tom Thumb, the famous midget exhibited in the States by P. T. Barnum. Figure 51 shows a popular set of the Bride and Bridegroom.

An early nineteenth-century woodcut gives conclusive proof that not all the cut-out sets were played with by children. Four young ladies fashionably dressed and with the latest hair-style are absorbed in a little stand-up model on the table. Two of them are considering alternative dresses to fit over her – a genteel and innocent pastime which could be indulged by purchasing a set such as *La Poupée Modèle* published by R. Ackermann of 191 Regent St, London. As the name indicates, this boxed game was an imitation of the French fashion doll, a frail framework for dressing mounted on a wooden stand. The set consisted of a cut-out figure of a woman 8³/₄ inches high, in a petticoat, together with three day dresses and four head-dresses, each consisting of two cut-out etchings, one showing the front and one the back, pasted together at the sides and open at each end to allow the insertion of the figure [52].

When I asked a specialist antiquarian book dealer in Amsterdam whether he dealt in such things as these early doll-dressing sets and games he smiled sadly and replied: 'Of course ... but where are they?' Where indeed are they? They are the very ephemera of children's play and among the rarest of collectable objects, as well as being some of the most charming. Easily broken or torn, dirtied with use and often including tiny accessories which could too easily be lost or mislaid, it is not surprising that complete sets are difficult to find and come to hand only occasionally in a family where they have been passed down as a treasure from the past. How many copies exist, for instance, of such a set as the Empress Eugénie doll-dressing cut-out [53]?

One of the foremost producers of cut-out dolls and games in Germany at this period was the firm of G. W. Faber. The London Museum has a boxed set with the German title: *Die Garderobe des Kleinen Lieblings, Neue Mädchen Puppe* (literally, 'Little Darling's Wardrobe for a New Doll'), which has been memorably rendered into English on the lid as 'The Ward Room of the Little Fondling: a new girl-doll'. The doll fits into a grooved wooden stand and the various frocks slip over her head. They are not engraved both back and front; instead

52 A Poupée Modèle: *Doll-dressing set published by R. Ackermann 1830; 8¾ inches*

53 *below left: A doll-dressing set based on the costumes of Empress Eugénie published about 1860 by G. W. Faber with hand-coloured lithographs; 9 inches*

54 *below:* The Ranks of the Female Sex, *1850, representing an ascending social scale from Beggar, Shepherdess, Servant, Shopwoman, Citess (Citizeness?), Nun to Officer's Wife, Singer, Court Lady, Princess, Queen, Empress, with two stand-up figures*

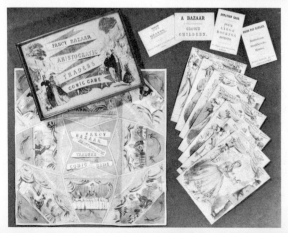

55 The Fancy Bazaar or Aristocratic Traders *published by E. and M. A. Ogilvy, London, 1865*

56 *opposite:* Interchangeable Features *or* The Joyful Young Girl in a 1000 Comic Attitudes, *published by G. W. Faber, 1860, coloured lithographs; 5¼ × 4¼ inches*

a flimsy plain backing is sufficient to hold the piece in position and it is only intended to be viewed from the front. A similar play-set, obviously from the same source, in the Victoria and Albert Museum collection (presented by the late Mr Raymond Barnett) is called 'The Ranks of the Female Sex' *(Stände des Weiblichen Geschlechtes)* and depicts various costumes from lowest to highest in the social scale [54].

'Interchangeable Features' was one of the popular varieties of this sort of game. The same German firm of G. W. Faber produced another fashion set which was mounted on wooden blocks out of which eight basic pictures could be composed. One of them, dating from 1860, shows a little girl clasping a very fashionably dressed doll of the period in her arms. 'The Joyful Young Girl in 1000 Comic Attitudes' [56], as it was called, was a delightful set with lithographs coloured by hand. Each picture was made up of six pieces in such a way that the figure synchronized and any head would fit any body or legs with comic effect and countless variations. Games like this had the virtue of being suitable for a solitary child, as were the cut-out dolls. A child could find quiet amusement for an hour with such a treasure, but a more uproarious form of entertainment was provided with a game such as 'The Fancy Bazaar, or Aristocratic Traders: [55] a round game for 8 Players' which was published in the 1860s by E. and M. A. Ogilvy in London. The game presents a wonderful picture of one of the social aspects of the age: the Charity Bazaar. A lithographed playing sheet, hand-coloured and showing various bazaar stalls selling fruit, grocery, drapery and toys is peopled by eight different 'Aristocratic Traders' – ladies of fashion pictured on cards, each of which represents one of the players, and fancifully named Baroness Goodchild, Lady Verysoft or Miss Silverstone, like characters from a Peacock novel. The game itself is a mild form of gambling and is played by turning up a little pack of cards which dictate who is buying or selling and how many counters must be forfeited to another stall or into a central pool. It ends when a card turns up naming a subject previously selected as the aim of this Charity Bazaar and the winner, one supposes, had some prize of sweets or a trinket.

There is a special magic for children in such characters. Many invent their own cut-outs from the pages of catalogues and fashion books. The designer Cecil Beaton confessed that his father ceased to bring in an evening paper because he found that his son was infatuated with the fashion plates of Bessie Ascough and would 'smear them with watercolours or oddly smelling silver and gold paints' – a pursuit which led his father to believe that 'the child was becoming peculiar'. Few children playing with or inventing fashion dolls are destined to become great designers themselves, but it is left to Cecil Beaton to bear testimony to the value of his child's play: 'My inward child's eye even as my adult vision always sought out the detail rather than the conception as a whole. A particular trimming on a dress seen in childhood could make a profound impression on me, and certain details have remained in my memory to this day with actual combinations of colour that have influenced my own creative work.'

57 Mechanical French wax devotional doll on couch

5

Crèche Dolls

Not everyone will agree that the Christmas crèche or *presepio* has a legitimate place in a collection of dolls, or in a book on the subject. Built with a wholly religious motive, it may be argued that such tableaux should remain in the Church to which they belong or as the centrepiece of a family Christmas. But if all works of art originally intended for a religious purpose were eliminated from museums it would mean the loss of much of the finest early painting, sculpture, textile and metal work. The greatest craftsmen in early Europe, in whatever fields their talents lay, were absorbed in producing work to decorate the great churches and buildings of religious orders and the makers of the first Christmas cribs were no exception. In examples of their work may be found the germ of skilful doll-making and puppet-making from various materials. They excelled at inventing new types of crib, and in so doing perfected fresh techniques of carving, modelling and dressing which later on were to be displayed in the production of fine play-dolls.

Mention of cribs is found very early in Christian history, but as Wilhelm Döderlein has pointed out in his book *Alte Krippen*, the term probably often refers to something quite different from what we now understand by it and meant merely a simple representation of the Christchild swaddled in the manger without attendant figures: a Bethlehem to which the villagers could flock in their own church and so learn the story of the first Christmas. For instance, early biographers of St Francis of Assisi recounted the story of the saint celebrating the feast of Christmas in a special way in 1223 at the little church of Greccio; he had a manger erected, an ox and ass led in, and a human baby to represent Jesus, to show the people who attended the celebration of the Mass how 'the Child in Bethlehem suffered for lack of the necessities for a new-born babe and how he lay in a manger between the Ox and the Ass'.

Indeed the earliest records of cribs come from Italy, and in 1478 the details of one commissioned for the family chapel of Jaconello Pepe in S. Giovanni a Carbonaro include the Child, the Virgin Mother with crown, St Joseph, eleven angels, Wise Men, Shepherds, sheep, dogs, oxen, ass and even trees. It was made by famous sculptor brothers, Pietro and Giovanni Alamanno, in Naples, and from this date onwards similar accounts show that the tradition became well-established and gradually spread to other countries of Europe.

Presepio making was an established trade in Naples by the end of the sixteenth century. Near the church of San Lorenzo, a street was called *Vico dei Figurari* after the *Figurari* or artists engaged in such work; whole families specialized in the art, with the womenfolk assisting in the sewing and embroidering of clothes for the little figures made by the men. Although wood was usually used for the limbs and bodies which were joined by wire bound with tow, the Neapolitans modelled the heads from terracotta, a hard un-glazed pottery of reddish brown colour which could be finely worked, baked, sized and finally finished with oil-colours which could well imitate sun-bronzed complexions. Figure 59 shows clearly how the head, neck and breast were made in one piece with holes at the base which could

*60 Street scene
from Neapolitan crib*

be used for joining to the body section. The eyes were usually inset glass and the clothes were made from materials and leather which faithfully reproduced the dress of the period. There was never any attempt to achieve historical exactitude and when Oriental figures were introduced they too wore contemporary, exotic dress. Animals too were made in terracotta but often their legs, horns and ears were reinforced with metal.

The simplicity of early groups soon gave way to increasing elaboration and the Holy Family with shepherds or Wise Men from the East gradually progressed to a literal interpretation of the Franciscan ideal with the whole world trooping into the humble stable of Bethlehem. Figure 60 shows part of a lively street scene where the silent adoration of the stable is replaced by the pulsating life of everyday: the butcher selling his wares and the beggars arguing. They are characters on a stage, gesticulating, laughing and grimacing. Indeed the power of the Neapolitan crib lay in its wonderful characterization, with the people, one feels sure, drawn from recognizable inhabitants of eighteenth-century Naples.

North of the Alps, the Bavarians and Austrians used the wood of the lime or linden for their carving, as did the inspired master craftsmen of the fifteenth and sixteenth centuries working on Gothic church statuary. Limbs were made to move either by wire or by ball-and-socket joints as in the artist's lay-figure, so that they could assume any position and be clad in real textile. Occasionally wax was used for the head and when the scale of the figures was very small, under five or six inches, they were sometimes carved from the solid wood and their clothes painted. Animals were usually made by this method, carved and coloured. An illusion of perspective could be given by large figures in the foreground and tiny figures for the distance.

The grandest compositions took many years to complete and went outside the subject of the holy birth to introduce other Biblical scenes such as the Flight into Egypt (with ample scope for beautiful animals); the Passion and Last Supper; the Crucifixion; the Boyhood of Christ in the carpenter's shop, or the Massacre of the Innocents. Specialist craftsmen, such as silversmiths or the makers of musical instruments or weapons, potters and glass-makers, were all able to contribute to the scenes with miniature wares. Whereas for some it was perhaps a personal act of worship it was for others merely a competitive test of skill and a remunerative occupation.

Figure 61 shows a Moorish king from an eighteenth-century Tyrolean group; the pose and carving are exquisite. He is about eighteen inches tall and is the work of an unknown carver. Here is all the charm of the Baroque with full panoply of ornament and embroidery and jewelled sword. He looks less like one of the Wise Men of old than the pampered black page of an eighteenth-century lady of fashion.

61 Moorish King:
eighteenth-century Tyrolean
wood-carving; 18 inches

62 opposite: Crib with wax-
modelled figures
from northern Tyrol, 1750

Figure 62 also comes from northern Tyrol and was made about 1750
for the 'Regelhaus der Servitinnen' at Innsbruck. The little figures
are made with wax heads, applied blobs of black wax serving as eyes,
and their arms and legs are carved from wood. The nuns of the order
made their clothing and they have been rearranged against a 'town
of Bethlehem' from a different Tyrolean set. The lustrous angels look
for all the world like the fairy queen of pantomime, and the Virgin
Mary, despite her traditional robes of red gown and blue cloak, bears
a family resemblance to some of the little ladies who inhabit eighteenth-century dolls' houses and is even about the same size: eight
inches.

The Sicilian crib-makers used an entirely different technique. The
figures tend to be smaller with heads carved from wood or modelled
from wax, but the bodies are made from quite crudely worked pieces
of wood fastened together and hidden by the outer clothing. This
clothing was applied by a method requiring great skill and artistry.
Pieces of cloth were dipped in a sort of size or glue-water and while
still wet were laid over the figure and arranged in the necessary folds.
When dry the material was overpainted and provided very natural
looking drapery. The animals were made in a similar fashion with
horns and tails of leather added afterwards. For the surrounding
scenery, buildings were simply fashioned from cork. Giovanni Matera
(1653–1718), one of the great masters of this technique, worked at
Trapani and figure 63 shows a typical scene made by him. The heads
are carved from wood and their expressions are very beautiful and
spiritual.

In 1839, a Mr Paxton, travelling with the Duke of Devonshire in

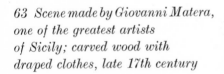

63 Scene made by Giovanni Matera,
one of the greatest artists
of Sicily; carved wood with
draped clothes, late 17th century

64 A little boy in Bavarian clothes from a puppet crib, with a removable head for change of mood; end of 18th century; 18 inches

Italy, wrote home giving an acount of a *presepio* he had seen in Rome and his views on 'this nonsense at Christmas':

> First of all there was a model of a stable on a tolerably large scale, in which were placed two small models of oxen lying down quietly, while Our Saviour is represented by a small doll lying quietly in the Manger wrapped in a little new hay. Close to the manger stands the Virgin Mother looking very complacently at the little fellow, while St. Joseph her husband stands opposite looking as if the child before him is a bastard. At a little distance stand the wise men from the East and at a greater distance are the shepherds in their caves singing 'O be joyful'. In some of the churches the figures are made as large as life, but when this is the case there are only three of them, viz. Jesus, Mary, Joseph. The humbug practised on the poor deluded wretches here is horrifying. I have seen in Rome into the inside of one hundred and forty churches.

In the last sentence one detects the unwilling sightseer, but the prejudices of Mr Paxton, like the misanthropy of Scrooge, are merely ghosts of Christmas past and the crib became a Christmas symbol in Christian countries throughout the world, although the early art was often translated into cheap clay or paper cut-outs.

Children also enjoyed puppet shows of the Christmas crib, when the Wise Men and the adoring shepherds could actually move across the stage and Mary could raise her baby in her arms. Figure 64 shows an unusual character from a puppet crib: a little boy in Bavarian dress with a replaceable head which can show him laughing or crying and is reminiscent of a doll with the same aptitude which later became very popular [203]. He measures about eighteen inches and dates from the end of the eighteenth century.

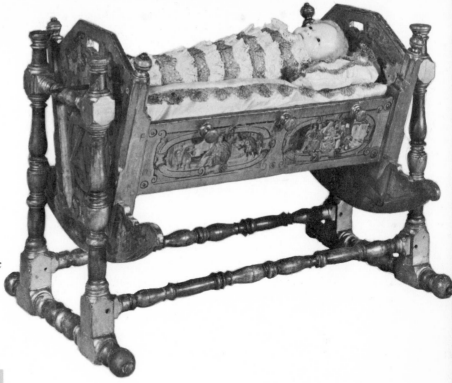

65 *Early wooden cradle with painted scenes on panels, 1585, with eighteenth-century wax doll*

66 *The 'Good Shepherd' doll. Wax with lambswool hair and inset glass eyes, from Grossigmain, South Germany; 18 inches*

Sometimes the birth of Christ is commemorated in the churches or monasteries of southern Germany by a model cradle and swaddled baby or even by a shrine of the Christchild enclosed in a glass case. Figure 65 shows a very beautiful early wooden cradle carved and gilded, with scenes painted on the side panels of the Adoration of the Shepherds, the Three Kings and the Circumcision. It bears the date 1585 and has protruding studs on each side by which the child would have been laced in, in the German fashion. The doll in the photograph is eighteenth-century and a replacement of the original. He is gently smiling with dark inset eyes in the finely moulded wax face and curly lamb's wool hair. German babies were customarily wrapped in a sort of thin, long, narrow pillow which was made to meet completely round them and to tuck up over their feet and reach to their chin; it was bound in place with wide ribbon tied in bows over their feet, middle and chest, but the little Christchild here has only simulated swaddling clothes made of frills of lace and gold brocade and he rests on a rich pillow and coverlet. It is difficult not to think of such figures as true dolls, for they are beautifully made and would be instantly acceptable to a little girl, with their sweet, babyish looks. But the modelling of the hands with fingers uplifted in blessing shows that such dolls were initially meant for the image of the Christchild. Figure 66, Jesus as the Good Shepherd, is a very similar eighteenth-century wax doll with dark glass eyes and lamb's wool hair, but he also shows little pearly teeth in his slightly opened mouth. He comes from Grossigmain, a small village in southern Germany. Little wax dolls, frail in type and sometimes 'home-made', were generally used in Catholic countries either for votive purposes or as commemoratives of Christian festivals.

Figure 57 shows a mechanized devotional toy: a girl with fair hair resting on a couch and surrounded by sprays of shrubs and flowers that certainly never grew in any earthly region, as the prettiest of them are made of minute blown glass balls painted brilliant green. In this toy there is a little lever beneath the wooden base of the case which works the figure. The child raises her arms and opens her eyes devoutly to Heaven. It is a pretty group, though the sentiment may seem cloying to us. It could perhaps have been given on the occasion of a christening, when it was often the custom to present one of the simpler Infant Jesus type of wax dolls. The workmanship is certainly French. There were several Parisian merchants of this period who advertised wax Infant Jesus dolls. Sometimes these tiny dolls must have been used in the true sense of a play-doll, for they would have made enchanting babies to decorate and fit into a homemade cradle, however frail and susceptible they were to damage and heat. Usually, however, they were used with a religious motive or with the underlying significance of a blessing asked for or received. The Worthing Museum Westwood baby doll [67] has been handed down within the family just as it was originally given by Thomas Westwood to his wife Eliza on 2 January 1844. The letter with it from a grand-daughter states that Thomas and Eliza had come to the conclusion that they would never have children of their own, but eventually there were seventeen children of the marriage, so it seems that their prayers

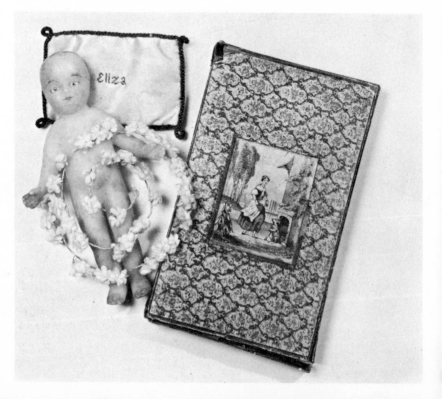

67 The Westwood baby doll with its original box; French; 1844; 4 inches

were answered! The tiny figure has inset blue glass eyes and is preserved in the original Parisian box with the little curl of artificial white flowers which first decorated it and the pillow embroidered in minute cross-stitch 'Eliza'.

Small wax dolls were also introduced in the second half of the nineteenth century as cherubic decorations for the Christmas tree. Lady Dorothy Nevill wrote in one of her reminiscences: 'What is known as the "old-fashioned" Christmas is really a modern festival. It was invented by Washington Irving and afterwards rehashed by Dickens. There is very little mention of Christmas day in old memoirs and going further back, Pepys merely touches upon it.' But for once her prodigious memory seems to be at fault for the decorated live fir tree was introduced into England during the early Victorian period by the Queen's consort Prince Albert. It was a German custom and he brought it from his native land.

A really pretentious Christmas decoration is shown in the mechanical wax angel from the Museum of Childhood, Edinburgh [68]. Wound up, this doll renders 'Stille Nacht, Heilige Nacht' and slowly flaps her white wings, which seem to have been skilfully built up from spotless duck or chicken feathers. The whole doll measures fifteen inches and she is of very pink wax over a papier mâché base. Her pale blue frock is trimmed with swansdown and she holds a little golden trumpet. She was made to be suspended by her back and the wings, worked by wires leading through a hole between her shoulder blades, caused her to revolve. Mechanical angels seem to spell the beginning of the commercialization of Christmas and the fairy doll with wand became the Christmas tree version of the angel and star of the early cribs.

68 German mechanical angel with feather wings and trumpet; 15 inches

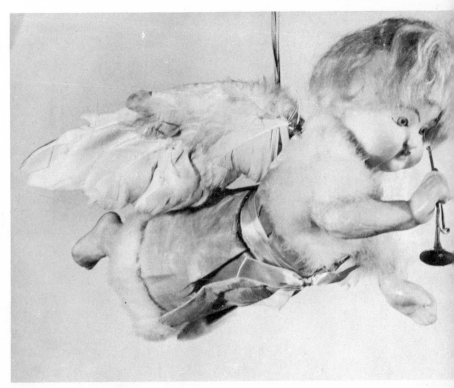

6

Wooden and Composition Dolls

As a medium for sculpture wood is wonderfully suitable for conveying the human face and it acquires with age a softness and patina which enhance the original line. Certain types are particularly suitable for doll-making, strong and durable so that they can be hand-carved or turned by machinery and bored for stringing or dowelling. Best of all, the finished work can convey to us accurately the original image which its maker had in mind.

One of the most sought-after types of wooden doll is that which has been popularly called the 'Queen Anne' or which in the United States is sometimes given the unwieldy but more accurate title of the 'Mary-Anne-Georgian'. A few examples do in fact precede the period of Queen Anne (who ruled in 1702–14) and very many were produced later, extending roughly to the first years of the nineteenth century. She is one of the enigmas of the doll world. Usually her manufacture is attributed to England, where, it is true, more examples have come to light than on the Continent of Europe, and it is evident that early settlers from England also introduced them to the United States. Some of these early jointed wooden dolls appear to have been made in an individual style with a quite unique cast of feature, but among the majority there is a traceable relationship which indicates that they were the work of a school of carving or turning, a district or group of people who worked in a continuing tradition and pattern and had similar quirks of style. So far it has not been possible to discover just who these people were or where they worked, but one day some positive piece of evidence may come to light.

The earliest type had a turned body, hand-carved features with paint and gesso finish and painted eyes. The head was rather large for the body and the cut-fingered hands rather small [69]. The most fascinating group were those following the Letitia Penn pattern, with inset eyes of dark enamelled ceramic and 'stitched' eyebrows and eyelashes; the convention was to indicate hairs by little black painted rows of 'stitches'. The doll's head and body were originally turned from one piece of wood to form a skittle shape and then the features were hand-carved and the jointed legs added in grooves cut in the base of the torso. Arms were most often attached by means of leather or cloth hinges tacked to the shoulder. Such dolls were made to be dressed and the details of head and bust were finely executed, while the remainder of the body was structurally simple and not finished off. Sometimes the high breast outline was beautifully indicated to conform with the low-cut neckline of the period.

A good example, typical of the excellent workmanship which flourished about the middle of the eighteenth century, is shown in the collection of the Museum of Childhood, Edinburgh [74]. It is a doll which has passed down in one famous family – as with so many of these fine dolls she can boast a pedigree. She portrays a type of beauty favoured at the period, with high forehead, exposed by plucking or shaving the front hair, and chubby full cheeks. Sometimes ladies of fashion resorted to artificial means to produce this fullness of face: little discs or balls were held in the mouth which went by the name of 'plumpers', but this is a doll which needs no such aid. Her mouth is

69 Wooden doll with leading strings; about 1710; 15 inches

carved as well as painted and her eyes are set in deep recesses. Her hair, long black curling locks of coarse quality, is mounted on a black material cap which is hidden by her little embroidered bonnet. She wears no drawers, which, in fact, were a rare accessory, but her pink silk stockings are tied with pink ribbon bows and she has soft shoes with flaps exquisitely made of blue silk with a soft kid sole and decorated with pink braid lacing. Her foundation garment is a smock or chemise of fine white linen which shows in a frill at her neckline and cuffs, while over it she wears a cream-coloured slip of coarse material bound with brilliant yellow, and a stiff pink underskirt which has been most beautifully embroidered in a patterned quilting stitch. A tiny pocket of fancy cretonne bound in green is tied to her waist along with a little hard-padded pin cushion; both of them go over her petticoat but beneath her frock. The very full-skirted dress of green silk is gathered at her waist and has long leading strings. A stiff corselet laced at the back is made of card and canvas with tabs at the bottom edge like a swallow-tail butterfly. A fine lawn apron or 'pinner' protects the gown, reaching to the bottom hem. It is obvious that hardly an item of her dress is missing or altered, and this doll and others of her period who have survived in such perfection are a wonderful guide to costume historians and sometimes illustrate an article of clothing of which an adult example has not survived.

The dolls of this type vary in size from over twenty inches to as small as six inches. Just as it is not known when the type originated or where, it is not clear why it fell from popularity. Whether it was usurped by increasing production of other more sophisticated types of doll in wax and papier mâché, or whether those who made the wooden babies ceased their business can only be conjectured. The tax on toys may also have played some part (see page 42). Their strongest claim to being English dolls is perhaps their style of beauty, which varies mysteriously from the arch, wanton expression of a wench from *Tom Jones* to the superior look of high-born nobility reminiscent of some portrait in an English Stately Home! Perhaps it was dolls of this very type which were sold at the London fair as Bartholomew Babies (see chapter 3). A comparison between the early and later types shows that the workmanship seemed to deteriorate; faces became less realistic and were carved with less care, and some of the later ones were made with a moulded plaster face on a wooden base – in an effort no doubt to reproduce them more quickly and cheaply for a growing demand.

Plate 75 is a portrait of an interesting legend: a doll reputed to be the handiwork of one Madame Bourget, a French milliner who was living and working in England at the end of the eighteenth century, dressing historical character dolls in beautifully embroidered gowns. Such dolls were said to have enjoyed a great vogue with fashionable ladies, who included them in their entourage along with pampered lap dogs and black boy servants. She returned to her native country in 1792, having made a fortune. So runs the story, but I have found no contemporary account to corroborate it, and a thorough investigation has proved that dolls such as this one (and a group in the Victoria

70 Wooden doll with masculine cast of features, dressed as a man in the fashion of 1760; 18 inches; the lace jabot is later addition

71 Hand-carved wooden doll, 1763,
32 inches

72 Nuremberg wooden doll,
ball-jointed and made of spruce;
19th century; 34 inches

73 *1830 period wooden doll with carved head, kid body; 34 inches. Note the curiously thickened neck — sometimes thought to represent a glandular affliction due to lack of iodine and occurring in some Southern German districts at the period*

74 *opposite: Wooden doll of about 1750*

75 opposite: 'Madame Bourget'
type doll, twentieth-century;
32 inches

and Albert Museum, London, which has long puzzled researchers and is said to represent Lady Teazle, Mrs Candour, Lady Sneerwell) were in fact made during the last fifty years, though not with intent to deceive. A curious legend has grown up around them and they have been installed in various museums as 'antiques'. They are certainly unlike any other eighteenth-century doll with their tall stature and the almost chinless wooden face with inserted blue glass eyes, rather bulbous and giving an impression of complete vacuousness.

One of the most difficult problems in writing a history of dolls lies in providing a sequence where there is no obvious connection. Contemporary with, but, so far as is known, unassociated with the making of these jointed English dolls of the 'Queen Anne' type were various famous doll-making centres in Germany. As we have seen, wooden dolls have been made in Bavaria since very early times and wood-carving is as traditional in toy-making as in most other branches of the decorative arts: house-building, church-decorating, furniture-making, as well as sculpture. There was not one school of carving but many, and the individuality which gave character to the German and Austrian puppet theatre evinced itself also in wooden doll heads. Many of the best wooden dolls never left Germany and it is still necessary to visit German museums to see them.

The oldest doll in the Focke Museum at Bremen which can be identified with certainty dates from 1763, when she was given to a daughter of Von Post, then Burgomaster of Bremen. She is hand-carved from wood and represents a person of some quality in a costume of the period with a velvet gown trimmed with fur and the *perlbintze* bonnet ornamented with beads of jet which at that time was the traditional headgear for a married woman. Note the beautifully carved and life-like hands [71]. This is also characteristic of another beautifully fashioned ball-jointed doll belonging to the Nuremberg Museum, unusually fine in profile as well as full face [72]. Her feet are carved like a pixie with pointed turned-up toes and red painted slippers; she is made of spruce wood and very probably represents Grodenthal work. The expression on her face, like that of one of the saints in the local churches, is sweet and elusive with a half-smile on her lips. The German carver craftsman could achieve with his wood what another artist attempted with paint, and with his knife cajole the very spirit from his wood.

Figure 73, also in the Nuremberg Museum, is a very large doll with wooden head and bust, though even larger sizes were made. She stands thirty-four inches high and though she came from Leipzig is thought to have been carved in Nuremberg with her immaculately detailed hair plaited round her ears (the tips of which can just be seen – a style popularized in England by Queen Victoria).

Few individual carvers are known, though occasionally their fame has lingered on and a few examples of their work have been retained in some local museums. For instance, at Eisenerz in the north of the Steiermark, a few dolls are still preserved which were made by the noted doll-maker and puppet-carver Matthias Tendler [77]. Tendler, who came originally from the Mürztal, made jointed dolls with marionette

76 Carved wooden doll with
shaped hips for costuming, 1805

77 Group of dolls and puppets carved by Matthias Tendler, Steiermark. The largest doll is about 2 ft 3 inches

78 Grodenthal work showing a doll bust and a group of puppet heads; early 19th century

mechanisms besides very complicated automata and at the time of the Congress of Vienna performed before the King and other important persons. He was so well known that he figured in Theodor Storm's novel *Pole Poppenspeler*. The trade of carving was carried on in his family by Tendler's sons, grandson and great grandson. In the group shown are acrobats and a large figure in the centre which is said once to have walked a tightrope, since a daguerrotype exists portraying the actual performance.

Puppet-making and doll-making were often closely allied in German and Austrian centres and the marionette show was, and still is, a popular and valued tradition. Figure 78 shows a group of puppet heads and a doll head made in the Grodenthal and exhibited in the Tyrol Museum at Innsbruck. It is interesting to compare them with [72] and to see how the tenderly realistic face of the earlier doll has become conventionalized, with the features drawn up smaller towards the centre of the face and the hair signified in an arbitrary parted fashion. This became the typical 'peg-doll' look and was accompanied by an odd elongation of the body which produced rather spidery looking wooden jointed dolls. Figure 79 shows an early example, from about 1820, dressed as a Quaker in actual remnants of Quaker materials: drab brown and homespun linen with sleeve cuffs and apron and deep collar over a full frock. The hands and feet have become almost rudimentary, though fingers are indicated and the shoes are dipped in coloured paint.

The 'Dutch' doll was in its origin not Dutch, nor German as a corruption of '*Deutsch*', but Austrian, and came from a small district in the Dolomites which has now passed into Italian hands. A valuable first-hand account of the Groden valley toy industry was given by Margaret Howitt in 1875 in a magazine published in England called the *Leisure Hour*. Travelling with a friend, she got into conversation with an old mountain guide, who told them of a wealthy village where the people could 'always eat meat' and afford to 'drink coffee cup by cup'. These people earned their money by 'painting *oggetti*' – a dialect word meaning 'dolls' – which puzzled the writer until she and her friend visited St Ulrich, the principal village of the Grodenthal and the centre of a toy industry which had been there since the early eighteenth century. A parish priest called Dom Josef Vian had recorded much of the early history of this district and it was possible for them to piece together the progress of the toy industry. High in the Alps – a district now famous for its winter sports holidays – the Groden valley was shut off without easy access to the outside world until in 1856 a carriage road was built linking St Ulrich with Waldbrück station. The people themselves were something of a mystery and seem to be of Italian, possibly Roman or Etruscan, origin. Perhaps their tall, strong stature accounted for the long-limbed figures of their dolls.

Certainly wood carving was an early tradition in the district, as

79 *Grodenthal doll dressed as a Quaker maid, about 1820; 22 inches*

can be seen in the beautiful carving in the church of St Anthony begun as long ago as 1682. The actual direction towards toy-making seems to have started in about 1703 when a carver called Johann Demetz became famous for carved frames made of the Siberian pine *Pinus cembra*, as well as figures of saints and crucifixes and all sorts of dolls for children. These carved goods were distributed by peddling the loads of wares southwards into Italy or north into Bavaria and new ideas were introduced from existing centres of carving such as Berchtesgaden or Oberammergau. Some local carvers set up outside the district and established Grödner methods in Italy and the Tyrol. The Dirschinger, a fast brook which runs through the valley, was harnessed to provide power to work the lathes of turners and, at the time when Margaret Howitt was there, not only dolls but various sorts of animal toys were made. An old woman fashioned animals from moist blocks of ashwood and an old man was hand-carving them from pear-wood, which is nearly as hard as boxwood. Strips of leather to which sand was stuck were used as pliable abrasives to smooth down the figures. In 1875 it was not usual for men both to make and market their own goods by going abroad; local dealers would collect their output and organize the foreign trade. One of the most famous and eminent of these dealers was Johann Baptista Purger and large warehouses owned by him were filled with piled-up bins of toys and dolls for distribution. Purger was recorded as displaying carved lay-figures in all sizes and made of pine, lime and maple at the 1851 Exhibition in London. He won awards at Exhibitions in Vienna in 1873 and Paris in 1879.

Many of the wooden toys, particularly carved animals, remained in white wood, but the dolls were thought to be more attractive with painted features, and sometimes with little yellow combs in their hair. They provided piece-work for most of the local people, especially in the winter when thick snow prevented other employment. The whole family would sit around the *panuc* or low table busy toy-making. It is ironic to realize that some of these very humble jointed wooden dolls from the cottage industry of St Ulrich found their way to Kensington Palace to be dressed by the infant hands of Queen Victoria [115]. A true rags to riches romance!

By the end of the nineteenth century the type had deteriorated in style and finish and the rather bullet-headed 'Dutch' doll, strongly built, with bold features and conventional black hair and red cheek blobs, had replaced the more delicate, sloping-shouldered outline of the earlier type. These Dutch dolls are familiar from many nursery stories. They were turned out in their thousands and the type proved a popular character for illustration in classic stories, such as the rhymed stories of the Upton Golliwogg books (see chapter 18), as well as in lesser works. They were easy to draw in many postures, like 'pin-men', and hardly beyond even the most limited artist. They were invaluable subjects for dressing up and the smallest were used for peopling countless homemade shops, schools and dolls' houses.

Perhaps the oddest rôle that a Dutch doll was ever asked to play was as evidence in a murder trial [80]. In the newspaper report of this

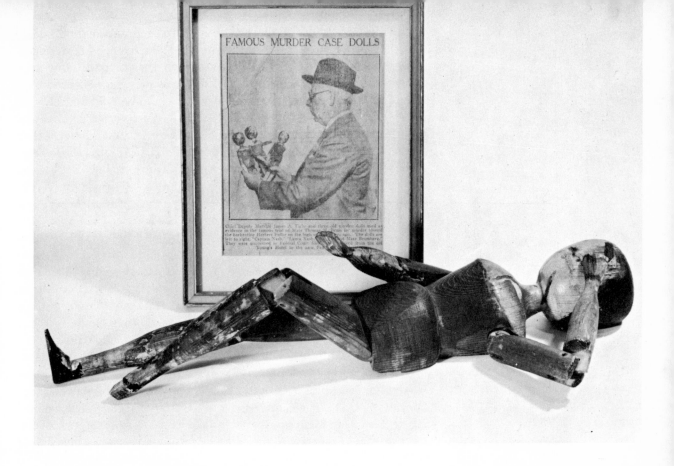

FAMOUS MURDER CASE DOLLS

80 A newspaper photograph of Chief Deputy Marshal James A. Tighe holding three murder trial dolls, and one of the actual dolls used in evidence with wounds marked in red paint, 1896

occasion, Chief Deputy James A. Tighe is shown holding three dolls which were uncovered in Federal Court Files at Boston, Massachusetts, in 1937 when they were being removed from Young's Hotel to new federal business premises. The recumbent doll shown was one of the three used to demonstrate to the Court the nature of the injuries which had caused the death of three victims of a seaman called Thomas Bram. In 1896 he was serving as first mate on the American barkentine *Herbert Fuller* and, driven insane by his love for the Captain's wife, Laura, murdered her and her husband and the second mate. The doll in the Edinburgh collection, given by Miss Ruth Cannon of New York, represents Bromberg, the second mate, and shows vivid red gashes at his head, throat and shoulders. Bram's defence was that the three victims had killed themselves, but the dolls proved that this was impossible because of the position of their wounds. Though sentenced to life imprisonment, Thomas Bram was later granted a pardon by President Taft. The dolls survive to illustrate this grisly tragedy and also demonstrate how excellently this type of doll was turned and jointed.

Some of the fine carved wooden heads made by hand in Germany were later obviously used as models for papier mâché heads and in a photograph it is not always easy to recognize the material of a modish painted head; but if we examine such dolls, the knife cut is clear and decisive in wooden heads while in reproduction, however painstaking, the impression is slightly blurred with a softening of the detail which marks the essential difference between a sharply gouged-out mark and the pressed-in hollow of 'composition'. Papier mâché presented a simply made plastic material and was the forerunner of other substances for mass-produced dolls. All that was necessary was the base or bulk material of soaked paper to which could be added a thickening and hardening agent and an adhesive. Recipes varied, but even in the 1920s a commercial formula listed the quite unsophisticated ingredients of wet paper pulp, dry plaster of Paris and hot glue *(Henley's Formulas, Recipes and Processes)*; this mixture was guaranteed to set as hard as wood within three hours, without cracking on the surface, and was capable of being coated with a wax surface or painted. The simplicity of mixing and of moulding was indeed the great advantage of papier mâché over other methods of doll-making. Even quite small children can master the technique. During the Second World War, when toys were very much at a premium in England, classes of five- to seven-year-olds made excellent puppets. It is true that their features were rather rugged and luridly coloured, but for young children this added to their attraction and they gave enormous satisfaction when they actually took the stage and came alive.

The method differs hardly at all from the making of papier mâché masks and heads three hundred years ago, if we can judge from an illustration in a Trades Book by Christopher Weigel printed in Regensburg in 1698 [81]. The engraving shows a family hard at work producing articles from *Pappenseuch* or soaked paper. A wooden tub of the mixture stands on the right with a wooden shovel. A woman is lifting a hollow mask off the mould or cast on a trestle in the foreground. It is interesting to see that the special feature of this bench, with a raised ledge all round it, is a hole with a spout at the end to drain away surplus moisture into an earthenware pot. Behind her, a man is painting on the features. Some of the finished work looks like doll heads of different sizes and other rather grotesque masks either for carnival use or puppetry. The curious animal swinging from the chain is probably the owner's shop-sign, and when this print was published his workshop was no doubt easily recognized.

Dolls of plaster of Paris (or 'alabaster' as it was more generally called at that time) were certainly on sale in eighteenth-century England and were most probably made in that country as the powder was mined there. In a little manuscript book of 1789, which was written by a girl of nineteen, Dorothea Herbert, one of the liveliest passages recalls an episode of her childhood. She was the eldest of an Irish family of nine children, and in 1777 she was taken on a trip to Bristol, accompanying her mother, who had been 'sent to drink the Bristol waters' for her health. When they returned, Dorothea brought presents for her younger brothers and sisters, and comments:

We had now another Addition to the Family which afforded the young folks much amusement – This was a large Alabaster doll I brought over. We christen'd her Miss Watts after one of the beautiful Miss Watts of Pill [a neighbouring village]. Mrs. Jephson sold us a curious little horse called Roebuck, no bigger than a large Dog

81 Pulp-doll makers from a copper plate by Christopher Weigel in a book of trades, 1698, Regensburg

82 *Costing but a few pence at bazaar or fair, cheap composition dolls were popular for 'dressing-up': two cadets in uniform, c. 1850; German; 5 and 6 inches*

83 *Papier mâché boy dressed in regional dress with* Lederhosen, *1900; 12 inches*

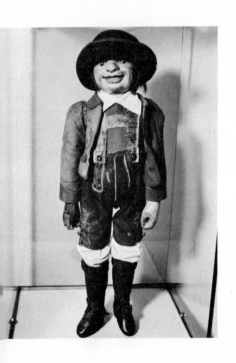

and between Roebuck and Miss Watts, the Jephsons and Miss Carshore, we passed our time most Enchantingly. Sometimes indeed we had bloody Battles about them – which brought on a general Flogging bout from our respective Mothers.

The Jephsons and Miss Carshore were other children and the whole bunch of them seem to have been as unruly and adventurous as they come. Their home was by that most romantic of lakes, Killarney, in Southern Ireland and their life was in a sense isolated from the rest of the world at that time: 'There were six or seven of us almost always in Mischief,' wrote Dorothea. 'Tom invented Pop Guns that often blinded us – Fanny the art of dyeng by which we compleatly spoiled a set of new scarlet Stuff Gowns we had just got. Otway and I were great Gardeners.' On one occasion they managed to replant a bed of laurels in the attic, 'having previously carried up large heaps of Earth in our Bibs and an old Backgammon box'. As they had torn up the floorboards to build the garden 'the whole Lobby Ceiling afterwards came down'! In the light of such exploits it is frustrating that no account is given of the games they devised for 'Miss Watts' and that no sketch of the doll appears among the water-colours illustrating the MS, which is today in the possession of descendants, the Mandeville family of Clonmel, Eire.

'Miss Watts' was obviously a fashionable-looking doll with adult features, but she was bought as a play-doll. The same must have been true of some of the handsome dolls produced in the first half of the nineteenth century with heads made of papier mâché or composition in place of brittle plaster, which had now assumed the subsidiary role of cast-making. The term 'milliner's model', or in French *modiste*, was given to many of these model dolls with coiffeured heads because they were admirably suited to dressing up in clothes illustrating the fashion of the day. The style of their hair, which was moulded in one with the head and bust, was not always so up-to-date since moulds were used again and again. The milliner's model gives an interesting three-dimensional representation of the little figures which pose so beautifully in etchings and engravings, coloured by hand, in fashion plates of the period, in some of the European periodicals for ladies.

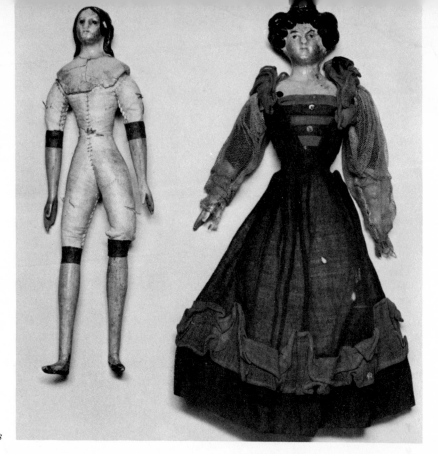

84 Sonneberg dolls of 1840/50
with leather bodies
and papier mâché modelled heads

Some of these dolls were no doubt used to illustrate current fashions by sending them abroad or exhibiting them in shop windows, but they survive in such numbers that it is obvious that they were also sold as toys. Even those made as fashion mannequins would of course have appealed to a child as coveted playthings if they fell into her hands later. Figure 84 shows an unclothed example and a shop-dressed model of the 1830s. The papier mâché head and yolk are fitted to a hard stuffed, hand-stitched kid body. The joint of the wooden legs and arms is neatened with dark blue tape binding on the torso. Such dolls were made in various sizes from six inches to two feet tall and are known to have been made at Sonneberg.

Foremost among the makers of German papier mâché heads was Adolf Fleischmann of Sonneberg. To display his prowess he exhibited a tableau of Gulliver taken captive by the Lilliputians for the 1844 Exhibition in Berlin and later repeated this *pièce de résistance* for the Great Exhibition in London in 1851 at the Crystal Palace, where it was much marvelled at and won him a medal. An example of the tableau is preserved in the Sonneberg Museum and shows little characters modelled from papier mâché and plaster grouped about a huge, realistic, recumbent Gulliver. Adolf Fleischmann was said to be producing as many as 360,000 doll heads a year in 1844 and the firm continued with mounting success throughout the century.

Cuno and Otto Dressel were another famous and long established Sonneberg firm specializing in the making of fine papier mâché dolls; they are the oldest doll firm for which records have been discovered, according to Elizabeth Coleman in *Dolls, Makers and Marks*, and were founded in 1700. Indeed this was a great centre for making all sorts of dolls and when the London toy-seller Cremer visited the town in 1875, he wrote that there was 'a most active manufacture going on of the larger pasteboard and papier mâché toys' and that 'Schools of Design' had been opened for increasing the modelling and designing 'fraternity'. 'The man who first takes up the task,' he wrote, 'requires little stock in trade – brains and clay.'

The method at that time was simple and, as it were, hand-done. Once a head had been modelled in clay and set hard, a separate master cast was made of the front and the back. A chalk line was drawn round the head, dividing it evenly in two. Then the head was placed face uppermost in a box of wet clay and thrust down to the halfway line. Liquid sulphur, which was usually used in Germany in preference to plaster of Paris, was poured into the box to cover the face completely. When cold and set, the box was turned over, the clay removed from the back half of the head and sulphur poured in to make a second cast. In this way two exactly corresponding halves were made; the prepared papier mâché dough was then cut into suitable squares and thrust into each mould; it was tooled by hand to make sure it took up the impression perfectly and was trimmed at the edge of the mould just like pie-crust. When both halves were dried and set they were smoothed off and stuck together to form a complete doll head. From this a circle was cut out with a sharp knife in the crown and holes were made for the eyes. When glass eyes had been stuck in with plaster, the circle was glued back and the head was ready to be finished with paint and features and a wig of hair. In cheaper models the hair could be indicated by modelling and painting and the eyes were merely painted on.

As competition increased and the doll factories were geared to mechanical production, many of the hand processes were discontinued. Although the head and limbs still had to be modelled in the first place (by a skilled sculptor who rarely gets any credit as he remains anonymous) the matrices for making the doll were of steel. Pierre Calmettes, in an account of French doll-making at the end of the century, explained that a liquid paste was spread into these hollow matrices and pressed down with weights by a 'contra-matrix'; he was describing the production of hollow bodies and limbs for use with the bisque-headed Parisian *bébés*. As early as 1829 the move towards mechanization had begun, with a patent such as that of Rondeaux and Henne for *carton*, which perfected a machine with a sort of central pounding arm for mixing up the ingredients. In this case the material consisted of five *livres* of dried leather and three buckets of water, which were later mixed with other ingredients. The fact that Calmettes nearly one hundred years later mentioned a paste composed of plaster of Paris, gum tragacanth and scrapings of skin leather from the glove factories of Paris indicates that this was an especially French recipe – thriftily employing the waste product of another industry. Perhaps in the future a scientific analysis of dolls' heads will be able to provide a few more clues to their identity and provenance.

7

Pedlar
and Needlework
Dolls

For five shillings (less than a dollar) it is still possible to buy a pedlar's licence in England, and, in the traditional fashion, fill a basket with merchandise of any sort to be sold up and down the country. But if you are lucky enough to find an early 'pedlar' doll for sale it will cost you many times that amount. I have deliberately used the word 'early' as this type of doll is now sometimes imitated or even faked, and it is very necessary for the would-be purchaser to be satisfied that it is a genuine work.

The trade of the pedlar, old as commerce itself, has almost died out with modern means of communication and transport, but it is still possible in country districts to meet an occasional gypsy woman with braided plaits and gold rings in her ears. She will offer to tell your fortune – 'cross my hand with silver dear' or sell you homemade clothes pegs, bunches of wild flowers or a card of lace from the basket on her arm. The pedlar was not, however, a gypsy but a very necessary go-between for the wholesale warehouse of the city and the isolated villages of the country. His visits and his gossip must have been as readily acceptable as his town-made luxuries in places where a strange face was quite an event. In the eighteenth and nineteenth centuries special centres existed in big cities to stock up the chapmen and pedlars. In 1708 for instance, a list advertising goods obtainable by dealers at the Bible in Gracechurch St in London included: 'Books, Broadsides or Half-sheets and Lottery Pictures, as Birds, Beast, London Crys etc. by the Gross or Dozen; also Labels for Chyrugeons Chests, Venice Treacle Directions and Rappers, Hungary Directions, Bills, Funeral Tickets, Affidavits for Burials in Woollen etc.' Venice Treacle was a nostrum prepared from various drugs in honey, Hungary was a spiced drink and the reference to woollen winding sheets was for burial without a coffin.

It might be thought that a trade which meant passing over bad roads in all weathers and in lonely places was more suitable for a man than for a woman, but pedlars often worked as a man and wife team, and pairs of pedlar dolls portray them. They probably each specialized in a rather different variety of wares.

A man and wife pair in Cliffe Castle Museum, Keighley, were made by Mrs Sugden of Eastwood House, Keighley, in 1820 and they are pictured against a design of the original house, now destroyed [85]. The man carries graters, bilboquet, wooden pattens which served simple country folk for shoes, and long hanks of wool and rope, while his wife, apart from her more usual millinery and needlework requisites, has a stock of novels of the day by such writers as Eustace, Moor, Young and Godwin and a miniature Wedgwood medallion, which perhaps gives a clue to the nearness of the Staffordshire Potteries. They are dressed typically, she in red cape and brown bonnet, he with hard billycock hat and buttoned topcoat.

In spite of the hardship endured, the pedlar's life offered certain attractions. It was certainly healthy, and independent, even if the living was a poor one. An old pedlar woman on her own was probably safe in that she became recognized as a local character, making her way over customary routes year in, year out, and even gaining a

*85 Man and wife pedlar dolls
made by Mrs Sugden of Eastwood
House, Keighley in 1820;
the house, now demolished, is
pictured in the background;
10 inches*

certain reputation for her healing powers. Some of them must have looked sufficiently witchlike, and the simples and remedies they could supply from their basket coupled with a passing knowledge of herbal recipes from the hedgerow were enough to establish them. Dorothy Wordsworth, sister of the poet, remembered one old pedlar woman who visited his home in Grasmere and in her journal for Friday 10 October 1828 she wrote: 'It was a most heavenly morning. The Cockermouth traveller came with thread, hardware, mustard etc. She is very healthy; has travelled over the mountains these thirty years.' It was thirty miles through rough mountain country from Cockermouth to Grasmere.

The pedlar certainly did not always have the reputation of an honest character. Shakespeare has immortalized one such fellow in the *Winter's Tale* (1611): the classic example of a rogue, Autolycus, using his respectable guise of pedlar as a cover for pocket-picking, and possessing a persuasive tongue for wheedling custom.

86 Pedlar doll pair with papier mâché heads from Stratford-on-Avon; 1840; 16½ inches

Figure 86 shows a pair of pedlars, the largest I have ever seen, which come from Shakespeare's birthplace. They were presented to Leeds Museum by William and Barbara Wilson whose great-grand-parents, named Salmon, made them in Stratford-on-Avon in 1840. They have heads of painted papier mâché and are dressed in beautifully worked linen smocks, typical of country folk of that period, with sheepskin wraps. As one might expect, their trays have various mementoes of the man who made Stratford famous: there are miniature commemorative mugs, prints of the town, a Shakespearean broad-sheet and even a perfect miniature of Shakespeare's birthplace in china.

Though the pedlar trade was common to all parts of Europe, the pedlar doll seems to have been uniquely British. It is not known when the vogue for making little models in imitation of the real thing began, or whose brainchild it was or for what purpose, if any. Examples are not often found which may safely be dated much before 1800 and my own theory is that originally they were made completely from home-made materials, singly or in pairs, as an economical cottage version of the very popular porcelain character figures which were then being made both by Continental and English potteries. The pedlar, both male and female, was a popular and colourful subject.

One very realistic, if simple version of the old crone in her poke bonnet with lace frillcap, print blouse and clean white apron, has a finely modelled wax face, little wire spectacles and arms of stitched

82

*87 Realistic old lady with
wax modelled face and
leather body; 1825; 9 inches*

*88 right: 'Applehead' pedlar
woman; 1830; 12 inches*

kid [87]. The base of the doll is merely a stiff card cylinder and in
the lamb's wool lining of her neat woven basket little items are glued
down: hanks of wool, a blue glass bottle, stay laces with metal tags,
rolls of ballads and cards of silk and ribbon, besides a few more pairs
of wire spectacles like her own.

Whatever their origin it is clear from the number and variety of
pedlar dolls that very many people enjoyed making their own, sometimes in the pattern of a living character they remembered. Figure
88 owes her character to a country-style method. Her head is made
of a dried apple with bright beads inserted for eyes. She is twelve
inches high and dates from about 1830. The fashion for pickled heads
made from apples was well-known among country people. A little
carving was needed to indicate the features, and then the head was
dipped in vinegar lightly salted, and air-dried on a stick propped in
a bottle neck. When dry and leathery, a process taking between three
and six weeks, the faces could be painted and the stick served as a
base for a rudimentary body. The wrinkled face gives enormous
character to this model, and she is dressed authentically with bonnet,
cloak and apron over her print dress. All her wares are homemade,
with the exception of buttons and needles and hooks and eyes and
'the smallest doll in the world' which peeps from the back of her basket.

If the earliest pedlar dolls strove after realism and really looked
the part, the later improvization of using a bought doll and dressing
it was probably more favoured, as the finished result was prettier.

89 A Charity Bazaar stall of 1850,
preserved immaculate under
a glass dome

90 Dutch doll made into
pedlar girl; 1860

91 'Fancy Fair — July'
from the Comick Almanack of 1837;
'Twelve Righte Merrie Cuts'

On the whole a wooden doll seems to have been thought most suitable – perhaps with some notion of social status similar to the 'above and below stairs' of the dolls' house. Figure 90 shows a typical long-legged 'Dutch' doll, the same type as those dressed by Queen Victoria as a child (see chapter 6). She is simply dressed in red cloak and black bonnet. On her tray is included a card of 'Fine Gold Wedding Rings', advertisements for Wilson's Sweet Babe (tobacco), White Windsor, finest quality soap, miniature framed engravings of Ellen Tree and Charles Wilkins – famous stage personalities – and a card of Superior Steel Pens (nibs). This is the fanciful cargo devised perhaps for a bazaar toy. With the hardships imposed by the Industrial Revolution, the Charity Bazaar was organized for many good causes and patronized by many ladies clever with their needle. Figure 89 seems to portray one such lady. She is far too fine for a pedlar with her lace-trimmed jacket and bonnet, and the booth over which she presides is elegantly rigged and full of pretty handiwork, tiny embroidered hats, delicate items of milk glass in miniature and fancy basketware. She is selling few of the everyday necessities which were the true pedlar's stock-in-trade. Note the round bottle of 'Verveine', a common herb whose root was at one time hung about the neck as an antidote to scrofula and was later used as an ingredient in many quack medicines. A glass dome has preserved the doll in perfect condition and her painted composition head maintains a complexion as fresh as the day she was made.

Vying with her in elegance, figure 93 dates from rather earlier, 1830, and comes across the channel from Jersey. This pedlar specializes in fancy beadwork and introduces a little note of exoticism with a sheet of French music 'Le Troubadour'. Toasting forks hang side by side with a rosary and crucifix and she also carries a packet of phosphorus matches, which a Frenchman is credited as having invented in 1790. One of the finest examples of the bazaar-stall lady [94] dates from 1835. She presides with a positively stately air over a four-legged table crammed with delightful gifts. Toys and trinket boxes, pot-pourri jars and pastille burners, engravings with gilt frames and fancy porcelain: this surely is the Christmas gift bazaar presided over by an earlier version of Baroness Goodchild (see chapter 4).

In the nineteenth century the pin-cushion occupied a far more important place on ladies' toilet tables than today and the pin was the indispensable item for the needlewoman. In her *Memoirs* Lady Nevill, has given an amusing acount of Queen Adelaide's mania for them. Her pin-cushions were 'elaborately decorated with devices and designs formed of pins stuck in quite an artistic manner. Their Royal owner knew all these by heart and when she wanted to use a pin would instruct her maid to take it from some particular curve, point or row, at the same time giving the strictest orders that it should later be replaced in exactly the same place. She never lost one without being seriously concerned, and would have it searched for for hours. A great subject for speculation with this royal lady was what had become of the millions of pins which had disappeared; the very thought of their fate gave her pain!' One is tempted to imagine that Queen Adelaide may have shared in the craze for devising ornamental pin-cushion dolls, which was a favourite needlework ploy of the nineteenth century. They were often made on the same pattern as the pedlar doll with a manufactured head attached to a body with a full or crinoline skirt. In this case, however, the skirt was stuffed hard with a sealed base to form a suitable 'cushion'. Sometimes emery powder was used for the stuffing, serving the double purpose of giving the necessary weight to hold the doll upright and of keeping steel pins rust-proof. Pins were often made with pretty glass or ceramic heads so that coloured patterns could be formed with them. Figure 92 dates from 1820 and has pins in a pattern made of groups of three around the scalloped skirt and singly around the hat brim. She is a pretty jointed doll made of wood and, despite her tattered state, preserves a sort of elegance. German porcelain heads with double stitch holes in the bust were particularly suitable for needlework dolls and a beautiful and exceptional example which belonged to the late Queen Mary was given by her to the London Museum.

A further refinement for the needlewoman was the little 'sewing companion': an idea for a doll dressed up in a costume which included needles, thimble, cotton and scissors, as well as pins. A recipe for the making of such a doll appeared in the *Englishwoman's Magazine* in the 1860s and the sort of doll obtainable then at Cremer's toyshop in Bond Street was advertised and illustrated [181]. The same idea was copied in *Peterson's Magazine* in America shortly afterwards with

92 A small, jointed wooden pincushion doll with pattern in steel pins; 1820; 9 inches

93 opposite: Pedlar doll from Jersey, Channel Isles, 1850

a rather crude woodcut reproduction and an account of how the doll should be constructed. It was suggested as especially suitable for a Christmas or New Year's gift. In *The Home Book*, edited by Mrs Valentine in 1867, a section on needlework dolls included instructions for making 'Work-table Friends', with dolls dressed variously as a French *cantinière*; a Charity School girl, with large school apron with pockets capable of holding thimble and cotton; an old market woman with a basket; a milkmaid with milk pails slung over her shoulder, represented by two reels of cotton hanging at the ends of a bodkin. All had solid pin-cushion skirts stuffed with bran.

The pin-cushion doll shown in figure 95 is made on a slightly different pattern with a little padded velvet head-dress in a basketwork frame. Her crinoline with a wired hem is made of grey moiré silk trimmed with black lace and deep pockets, while the muslin blouse is tied with pink ribbon elegantly cut with 'pinking' scissors. The necessity for a stand is fulfilled by stiffening the skirt with a stout card. This may give a clue to the date, as it has the unlikely heading 'Subscription card for the Education of Native Females in India 1845'.

95 A needlework doll, perhaps a 'Dressmaker's companion' with pockets and pin-cushion hat; 8 inches

96 Small woodcut of 'Fate-lady from The Girls' Companion *edited by Mrs Child (1847)*

In the *Girl's Companion* of 1847 Mrs Child gave a pattern for making a 'Fate-Lady' or fortune-telling doll, which was another popular needlework diversion and also a play-doll in the sense that it taught useful lessons in a very pleasant way [96]. A small elegantly dressed doll holding a straw wand was mounted on a disc of card over a small pill-box. She was fixed on a wire so that she would revolve freely when twirled round and point out a fortune with her wand. Some of the suggested fortunes were kind, some mean, but all in verse:

Two dunces her fast friends shall be
Herself the dullest of the three.

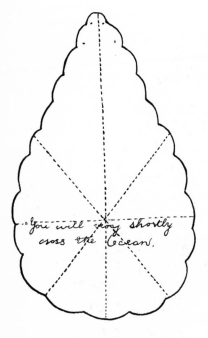

97 Diagram of single leaf from a scalloped skirt of a fortune-telling doll similar to 98

98 opposite: A fortune-telling doll with skirt of folded paper leaves which belonged to Queen Victoria as a child

I have never found an example of this particular type of fortune doll but there are many variations on the same theme. Prettiest of them are perhaps the dolls dressed with a full skirt made up of pleated coloured papers with fortunes written on each leaf-shaped section [97] closely packed to form a crinoline and fastened at the waist. The papers, of pastel shades and cut with a deckle or scallop edge, opened out easily when the doll's wand indicated the chosen fortune. One of this type belonged to Queen Victoria as a child, though it must have been well beyond the powers of any doll to tell that particular child's fortune! [98].

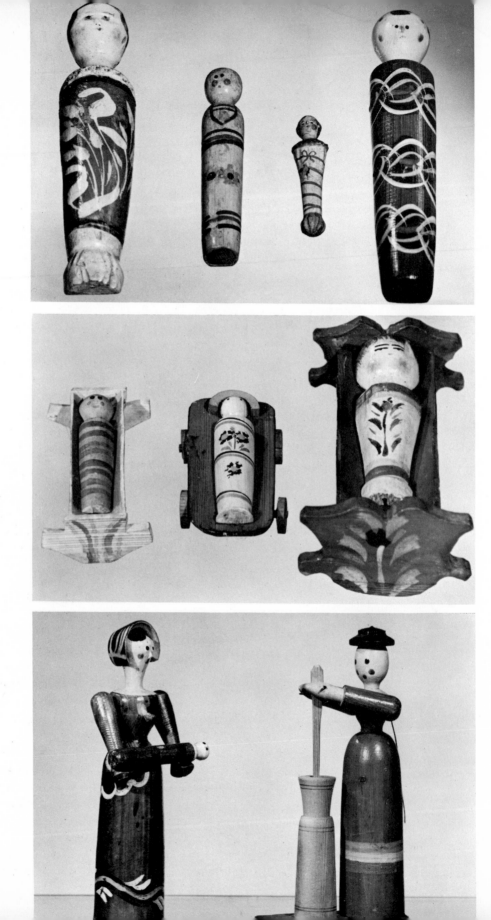

8

....

Folk Dolls

99 *Wooden babies, lathe-turned and painted, from Bohemia and Moravia; early 20th century*

100 *left: Wooden babies in cradles from Skasov, others from Krouna near Hlinsko*

101 *Rocking and churning mechanical dolls in turned wood; one from Skasov (left), the other from Krouna; early 20th century*

The very essence of the folk-toy was its isolation: it was particular to one country, one special district or tribe or even to a distinct occasion. The gradual standardization of the peoples of the world, the merging of frontiers, if not geographically at least in knowledge, has led to the gradual disappearance of folk art. In some countries a revival of the old traditions has been sought, folk-toys have been made again to represent old costumes, early customs and occupations, but, charming as they are, they cannot help but appear self-conscious because the original ceremony or superstitition for which they were made is either forgotten or ignored. Eastern Europe is a good example of an area where the folk-doll tradition remained a live one and therefore this chapter will concentrate on Czechoslovakia and Russia where the folk-doll tradition is seen at its best.

The Czechoslovakian toy maker, Emanuel Hercik, realizing that many of his country's splendid folk-toys were doomed to extinction by modern progress, set about providing a permanent record of some of the most notable patterns he had discovered since he had begun to study them in about 1919. These he illustrated in all the beauty of their original bright colours and strong shape in a book published in 1951 with the express purpose of encouraging a resurrection of the old toys, and of leaving modern designers a record of the old models in his own collection, which now has a permanent home in the National Museum of Prague.

One of the oldest types of doll, which has been traditionally made in Bohemia for centuries, is the familiar model of a swaddled babe that appears in early engravings and was made variously from moulded clay, painted papier mâché [109] or lathe-turned from a round log of wood with details either carved or painted. The fundamental shape led Hercik to call it a 'rolling-pin' doll. Some more modern types of this swaddled doll are shown in figure 99, where the epithet 'rolling-pin' really is suitable. They are lathe-turned, long slim shapes like the Japanese *kokeshi*, formalized and less baby-like. The swaddling bands become a painted pattern and soon the 'rolling-pin' becomes an embryo 'Dutch' doll, merely lacking the addition of jointed arms and legs, like a tadpole about to turn into a frog. Still they were ideal to wrap up and cuddle as a little child would wish. Sometimes they were made complete in their little cradle of wicker or wood, beautifully and gaily patterned [100].

The Bohemians were infatuated with colour. Probably they were influenced by Bavaria across the border and it is known that there were South German settlers in Bohemia during the eighteenth century. Their folk art is a riot of colour and pattern, vying in gaiety with the pretty Japanese folk-toys with which they often have curious parallels. Even the delicate little chip-wood boxes in which small toys and dolls were packed up and exported were ornamented with traditional flowers and patterns – just as the Bavarians decorate their houses, inside and out, their wooden furniture and the utensils of everyday life. The figures in 101 show local variations on the 'rolling-pin' theme, where the baby doll has become a Mama doll to make novel working toys. Sometimes the rolling-pin doll was made with a

*102 The devil carrying off
a naughty child. A fairground toy
made from wood and edible pastry;
Pribram, 1900*

hollow body in which a few tiny pebbles were inserted and sealed up so that a baby could use it as a rattle. The attraction of all these dolls lies partly in their easily graspable shape, but principally in the rich and varied colouring of their dress. The lady dolls wear little flat hats like Mrs Noah (who was, of course, nothing but a miniature 'rolling-pin') or poke bonnets or round crowned hats with painted flower or stuck-on feather. One type made for export to Austria was known as *Tyrolka:* in the fashion of Tyrol costume they wore green hats and white frocks decorated with short blue and red aprons. A doll finished and ready for painting was given an all-over undercoat of flat white base and then brilliant dabs of colour were added for the final finish. They were sold especially at the big fairs which precede Christmas.

A Czechoslovakian friend remembers such fairs from her childhood, with their sweetmeats and toys and the gay procession through the streets celebrating the return of St Nicholas. At the end of the procession through the village there always danced a few men or boys dressed as devils and, on one occasion, as a little girl, she was too timid to venture outside the house. One of the lads, seeing the little face peeping from the window, danced forward and tapped on the pane. She has never forgotten her moment of terror and it is evident that the devil dolls sold at the fair depicting naughty children being carried away must have been a mixed source of pleasure. The dolls in figure 102 were made at Pribram, centre of the old silver-mining industry, where the miners employed their spare time in making little model miners of wood who wielded their pick-axes by means of a working lever.

The famous German maker of dolls, Käthe Kruse, told the story of how, when she first thought of making a rag doll, she began with a potato wrapped in a cloth, tied at the neck to form a head. This or similar quite primitive methods must have been used in Europe for cheap home-made dolls from early times. The Victorians even quieted baby with a little dolly or 'comforter' made of a sugar lump tied in a clean rag, which could be sucked as well as fondled! Figure 103 shows the next development of this simple type. Features are painted on the round face (stuffed with something rather softer than a potato) and tubular arms and sometimes legs are added to the doll-on-a-stick. It resembles the 'dolly' of soft leather used for a drum stick. The knotted kerchief doll looked uncommonly like a peasant and sometimes the knot would be slipped over a grown-up's index finger and the hand, covered by the handkerchief, provided the simplest form of puppet to amuse a little child.

The most famous form of peasant doll in Russia, now known throughout the world, was the *Matryushka*, or wooden nest of dolls skilfully lathe-turned and made to fit exactly one within another [104]. It is not known how the idea originated or whether some allegorical representation of the child in the womb was intended. Such dolls varied in size and in the number of dolls fitted within each other. The principle is the same, however, and usually the set contains about seven dolls ending with a tiny solid creature no more than half an inch high. In the last century they were coloured with dyes over white

103 Stuffed rag dolls from
Moravia and Slowakia;
beginning of the 20th century

104 Russian nest dolls or
Matryushka, c. 1850

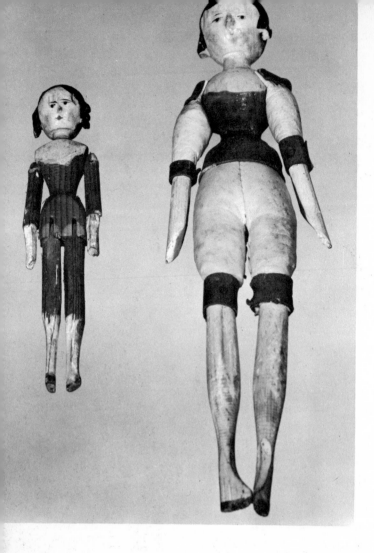

106 *Glass doll goblet which has to be emptied of liquid before it is set down*

105 *Prague wooden dolls from the first half of the 19th century. Note the shaped hair line and leather joints of the larger model*

wood; the modern counterparts are brightly varnished. They are always peasant people and the larger 'boxes' of the set are depicted as carrying market goods like a rabbit or a goose, a bag or tied-up kerchief. Other later variations show a family of frogs with pale bellies and painted-on arms and legs, or the first container may open to reveal a set of half-a-dozen little tumbler dolls, or a set of skittles and ball. In September 1966, there was a report of such a set of dolls being used as a spy instrument to smuggle NATO secrets from Paris to eastern Europe. On a less sinister level, children used to hide a sweet inside one case and make their sisters guess which held the prize.

The higher strata of nineteenth-century Russian society are depicted in the little carved ladies and Hussars made of wood and painted by the Bogorodsky carvers of Moscow province [107, 108]. They are fine examples of carving with a single knife from a tri-hedral block which provided a solid stand for them. In technique they resemble the Nara dolls of Japan (see page 223), cut by the *ittobori*, or one-stroke style.

In a continent as vast as Russia it is obvious that very many types of doll-making could develop quite independently.

107, 108 *opposite and over page: Dolls carved from trihedral blocks by the Bogorodsk carvers of Moscow province; mid 19th century*

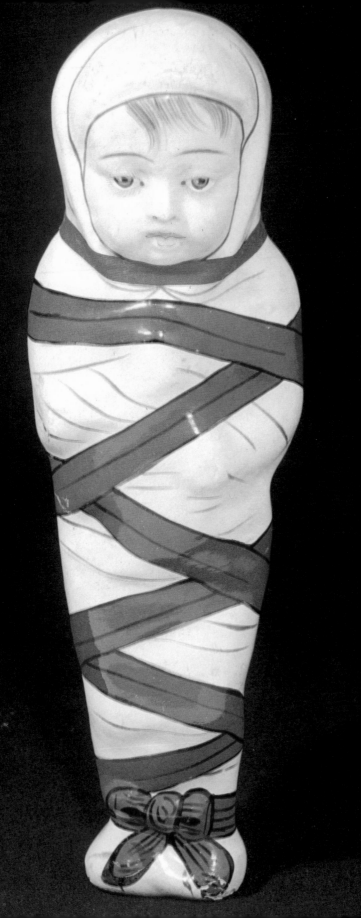

109 opposite: Papier mâché swaddled doll from Russia; late 19th century

In the northern forests, besides the 'moss men' (see page 27), children played with stick dolls: a wooden doll mounted on a long stick which could be prodded into deep snow to make it stand up. The delightful swaddled doll [109] measures twelve inches from top to toe and is of gaily painted papier mâché and quite light in weight. It is not known in which part of Russia it was produced but it was clearly made commercially and perfectly represents the peasant baby, safely wrapped round and transformed into a warm cocoon which could be laid on a shelf or in a hammock or wooden cradle while its mother worked. In Russia, where winters are very long and very severe, it was sometimes the custom to sling the baby's cradle round the central stove of the house for warmth.

110 Hand-worked Russian needlework dolls of about 1814, made in a traditional pattern

The small handmade rag dolls in figure 110, a little man and woman in a sort of regional costume which varies little from example to example over a period of two hundred years, come from the Crimea, and are, perhaps, the bride and bridegroom models presented at a wedding – a custom often traced among peasant folk. They are exquisitely made with embroidered features and details. A few years back a similar pair at an auction in a leading London sale room fetched a high price as they were catalogued as English 'Elizabethan'. The dolls pictured here were sold at a Red Cross sale in 1915 when it was claimed that they were already over one hundred years old.

9

Dolls' House Dolls and Miniatures

Some of the earliest dolls to have survived in the western world are those who have actually lived in their own residence since it was first made some three hundred years or so ago. I refer, of course, to the dolls' house dolls. Set among the furniture and furnishings of their period and dressed *à la mode*, whether fine lady or gentleman or serving maid, they present a miniature three-dimensional tableau of life as it existed when they were made. Looking into some of these early rooms we feel, uncannily, that we have slipped back in time and are seeing life through the eyes of a Dürer or a Rembrandt. The idea of making a collection of miniature furniture and all the domestic appliances of a household in a house-shaped cabinet or dolls' house seems to have originated in Germany. Nuremberg, an historic centre of the German toy industry, possesses fine dolls' houses which have never left that city. They were built and furnished early in the seventeenth century, remained in Nuremberg families, and are now a cherished part of the collection in the National Museum. Tall and solidly built, with ornamental gables typical of a fine patrician town-dwelling of the period, they are equipped with all the necessities of life, from the fine horses in the stables below, with special quarters for the coachman, the cool cellars full of wine and provisions, and the well-filled linen cupboards above stairs to the kitchen with its open fire stove and wide range of cooking implements. There is an atmosphere of exalted domesticity and comfortable living: the home, beautifully organized, of a seventeenth-century lady justly proud of her possessions and her skill in management.

A fine example, dated 1639 on the dormer window in the roof, is particularly rich in delicately carved panelling and, rather unusually, has an interior system of stairways leading from lower floors to upper rooms [124]. There is also the pleasant convention of a little balustrade to each of the top rooms which would prevent any pieces of furniture falling out. These houses seem to have been meant to be played with, at least in an instructional way – a pleasant manner of teaching little girls their domestic duties and making them familiar with the quite complicated management of a household which had to cope with all its own laundry, cooking, spinning, weaving, besides ordinary needlework and dairy craft.

Not least of the delights of such houses are their fine proportions: the rooms are large, giving a spaciousness to the furniture, and the little dolls, between four and six inches in height, are in perfect symmetry. They are made of wax with finely featured faces and delicate hands and legs and bear a strong family resemblance to some of those little wax figures who people the early Tyrolean crèche scene [62]. No doubt some of them came from the same source. The dolls are not haphazard figures introduced into the rooms but little personages, if not 'made to measure', at least clothed and equipped with a character fitting the part they played in the life of the dolls' house.

Very similar figures were used in dolls' houses of the corresponding period in Holland, but from examples now preserved in museums in the Hague, Amsterdam and Utrecht, we find that the houses themselves were rather different from the German models and seem never

111 Wet nurse and baby from the dolls' house; Dutch; 1670

112 *Sitting room in the doll's house of Margaretha de Ruyter; Dutch; 1670*

to have been intended for the use of children. The comparison reflects the different status between the two owners: domestic aim and outlook in the German with its gaily painted and carved house, the collector's pride and fervour in the rather more ostentatious Dutch version, where dolls' rooms were housed in fine walnut cabinets. The contents themselves display a far richer treasure. Fine miniature silver 'toys' (the general seventeenth-century term for small decorative pieces) – replicas of costly Delft ware, oriental porcelain, delicate glass and framed paintings or engravings – display the taste of the Dutch burgher for exhibiting his wealth. The atmosphere in these Dutch houses seems to us now to savour more of the museum than of the home and reflects the culture as well as the luxury of the period. The vogue for such collections in miniature must have existed from early in the seventeenth century, which was a splendid period for Dutch silver. The famous dolls' house at the Hague was assembled by Sara Ploos van Amstel, a married lady of Amsterdam. In an inventory of possessions drawn up on her death in 1760 it was called

'A Cabinet of Art Curios with all those Household Articles appertaining to the same'. She had bought three earlier cabinets in 1743, which are recorded as having also been in an auction sale in 1700, and combined the contents in a fine new cabinet which she had specially built to order at a cost of about £23 or $56. This is the present cabinet and is of fine walnut with two folding doors closing on nine rooms, and with three drawers underneath. As she made notes of the additional pieces of furniture and furnishings, she has left an invaluable page in the history of dolls' houses. The little wax dolls themselves seem to have cost about six shillings or a dollar each.

The fashion of collecting seems also to have been well-established in England by the beginning of the seventeenth century. Dutch silver was brought over from the Continent and the English copied the vogue and produced miniature silver every bit as beautiful, often with coat of arms complete for the family for whom it was made. The earliest English baby-houses seem to have followed the Dutch pattern of a cabinet on a base with doors opening to reveal the little furnished rooms. A very interesting example was given by Queen Anne to her god-daughter, Anne Sharp, daughter of an Archbishop of York and born in 1691, and it remains today in the possession of her descendants. It is considerably simpler in its contents than the magnificent Dutch houses and in addition to a few wax dolls it also has some little wooden characters, typical of the period, with round, disproportionately large heads and carved spatulate wooden hands. Some of the dolls still bear the names given to them by their first child owner and pinned to them on written labels [113].

The English, having discovered the dolls' house, made of it something peculiarly individual and representative. Splendid houses still exist that are as unique in themselves as the stately homes in which they are often lodged. Jonathan Swift, who knew both London and Dublin well, may well have drawn on some personal recollection of a dolls' house in his invention of the Lilliputians – a pygmy race under six inches tall. Certainly a reference in his book to an 'entire set of silver dishes and plates and other necessaries ... which were not

113 Some of the inhabitants of Ann Sharp's Baby House of 1700 (reading from left to right) Roger ye Butler, Lady Jemima Johnson, Mrs Lemon, Hannah ye Housekeeper, Lord Rochett, Lady Rochett, identified by contemporary hand written labels pinned to them

114 *Dolls visiting a dolls' house of 1851*

115 *Group of small wooden dolls dressed by Queen Victoria as a child, with a mechanical toy*

much bigger than what I have seen of the same kind in a London toy-shop for the furniture of a baby-house' shows that he was not ignorant of such things. The adjective 'Lilliputian' was speedily assimilated into the language and was applied especially to very small dolls. An advertisement in the *Independent Gazeteer* of Philadelphia on 6 May 1785 for toys sold at John Mason's shop included 'DREST DOLLS, NAKED DITTO and LILLIPUTIAN DOLLS' besides 'two new HOUSES with fine gardens'.

Ireland, too, had its dolls' houses. A fine eighteenth-century example, unfortunately quite empty of furniture or dolls, exists in the Guinness home at Leixlip Castle in Southern Ireland. Dorothea Herbert (see page 76) wrote in her *Journal* for 19 July 1772: 'I stood Godmother for Mr Valentine Smyth, Got a fine Babyhouse on the occasion from his Mother Mrs Larry Smyth of Carrick on Suir.' With maddening nonchalance she gives not one further detail, but it may be assumed to have been something much less grand than the Guinness model.

There is a curious hiatus in the history of dolls' houses about the end of the eighteenth and beginning of the nineteenth century, but we soon find, when we enter the second half of the nineteenth century, that the little jointed wooden peg dolls have taken up residence. These are those same little people whom Queen Victoria, when she was a child, dressed to impersonate characters from plays and from high society, with the help of her attendant Baroness Lehzen. The *Strand Magazine* for 1892 (just at the time when the Sherlock Holmes stories were first appearing in this magazine) carried a highly eulogistic account of some of these dolls, one hundred and thirty of which passed to the London Museum [115]: 'An hour spent among the dolls that Queen Victoria played with as a child is not only a liberal education in the evanescent influence and fashions of the early part of this century, but an *abiding study of her imaginative infancy*,' wrote Frances Low. 'The Princess must at an early age have been an expert with her knitting needles for the ballerina wears neat little pink and blue stockings and nicely fitting white shoes.'

The elderly Queen who corrected the proofs with down to earth candour perhaps saw through such fulsome flattery and wrote 'No! Baroness Lehzen did the *minute* work!'

Queen Victoria was only one of many children who enjoyed such pursuits. An account published in *Harper's Bazaar* on 28 January 1871 described another family dolls' house:

Thirty years ago we could get nothing better than jointed wooden dolls with dots for features; but as there was no alternative between these and gigantic bran creatures with waxen heads, we contented ourselves with the ugly wooden ones. They were beautifully dressed by our friends and acquaintances. Some were given to a tailor who turned them into general officers, blazing in scarlet and gold, clergymen in gowns and bands, and lastly footmen in every conceivable livery! They swarmed everywhere; and the real cook often rebelled against the constant demand for a christening cake. We had about fifty dolls altogether...

One small type of doll, now rarely found, probably made only for a short time and by a few factories, represents the transition between jointed wooden dolls and the small dolls with porcelain heads, arms and legs which appeared in large numbers from the middle of the nineteenth century, turned out by busy German manufacturers. The upper sections of the wooden arms and legs were jointed to the body but slotted at the elbow and knee to receive a solid lower arm and leg of moulded porcelain with a little projection to pivot into the socket (see sketch). The glazed china head was moulded solid with a hole at the neck which could fit on to a wooden peg at the neck of the wooden body. An example in the London Museum, $5^1/_2$ inches high, seems to have been a coronation souvenir of young Queen Victoria, with a hole in one hand intended for holding the sceptre. Its date must therefore be about 1837, her coronation year.

The use of ceramics for doll-making made it possible to produce a far greater variety of small dolls and most of the methods used for large dolls were also adapted to miniature types. Head, arms and legs, glazed or unglazed, could be attached to a small body of wood, stuffed calico or leather. The parts of such little dolls make an interesting study in themselves: few are ever marked to give a clue to the factory which made them, but characteristic identifying marks can be traced in their design. Sometimes they had painted shoes and socks, sometimes part of their clothing was indicated in the actual modelling, such as ribbed stockings or tartan patterned socks. Their hair — beards and moustaches, too, for some of the males — might be shown by colouring under glaze or by raised modelling. Particularly with the unglazed or parian miniatures pretty details of ribbons, bonnets, nets and combs were shown and may help to trace at least a common factory, even though the maker is unknown.

In the second half of the century, when bisque doll-heads had become popular, miniature versions of these were also produced and they are generally admired as the prettiest of all, as they have the advantages of bright glass eyes and real hair [116]. The bisque type were often made with porcelain bodies with wired joints and were skin-tinted with delicately marked features.

The type of small doll made all in one piece with head, body, arms, legs moulded together earned itself the name of 'Frozen Charlotte' in the United States, because of a popular ballad of the 1830s about a girl who froze to death on an icy night. Miniature models no more than an inch long were popularly used in England in the traditional plum pudding at Christmas dinner and provoked a good deal of teasing and merriment. In those days such trophies were cooked in the pudding, but I think the custom is dying out. When Christmas was over the tiny dolls were cherished in matchbox beds with bright snippets of velvet and ribbon for a cover.

There were, of course, many uses to which miniature dolls could be put: they were handy enough to carry round in the pocket or pinafore and I know of one elderly collector of porcelain who confessed to the joy he and his sister had in buying sets of cheap dolls which could be dressed as Robin Hood and his outlaws or King Arthur and his Knights, or indeed to illustrate any book which was currently their favourite. Figure 125 shows a whole cast of miniatures dressed to perform a play or pantomime. It is not difficult to visualize a family of children taken to one of those splendid London Pantomimes at the Drury Lane Theatre in the 'eighties setting out together on their return to re-enact the scene they had just seen. At one time there was surely a theatre to accompany this colourful party. Here the children could live over again the delights, the excitement and glamour of the flying ballet, the slapstick comedy and, perhaps with candles lit in the

116 Group of small dolls' house characters; bisque head with glass eyes for the 'family', cheap quality stoneware with painted features for the domestics

dark drawing room, the glitter of the famous pantomime.

Naturally the most frequent use for Victorian dolls was in peopling dolls' houses. Even at this time dolls' houses were less often bought from a shop than made privately. Sometimes the order went to an estate carpenter or village handyman; often a talented amateur had a go at constructing an architecturally ingenious house in imitation of a building familiar to him or even his own house in replica.

Many such houses still survive from the eighteen-sixties but it must be rare for one to be preserved complete with a record of the building and furnishing costs. York House [117] was created by Mrs Francis Boase, a great-aunt of the present owner, Mrs Trew of Reigate. She was the wife of a doctor living at Penzance in Cornwall. A photo of the period, tinted by hand, shows her looking not unlike one of her own dolls, seated very upright on a tall-backed chair, book in hand and her feet on a velvet footstool. She wears a full alpaca dress and heavy black mantle of lace over her shoulders with a gold brooch at her throat. Her fair hair is parted severely in the centre and braided over the crown.

117 'York House' drawing room, 1864

For the house, Mrs Boase employed a Mr Tregarthen – there are Tregarthens still in Penzance – who for the sum of £5.15s built a typical mansion of the day, a four-square memorial of Victorian respectability, measuring 3ft 10ins in length, 1ft 6ins deep and 4ft high, with stucco finish, square coigning at the edges and battlemented roof. Inside, its form was very simple, lacking either entrance hall or stairway, but divided into four large equal rooms: drawing room and bedroom upstairs, dining room and kitchen below. A thin notebook with Almanack for Leap Year 1864 carefully records in faded ink details of all that was spent in fitting out the house, which was actually built in 1862. We are not told on which room Mrs Boase began her work, or whether she prepared all four rooms before filling them with furniture and inhabitants but the list for the drawing room comes first and the very top entry is 2s6d for papers. The papers must have been sold especially for dolls' houses and have delicate, small, patterns. The one for the dining-room is particularly splendid with some gold tracery in its design.

Though children have played with the house, tidied it and rearranged it during the hundred years of its life, it was not originally built for them. Whereas with the majority of houses of this period the whole front of the façade opened to show the interior [114], this house is made to open from the back and the back wall is accordingly papered and embellished with pictures and ornaments so that it looks finished and complete to an onlooker peeping in through the tall lace-curtained windows in the front. The house is unlit, so the windows served to let in extra light.

Originally there was a garden with potted flowers (3s), a summer house (8d), garden tools (2s), and two strawberry plants (1s6d), but this has vanished during one or other of the house's moves although it survives in the pages of the notebook. Most items cost only a few pence, but the more expensive luxuries were the larger pieces of furniture such as the set of four chairs for the drawing room at

118 'York House' dining room 1864

2s each, now pleasantly aged with their blue silk covers a little worn and faded. There is an ingenious German piano which still works with little dancing figures jigging up and down as the keys are played (3s6d). The fireplace in the drawing-room cost 2s and the mirror above it 2s6d; pictures were quite an expensive item as there are many of them, mostly with a religious subject, and a wealth of ornamental vases. The services of Mr Tregarthen were employed in making the console table and also the fine carved four-poster bed for which he charged an additional 6s, besides his original £5 15s for 'constructing and labour'. Not many of the pieces of furniture are handmade, though there are some little items of expenditure such as black and red silk for Ottoman (4d) and red moire for chairs (10d). On one occasion Mrs Boase must have made the long journey to town, as she lists 'Sundries from London' (£1 16s). As this last entry appears under the heading of 'Kitchen' it accounts possibly for some of the numerous pots and pans and dishes (including miniature Leeds and Wedgwood ware).

Against the background so lovingly composed, a family of dolls was gradually introduced and dressed in character, forming a social hierarchy reflected in a slightly different type of doll according to whether they lived above or below stairs. None of the dolls was expensive. The mistress of the house, a long-legged wooden German doll, with wax-coated face and a coiffure of real applied hair, cost 6d; China dolls for the drawing-room cost 1s4d and for the dining-room 2s 2d. The kitchen folk were only 1s and made of rather cheap stone bisque and the baby in the bedroom in his 1s cradle cost only one penny. The parian twins in the dining-room would seem to be a rather haughty pair of resident aunts – a force to be reckoned with in most Victorian households.

Perhaps Mrs Boase herself was a little surprised or even alarmed to find that when all was totted up she had spent a total of £18 1s1d: a sizeable amount in 1864! Perhaps she felt it was high time to rule a final line in her neat little book. More likely she was unable to resist from time to time adding some small extra. The greatest charm of her house is that it is now as it was when first built, scarcely altered in any detail, and must represent very closely the sort of rooms she herself lived in. The work-table in the drawing-room (1s 6d) is well stocked with scissors and fittings (4s); the family portrait album with ornamental clasps (6d) lies ready on the occasional table. The larder is well stocked with plaster model food dishes of hams and fish and poultry (listed as 'Bag Meats 2s 6d') and the inevitable singing bird's cage is hung in the dining room. The sixpenny china dog originally listed in the drawing room has judiciously found his way to the dining room (and found some friends *en route*) and the cat with her sixpenny basket of kittens has been quite properly transferred from the bedroom to the drawing room. It is an undisturbed idyll of domesticity.

The very fact that small goods in such variety were obtainable for furnishing these houses shows how popular the hobby had become. It was a pastime in which the whole family might join.

10

....

Automata and Mechanical Dolls

Man, having made figures in his own image, always dreamt of making them move: to walk, talk, perform. It is the theme of many stories and legends from remote time. Greek mythology gave the god Vulcan the powers and magic art of making not only lifelike figures, but ones that could move about by the mobile force of that fascinating metal 'quicksilver' or mercury. Magic, indeed, was often the underlying principle of such ambitions and the desire to impress, mystify or mislead, or to give an oracle utterance, like the speaking heads of Egypt, was all calculated to persuade a gullible and superstitious public. The wonderful inventions of Hero of Alexandria (285–222 BC) in providing apparatus which made birds sing, model priests pour libations or little theatre scenes work automatically were based on physical properties. Though no examples of his working figures survive, he left works which exactly describe and illustrate his methods using hydraulic, pneumatic and mechanical action.

But it was with the invention of clockwork machines and the steel spring that automata really came into their own. From the *jacquemarts* or mechanical figures which struck the hours in some early clocks, it was only a step to the evolution of performing figures which possessed an identity of their own, worked by clockwork but unassociated with a timepiece.

By the eighteenth century, there was great competition in inventing ingenious mechanical figures who could give a variety of clever performances. Musical automata were obviously popular but, looking at some of the earliest examples, one realizes that they are less working figures than musical instruments hidden in the outer casing of a human shape. The famous flute-player and tambourinist of Vaucanson (1738–82), which so enchanted audiences all over Europe together with his diverting mechanical duck, were based partly on his knowledge of mechanics, but more especially on his skill as a musician. The fantastic dulcimer player, which was made in 1780 by two Germans, the cabinet-maker Roentgen and the mechanical wizard Kintzing, and which belonged to Queen Marie-Antoinette, is now displayed in the Conservatoire des Arts et Métiers in Paris, as charming as the day she was made. Her performance was so exquisite that special music was composed for her by Gluck. Yet another musical lady produced by the Frenchmen Jacquet-Droz and Maillardet in 1784 was still being exhibited to enraptured audiences in England in 1827. In company with a rope-dancer, a magician and the Juvenile Artist, she was shown at Hull and an on-the-spot witness reported: 'She plays upon an elegant organ a variety of pleasing airs. The fascinating sweetness of her countenance and the lovely motion of her eyes never fail in securing admirers. She bows gracefully to the audience, her bosom heaves as if naturally influenced by the lungs and every note is produced by the brilliant touch of her fingers, with the exceptions of the flats and sharps which are *played by her feet!*' The wonderful creature had a repertoire of eighteen different tunes.

'The Juvenile Artist' referred to was probably also the work of Jacquet-Droz, father and son, who were responsible for some uncannily lifelike 'androids', including a child writer and a child draughts-

119 'Juvenile Artist': a writing child made by Pierre Jaquet-Droz in 1774; 27 inches

man. These were sculpted out of wood and were about twenty-seven inches high with natural hair and lifelike eyes. Although they took no one in, there was an air of mystery about such figures made to look, in every detail of size and appearance, as near as possible to a living, moving child. Neuchâtel Museum possesses two originals [119].

The mechanism of such figures was unbelievably intricate. A family living in Philadelphia this century possessed the derelict remains of one such mechanical scribe which they had always thought to be the work of Johannes Mälzel. Thanks to brilliant restoration work at the Franklin Research Museum the figure was mended and set in action. When the mechanism worked once more and the doll was reconstructed, with a modern pen in its hand, it was able to identify itself, for it traced out a little verse in French with beautiful scroll work and copperplate writing, and signed it at the end:

> *Enfant chéri des dames,*
> *Je suis en tout pays*
> *Fort bien avec les femmes*
> *Même avec les maris   (Ecrit par l'Automate de Maillardet)*

Maillardet was a contemporary of Jacquet-Droz with whom he worked.

Johannes Mälzel, a German born in Regensburg in 1783, is credited with the honour of first inventing a doll with a synthetic voice. Many mechanical experts had worked on the problem of reproducing speech sounds during the eighteenth century, including Baron von Kempelen, who produced speaking machines which could utter the different vowel sounds. Mälzel was associated with von Kempelen and seems to have worked on the same principles on a scale diminutive enough to use in a doll. Only one tantalizing clue seems left in a reference to a 'child mannequin made of wax' by the English inventor Robertson, in a letter written by a friend who said it 'pronounced every letter of the alphabet perfectly. The manner in which it afterwards said a lot of words was quite intelligible. It was an absolutely astounding thing...'

A detailed description and a drawing of the actual mechanism of the Mälzel doll was provided by M. Muller of Pau for *Automates* by Chapuis and Droz (1949) the authoritative book on the subject, but this clue, too, seems to have vanished, as this single surviving doll has disappeared. Mälzel won an award in 1823 at the Paris Exhibition, perhaps for this very type of doll, for which he took out a patent in 1824. The principle was a bellows action which was alternately pumped by the left and right arms sending sound through a reed to a voice box behind the mouth. The valve controlling the air made an explosive double sound, 'Pa-Pa', and then, muffled by another small apparatus, repeated the sound as a muted 'Ma-Ma'.

In the late 1820s, Mrs Child, in editing a little anthology for girls, *The Girl's Own Book*, included a conversation between a fictitious aunt and her niece about a visit to London. The very first question asked by the child was 'Did you go to see Mr Mälzel's automatons?' – a naïve plural which Aunt Susan properly corrected to 'automata'.

The account of these wonders is even more surprising as, after referring to the 'Chessplayer dressed like a Turk' (which is known to have been made by Baron von Kempelen and purchased from him by Mälzel in 1825 for public exhibition), and to the Trumpeter, which is recorded as having been made by Mälzel in 1808, she goes on to describe a mechanical circus. This has a fountain in the middle complete with riders on horseback, a marksman firing at a bird, a famous vaulter leaping hurdles, a Clown and a Harlequin. Finally, she describes the Rope-dancers:

> To me they are most wonderful of the whole. These two little figures performed all manner of feats on a rope suspended across the room. Sometimes they were seated firmly with arms outstretched, sometimes they turned heels over head; sometimes they hung with head downward and sometimes they were suspended only by one foot. This was all done so naturally that it really seemed as though the little creatures were alive. I felt half afraid they would tumble and break their bones. By moving the limbs of these figures they could be made to utter quite distinctly 'Mama', 'Papa' and 'la, la'!

We feel almost tempted to remark with Ann, the child listening, 'This is so very wonderful, that I should not believe it, if you did not tell me that you had seen it.' But even accepting a little journalistic licence, it is possible that Mälzel went on to adapt his ideas for speaking and performing dolls and there are other accounts of this period which refer to the wonderful exhibitions of automata.

Mechanical walking dolls seem to have been attempted even earlier than talking dolls [120]. Another engraving, designed by the French artist Cochin, and engraved by Madeleine Cochin, shows a candle-lit room full of people exclaiming with pleasure and all intent on watching a little dressed walking doll about a foot high who is walking forward

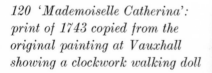

120 'Mademoiselle Catherina': print of 1743 copied from the original painting at Vauxhall showing a clockwork walking doll

121 *Mechanical doll made by Pierre Gautier*

in the centre front of the picture. A magic lantern showman at one side leans forward on his instrument and one guesses that this is the grand finale of his show. The verse beneath the engraving, with philosophy typical of the period, says it is often the lot of man to be 'worked' by the unknown 'powers-that-be' just as little 'Catin' is moved by a hidden spring. An eighteenth-century print from a set of the 'Cries of Paris' by Bouchardon showed a child displaying *Petite Catin* and the long, voluminous skirt which conveniently hides her works has a hem just sufficiently high to show a glimpse of a little guiding wheel in the front and a larger driving wheel at the back. That children did play with clockwork toys at this period is obvious from a remark made in a letter from a Mrs Carter to a Mrs Montague (December 1775) when she writes of an overworked friend that they are 'treating her as children do a clockwork toy, which they never think has diverted them long enough till they have forced and broken the springs'.

There are still examples in present-day collections of walking dolls of the eighteenth century. One made by Pierre Gautier and signed by him as early as 1764 seems to play a guitar with her right hand as she moves forward and revolves. In the Cavailles collection is another which is presumed to be his work: her mechanism is a heavy base with two front wheels which are worked by clockwork [121]. Alexandre Nicholas Théroude was another toy-maker who specialized in walking mechanical dolls and his advertisements appeared as early as 1842.

All these dolls seem to have been worked on a wheeled framework, but in a letter from one Bruguier, one of a family of makers of automata and singing birds, he speaks of a walking doll made by his eldest brother, Charles Bruguier, who lived in London from 1815:

'One was a little doll who walked like a real person *putting one foot after another* and turning her head. The mechanism which worked her was entirely hidden in her body which was left unclothed to demonstrate this fact. The little figure could walk on any table and she carried a rake which gave her the necessary balance.' This model was made in London in 1821 and the customer was very satisfied, as she had asked many clever mechanics to attempt to make her such a doll without success.

It is interesting to discover that at the same time as the French and German mechanical wizards were treating the English public to these performing joys, it was possible to buy, in London shops, quite simple handmade working toys which convey considerably the spirit of the time. Figure 122 shows three working dolls from the collection of Miss Blair Hickman. They carry labels on the base which show that they were sold at 'EDLIN'S RATIONAL REPOSITORY OF AMUSEMENT AND INSTRUCTION', 37 New Bond Street, next door to where the auctioneers Sotheby & Co. now have their London sale rooms. In 1811, Edlin of New Bond Street was listed in a London directory as a turner and silversmith, so it is obvious that he branched out along other lines during the next ten years. Nothing is known of John Hempil who signed the toys and he may either have been actually employed on the premises or have been an outside contributor with a home workshop. The dolls are made of carved wood with plaster-applied features and they depict 'Spinning', 'Taking snuff' and 'Influenza: Powerful Symptoms'. The chairs and base stands are simply

122 Working model dolls made by John Hempil of London in 1820: 'Spinning'; 'Influenza'; 'Snuff-taking'

made of soft wood painted over quite crudely, but the figures themselves are cleverly sculpted from plaster over a wooden base reinforced with strips of leather which act as hinges at neck or shoulder. Where the joints are made to move, as in the right arm of the snuff-taker and the spinstress or the influenza victim, a small wire spring of about the same diameter as the arm is used. Strings threaded through the hollow core of the body and worked by a thin wooden lever attached to the base-board by a leather hinge make the fat lady with influenza wave her fan to cool her heated brow as the be-wigged quack feels her pulse. The characterization is very amusing and was based perhaps on the *Tour of Dr Syntax*, written by William Combe and illustrated by Rowlandson and extremely popular at that time. The toy is dated 1 July 1819.

The 'snuff-taker' is a little more complicated and is worked by three levers. At first I thought that the front lever was not working until I found that her eyes were slowly opening and shutting. It is a sinister sight: the eyes are not made of glass but of carved balls of wood from which a plaster covering has peeled, giving them a gruesome, baleful expression like a chicken blinking at the daylight. The whole face is rather witchlike and reminiscent of certain character-designed pedlar dolls (see chapter 7). It would be interesting if any collector were to find a contemporary John Hempil crone among her pedlar dolls. The middle lever moves her right arm across to take a pinch of snuff from a box no doubt originally held in her left hand, and the third lever turns her head from side to side. So, in sequence, she probably took snuff, sniffed with each nostril in the approved style and then closed her eyes in appreciation.

The third doll has an even more complicated mechanism. A wooden handle at the side turns an ingenious roller concealed under the platform base. This winds three separate strings simultaneously, one working the treadle of the spinning wheel beneath the old lady's foot, the middle one keeping her hands busy with the thread, which is carried by tiny holes through the plaster, and the third inclines her head as she works. This, too, is attached to the body by a wire spring so that she would not jerk but sway in her movement. A limb or head worked by a string would adjust to its original position by the wire spring-joint.

The pretty fragments of material of which the dresses and shawls are made and the fine lace of the bonnets have become dusty and faded in the course of one hundred and fifty years, but must have once looked very pretty and gay, with minute floral patterns, spots and stripes. The three toys in their original state must have looked very lifelike and amusing. It is difficult to picture them as new, but they possibly stand as unique examples of the work of an early nineteenth-century dollmaker.

The search for perfecting a realistic walking doll continued throughout the nineteenth century and the diversion of the *salon* became the plaything of the Victorian nursery. The mother teaching her baby to walk is at pains to give it the idea of balance, holding it lightly by the hands until it can stand upright and feel the weight of its body before

123 Wax-covered papier mâché baby doll in 'walker'; German; 7 inches

124 opposite: dolls' house from Nuremberg; 1639

125 overleaf: Theatrical group of miniature dolls dressed by children, probably representing a pantomime cast of the '70s

127 Mechanism of the
Autoperipatetikos *(revised model)*

mastering the first few staggering steps. The maker of a walking doll is faced with this same complex problem of balance for, however cleverly he may simulate the mechanics of stepping or moving forward, the little figure must be steadied on its way and can never, like the human baby, master balance of its own accord. Sometimes eighteenth-century dolls were supported on leading strings (like babies of the period), an early version of 'reins', on which they could be dangled along the ground as though walking, and by the end of the next century a mechanism had been mastered which could propel a doll forward if she was held by the hands.

One of the cleverest walking dolls, the *Autoperipatetikos*, was invented by an American, Enoch Rice Morrison of New York City, and a patent was taken out in England in 1862 by a mechanical draughtsman, A. V. Newton, who left a very elegant design of the doll and its mechanism. Head and dress varied and some examples are found with parian heads, some with highly glazed porcelain heads with black or blond hair, and, rarely, with a moulded wax or papier mâché head. The head was mounted onto a stuffed bust with kid arms, and the skirt of the doll concealed a bell-shaped hollow cylinder over a wood base. One labelled box represented a male character clothed in a zouave costume. The mechanism [127] was very well made and beautifully articulated with a strong spring that has in most cases lasted to this day after countless windings. Except when the model has been neglected and the works have become damp and rusted, *Autoperipatetikos* trots along as well as the day she was first made. 'Trots' in fact is rather misleading as the movement is more one of gliding or skating over the surface. A little perpendicular bar comes down inside the leg and through a hole in the centre of the sole projects just sufficiently for the foot to be raised off the ground; at the same time, the other leg swings forward and a little bar in that sole in turn protrudes as the first leg follows through its forward step. If one visualizes someone walking on stilts, that is the action which this doll really imitates. The feet are set sufficiently wide apart for the doll to balance, but even so, the first models apparently played up sometimes, as the winding instructions on the box end with the foreboding advice: 'If it should stop at any time, turn the feet toward you and see if the inside leg is not caught against the feet. Do not wind too tightly.'

It seems that the first patent was improved upon. The toy shown in figure 128 works in exactly the same manner, but the feet are made of strongly pressed gilt tin and are much steadier than the little black boots of the first models, if not so realistic in appearance. An alternative to balancing the actual doll was to provide a wheeled support which they could push along as their legs walked [126]. This was a principle used by the American inventor, William P. Goodwin of New York, who in 1868 patented a doll with a spring-wound mechanism which moved the legs very realistically as she pushed a pram. The *Scientific American* of 1868 reported: 'Some of the most ingenious and interesting mechanical toys that have been invented are the walking boys and girls just being introduced in Broadway. The figures are constructed so that they literally walk, taking up the feet by bending the knees in most life-like manner.'

128 Autoperipatetikos *with china head modelled after Empress Eugénie*

*129 Pull-along mechanical Pierrot
on platform of 1880; French;
10 inches*

*130 right: 'Magicienne' by
Decamps,
using Jumeau doll heads;
2 ft. 3 inches*

It may be seen that by the 1860s the dollmakers had begun to realize the attractions of surprise or 'novelty' dolls in a competitive market. Some of the most famous doll firms in France were looking for ways in which ingenious mechanisms could make their luxury dolls perform even more realistically, thus endearing themselves even more to their customers. Existing makers of automata began to realize how profitable the doll market was, and either lent their services to doll firms or acquired doll parts to make up automata in new guises with beautiful bisque heads and, often, musical box accompaniment.

M. Jean Roullet was the founder of a famous firm of automata makers in 1865. He won a bronze medal at the Paris Exhibition of 1867 and was famous for the fine performing characters he produced and for articulated animals. In the 'eighties he went into partnership with his son-in-law Ernest Decamps, who had married his daughter Henriette and whose son, Gaston, the present head of the family, is still producing automata and robots along the same lines as his father and grandfather. The bisque heads made by Simon & Halbig or Jumeau saved the maker of automata a great deal of time as it was simple enough to adapt mechanisms which had been used earlier for negro fluters, monkey conjurors or instrument players, snake charmers and acrobats into pretty little boys and girls duplicating the same actions for different purposes. The actions of the squirrel which popped up from a tree-trunk and slowly nodded to music, or the rabbit which appeared similarly from the heart of a cabbage, could be simulated by a doll appearing from a basket of sweetmeats or from the cupped petals of a rosebud.

131 Decamps catalogue pages printed in 1911 in Paris

There was an infinite number of charming variations on these performing dolls and partly because people have cherished them for their beauty and interest, but also on acount of the skill and craftsmanship which went into their making, many examples are still preserved today in working order. Dolls holding an Easter egg or bird cage, little waifs of Paris selling flowers or cherries from a basket, prodigies who perform on piano or violin, pretty girls conjuring at a table, playing with dolls, blowing bubbles from a pipe, or dressed up as Red Riding Hood: all came from the famous Roullet-Decamps workshops with a strong winding key and tinkling musical movement to give pleasure for many years.

M. Decamps has kindly allowed me to reproduce some pages from a catalogue issued in 1911 which showed models then current, though many of them were based on similar pieces planned years before. An early photograph of him at work in his studio (reproduced in *Automates* by Chapuis and Droz), painting the heads of some of his famous acrobats, showed him using a sort of frame of sticks on which he perched heads, legs and arms while he finished them by adding features. Later these would be incorporated with a working body and dressed. When bisque came to take the place of papier mâché, dainty porcelain legs and arms were fastened to wires by plugs and the movement of each little performer was synchronized to the strains of the musical box on which it was mounted [135].

In 1845, another Parisian maker of mechanical dolls, Jean Rousselot, had taken out a patent for a simple walking doll which moved on a little platform on three wheels. The doll had a china head and its arms moved up and down as it rolled along, but the body was no more than a cylinder of strong card which hid the clockwork mechanism and provided a base for its dress. Figure 132 shows a similar, but later version of a 'walking' doll which had persisted from the early *Petite Catin* right through to the beginning of the twentieth century. In this case she has four wheels and her pretty bisque head swivels from side to side. She is nine inches high and has fixed blue glass eyes, flaxen hair and composition hands. Her cheap dress fabric is sadly perished but she still works.

132 Clockwork walking doll with cylinder body on wheeled base; German; 9 inches

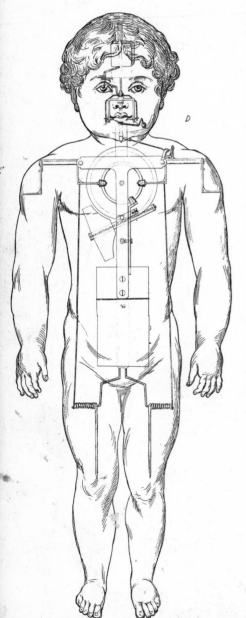

By the end of the century there were various clever walking dolls. Jules Nicolas Steiner, who was originally a clockmaker in Paris, first took out a patent for a mechanical doll in 1855 [133]. Whether or not this quite extravagant model was ever marketed is doubtful, but he obviously worked on the idea. He was awarded a Silver Medal in the Paris Exhibition of 1878. In 1890 he patented 'Bébé Premier Pas', which was meant to imitate the first steps a baby takes. The doll with a strong wind-up mechanism could step forward when held by a hand or from the shoulders. Figure 134 seems to be an earlier version of this doll. She has a very beautiful face of the finest quality unmarked bisque with slightly open mouth and teeth, fixed blue glass eyes and a wig of tightly curled fair hair. A heavy gold key on her left-hand side with an on-off lever winds the mechanism which causes her to turn her head from side to side, move her arms up and down and her legs backwards and forwards. She utters a plaintive cry with a double note and is dressed in a grey frock trimmed with black velvet, scalloped edging, and buttons with a pink band. She wears long white drawers and white petticoat with a pinned-on handkerchief. Her composition arms and legs are rather small in proportion, while her torso, because of the machinery, is a very curious lumpy shape. A similar model in Edinburgh has exactly the same mechanism and movement, but her head is a different model, early bisque with lamb's wool hair.

Another rare walking doll in the Edinburgh collection is quite different in type and so rare that one is led to believe that few were produced [189]. She bears the Dep. 10 mark, is eighteen inches high and follows a patent taken out for a walking doll by Fleischmann and Bloedel in 1895. Her head is German bisque with lovely grey-blue eyes, dimpled chin and mouth open to show two white teeth. The body has been cut away to display the heavy and powerful mechanism, a clockwork motor wound from the doll's left side driving double chains which work wheels in the feet. The head moves from side to side as she walks and her arms swing up and down, attached by long wires to the clockwork. The bellows for her voice are attached to a solid wooden block which is screwed in place with three screws in the doll's back. A knobbed lever on the right-hand side stops and starts the mechanism and the rather thick carton body fabric and straight legs are moulded in one piece.

*133 Steiner patent for
a walking doll, 1855*

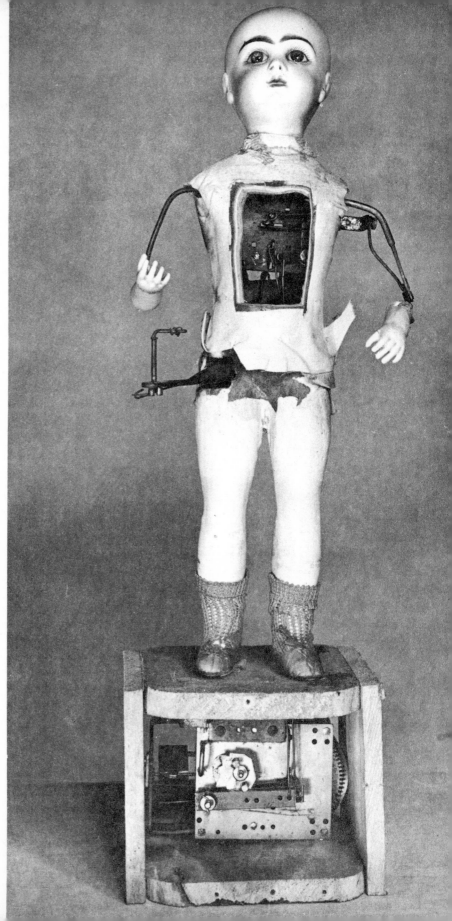

134 Clockwork walking doll,
unmarked but probably Steiner
(see 133)

135 Base of 'Le Cerisier' made by
Decamps with a musical box.
The head marked 'Jumeau dep'

11

....

Wax Dolls

A 'Comical Figure which drummed, opened and shut its mouth and rolled its eyes, stood between two lifelike children in waxwork' to summon the audience to a waxwork show called the 'Temple of Diana' at old Bartholomew Fair in London in 1699. It is one of the earliest records of the popular appeal of this form of entertainment. Among the famous personalities who practised the art of wax sculpture was one 'Mrs Salmon' whose handbill in 1711 advertised: 'Mrs. Salmon's Waxwork – Royal Court of England – the moving waxwork: 140 figures as big as life, all made by Mrs Salmon who sells *all sorts of moulds and glass eyes* and teaches the full art.' At that time she showed at *The Golden Salmon*, St Martin's, near Aldersgate, but the exhibition moved to a house in Fleet Street and was one of the sights of the town until the old lady's death in 1760 at the age of ninety. The collection then changed hands many times until vandals plundered and broke up the figures in 1827. She was famous for such historical characters as Alexander the Great, Henry VIII, Caractacus and the Duke of York. A contemporary visitor remembered a model of the seer 'Old Mother Shipton', who would aim a kick at the visitor as he departed.

Wax is recorded from the very earliest times as a modelling material and has obvious advantages in that it may either be used in a liquid melted state to take the accurate form of a mould, or sculpted by hand in the block. It was used variously for effigy and votive figures, for shaping the religious characters of the crèche scene or for the diminutive figures who peopled the first 'baby-houses'.

It was the sculptor Nollekens who, at the end of the eighteenth century, referred playfully to the effigies surviving in Westminster Abbey as 'the wooden figures with wax masks all in silk tatters, that the Westminster boys called the "Ragged Regiment"'. 'The Play of Dead Volks', as they were also called, represented princes and others of high quality, the past kings and queens of England, buried in the Abbey. They were made life-size to resemble the deceased as nearly as possible and were exposed at the funeral of great personages in open chariots with their proper ensigns of royal honour appended. (Now once again they are shown in something of their former glory, restored in 1952 by a brilliant feat of scientific skill and research.) Macabre though it may be, a corpse provides the ideal model for a plaster cast and a wax mask prepared from such a mould produces an exact replica of the features and expression. Real hair used for the wig contributes even further to the lifelike appearance and wax itself subtly imitates the human complexion, expecially as it is possible to introduce delicate colour tints. Perhaps waxworks and funeral effigies may seem hardly relevant to the subject of dolls, but the methods used were later deployed in much the same manner to create some of the most beautiful play-dolls.

By an odd coincidence, the very year that Mrs Salmon died, 1760, saw the birth in France of a child of genius who was destined to be one of the greatest wax-modellers of all time: Madame Tussaud, who also lived to be ninety years old. She was taught the craft by her uncle M. Curtius. After the French Revolution, in which she was actually employed to make wax masks of some of those beheaded by the guillotine, she set up an exhibition in Paris and this was brought to the Strand Lyceum, London, in 1802. Her original figures were destroyed by fire and the historical collection of costumes and personal mementoes of famous persons also perished. The tradition has been preserved and today it is still considered the eventual mark of fame to be represented in wax at the modern 'Tussaud's' in Baker Street, London.

Figure 136 shows a very beautiful doll or miniature portrait figure which is said to be the work of Madame Tussaud herself and a self-portrait at the age of about twenty-eight (1788). An interesting German doll [137] shows a head that was made of poured wax, much as the Tussaud doll, but in this case was reinforced by a thin fabric which was inserted before the wax was fully set or between successive layers of wax. Thought to date from about 1750, she is twenty-six inches tall and wears a splendid gown of turquoise taffeta trimmed with little bows and lace. Her arms and head are nailed to the stuffed body and legs. She is as German in character as the Tussaud doll is French: plump and homely with brown glass eyes, her face is the face

136 Miniature wax portrait thought to be Mme Tussaud designed by herself c. 1788 when she was 28; 24 inches

137 Poured wax doll from Nuremberg c. 1750; 26 inches

138 Wax doll in original dress; German; c. 1730; 19 inches

139 right: 'Stulpnase' or 'Bagman's Baby'. Wax over papier mâché; German; 1820; 10 inches

encountered every day in Bavaria. Her hair is modelled from the wax and is neatly ordered and tightly trained from the forehead in the severe fashion of the period. A more obvious play-doll in the same collection is nineteen inches tall [138]. She bears a family resemblance to the last lady and could almost be her daughter, with dark brown eyes, a pert expression and a half-open mouth revealing the tip of a tiny red tongue. Although the attribution gives 1730, her pretty green silk dress is hardly faded and beneath it she wears a hooped underskirt trimmed with little red rosettes and embroidered slippers.

The term '*Stülpnase*' or 'turned-up nose' is sometimes used to describe German dolls, as they often have this rather endearing characteristic. Figure 139, a cheaply made little person, not only has a turned-up nose, but a slightly rubbed-off one. She dates from the beginning of the nineteenth century and is of the sort sometimes referred to as a 'Bagman's Baby', as she was cheap and hardy enough to be included among the hawker's stock-in-trade. She is gaily dressed in a quick, professional way with coloured scraps and ribbons. Her scanty curls are attached from a centre slit in her crown: a simple method often used in cheaper dolls and one which often proves fatal, as the wax tends to crack down very easily from the incision.

By far the highest proportion of nineteenth-century German 'wax' dolls were made by the method used for this one and were not truly wax at all, but had a head made of hollow moulded papier mâché or carton. The wax was only an extension or improvement to give an attractive finish to the complexion. When the thin wax surface cracked, and little fingers picked at it, the brilliant colour of the underneath surface quite often showed through, for the papier mâché head (made by the process outlined in chapter 6) was painted before being dipped into vats of liquid wax, and the colour showed through the transparent coating. Thus Negro babies with a dark brown undercoat look as though they are made of milk chocolate with their final wax layer. Finally lips, eyebrows and cheek colour could be added by hand and a made-up wig fitted or hair slotted in the surface. The poor relic shown on page 7 shows the type perfectly, as she is stripped to essentials and we can see where the disc was cut from her papier mâché crown in order to fix in place the squirrel-like brown eyes of blown glass. Similar dolls were made on more de luxe lines [156].

Both process and finish were improved in a doll of about 1875 [140]. She has sleeping eyes worked by the counter-weight principle and chubby arms and legs of wax-coated moulded composition. She is in perfect condition and her owner explained that she belonged to a Quaker family where the children were not allowed to play very much with their dolls but could stand them up and sing hymns to them! She is brilliantly dressed in a scarlet wool frock with black and white trim.

140 Wax doll of 1875; 12 inches

141 Wax doll with flirting eyes; German; 1880; 12 inches

142 right: German 'pumpkin-head' wax doll; 1850; 18 inches

Another doll, similar in size to the last, is one of the most engaging I have ever seen [141]. Dating from the late 1880s she has an indisputably French look about her. The toy-seller Cremer, famous in Victorian London, once wrote: 'If you quiz the ankle of Mlle Maquette you will find it lacks the fine turn of ankle of her symmetrical rival.' *Maquette* in this sense meant a 'small rough model', the German as opposed to the French. In this doll the fingers are gesturing, and the boots are exquisite, painted pale tan with gold tips and buttons. The lacy dress with red bows seems to be original and gives a last touch of Parisian *élan* while no photograph does justice to her sparkling eyes set by the 'flirty' method which allows them to glance from side to side. Yet a very similar doll of possibly a little later date had the indisputable trade mark of Cuno and Otto Dressel of Sonneberg and it must be conceded that they are German in origin with a Parisian wardrobe.

A variation on the wax-covered papier mâché or carton base incorporated a moulded hair style and ornament or hat in the actual design, as against the bald wax-covered pate which needed to be covered by a wig. There was ample scope for fancy headgear and ornate hair grooming, as the colour could be applied beneath the wax. The term 'squash' – or 'pumpkin' – head has been fittingly used for

*143 Cheap character dolls with
bonnet heads: coloured papier
mâché beneath wax coating;
German; pre-1850; 8 and 10 inches*

the type whose brushed back golden hair makes the head resemble
such fruit. This type dates generally from the 1840–60 period and was
made in various sizes. Figure 142, eighteen inches tall, has wooden arms,
small in proportion to her height, and painted wooden button boots.
Once again she is a typical Germanic type and her fair hair is held
back in five moulded ringlets by a painted blue comb. Her dress is
shop made and has blue ribbon prettily trimmed on the white muslin.

This moulded method was a favourite for small dolls of cheap
quality, such as those which were stuffed with hay or straw and which
held a little voice-box squeaker in their middle. One of the dolls in
figure 143 has a flowered hat and the other wears a deeply moulded
bonnet and is also fitted with tiny wire spectacles. The simply made
one-piece wooden arms and wedge feet denote a sort of 'bazaar standard' German plaything.

In the last years of the century in Germany another cheap method
of making wax dolls was to provide a thinly moulded shell of wax into
which a lining of plaster composition was poured to give it substance,
but dolls of this type were not very durable and are often found
damaged; being poorly made they have little to endear themselves to
the collector unless they have been prettily dressed.

133

The export from German centres of toy-making such as Sonneberg, where the whole population was involved in the trade either as factory workers or as piece-makers at home, was enormous by the middle of the nineteenth century. An English writer commented:

We said that all little girls liked dolls. An exception should be made in the case of those who help to produce them. The work both in this country and others is so poorly paid that those engaged in it cannot help detesting dolls. In Sonneberg, for example, the average earnings are only three shillings a week for children, eight shillings for girls and women and sixteen shillings for men. The hours worked in London are also very long.

If German dolls were cheap and popular, those made of wax in England had the reputation of being very fine and expensive, and, one must conclude, exclusive. Though cheap dolls of the 'penny wax' variety were made and marketed, they were simple little objects more like animated candles, with eyes of coloured beads or blobs of wax. A report on the 1849 Paris Exhibition stated: 'For a long time wax busts have been obtained from England. Those that are made in Paris are less delicate but modelled more truly.'

The wax dolls for which England became famous were those made by the poured wax method used by the famous waxwork makers of the past. The head and limbs of a doll had first to be modelled and

144 Etching by Queen Victoria showing the Princess Royal as a baby

145 Small Royal dolls representing the Prince of Wales and the Princess Royal and originally belonging to them as children, c. 1840; 6 inches

then two- or three-part casts were made for each one. Liquid wax would be poured into these moulds and when set to the required thickness of shell, the surplus could be poured off for re-use. Finally the head and limbs could be trimmed by hand to remove any mould mark and to delineate and emphasize features. The work needed personal care and artistry at every step.

A display of wax dolls put on by one of the most famous exponents of the art, Madame Augusta Montanari, at the 1851 Exhibition in London, provoked this official comment from the Jury: 'The dolls are adapted for children of the wealthy rather than for general sale. Undressed dolls sell from ten shillings to one hundred and five shillings. Dressed dolls are much more expensive.' The 1851 Exhibition at the Crystal Palace had been especially built to put on show the industry of all nations. It was a royal occasion opened by Queen Victoria and her consort and attended by the eldest of her children.

Queen Victoria set a fashion in large families and she may also be said to have set a new vogue in dolls, for several famous makers of the period lay claim to being the Inventor of the Royal Model Doll, including Madame Montanari, Henry Pierotti, Charles Marsh and Charles Edwards. An etching made by the Queen herself in 1841 [144] shows a nurse holding up the Princess Royal. The Queen was certainly something of an artist and she enjoyed keeping a record with her pencil as well as writing a diary.

A room in Buckingham Palace was fitted for printing... This is probably the earliest picture known of the Empress Frederick of Germany, Princess Royal at the time, when the princess was only three months old. Every line, every item betokens how anxious the Royal artist was to obtain a faithful drawing of her first child, whose name 'Victoria' is written underneath...

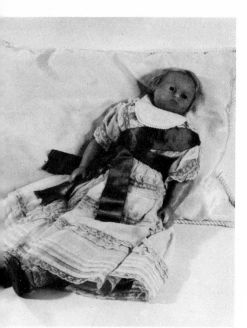

146 *Royal baby doll made by John Edwards, c. 1850; marked with cipher E on shoe; 15 inches*

This passage was included in an article written in the first volume of the *Strand Magazine* in 1890 when the old Queen was firmly settled in the affections of her people and the Princess Royal, born in 1840, had been married for years! At the time, matters seem to have been viewed differently and an amusing, but impudent cartoon of 25 April 1843 headed 'Tender Annuals' showed Prince Albert as a gardener with two small children in glass forcing frames and about to transfer a small baby from a flowerpot. A youthful Victoria watched over the fence and a truculent John Bull cried 'Hollo, Hollo young man, come, come! I shall have such a stock o' them sort of plants on my hands, I shan't know what to do with them!' A row of little pots numbered 1844–51 echoed the nation's fears of an annual addition to the Royal Family and the consequent drain on the taxpayer's purse. The fears were underestimated, since by 1856 there were nine royal children – ample models for an army of baby dolls!

Figure 145 shows two small dolls of the eighteen-forties which belonged to the Princess Royal and show her with her brother Prince Edward. They are simply-made with applied eyes of coloured wax – the larger almost life-size models of royal babies do not seem to have appeared until rather later.

Madame Montanari was the only maker of wax dolls to receive a Prize Medal at the 1851 Exhibition, but an engraving published at the time (Clark's 'Crystal Palace') shows people looking at a glass case full of rather small dressed dolls with miniature furniture. The entry was described in the following terms:

> This stall consists of a series of dolls, representing all ages, from infancy to womanhood, arranged in several family groups, with suitable and elegant model furniture. These dolls have the hair, eyelashes and eyebrows separately inserted in the wax and are in other respects modelled with lifelike truthfulness. Much skill is also evinced in the variety of expression which is given to these figures, in regard to the ages and stations which they are intended to represent. The younger dolls were modelled as likenesses to the children of the Royal Family.

Perhaps the Montanari family had originally come from Mexico to London, since it is apparant from his prize winning exhibit at the 1851 Exhibition that Napoléon Montanari (Augusta's husband) had had first hand experience of the country. He showed full-sized models in wax of Mexican Indians 'from the living originals', and since many of these had long hair and beards it was perhaps from such works of art that the technique of embedding hair in the wax was adapted for dolls. After Madame Montanari died in 1864, at the age of forty six, the business was carried on by her son, Richard Napoleon (born 1840) who became famous for his 'rag dolls'.

The Pierotti family, who worked at roughly the same period as the Montanaris, must have been business rivals and they still compete for the favour of collectors. Henry (or Enrico) Pierotti is not listed in the London Trade Directories until 1853, but the family is said to have been established there from about 1790, when Henry's father Domenico first began making dolls. He had originally come from Italy as a boy and it is interesting to note that his trade was that of a modeller in papier mâché especially involved in making panels and relief patterns for ceilings etc. (See 'The Pierotti Wax Doll' by Lesley Gordon, *Spinning Wheel*, 1957.)

It was Henry who claimed to be the inventor of the Royal Baby doll. There had been baby dolls before, such as wax baby dolls from Sonneberg with eyes made to shut by a lever and little curls painted above the ear on a wax-coated carton base [147]. But this did not compare with those advertised by Pierotti: 'With Human Hair implanted through the composition to form the wig. Hair, Eye lashes and Eye brows warranted to repair equal to new, by sending them where purchased. *La Sola Monifactura in Londre.*' In *The Doll and her Friends: Memoirs of the Lady Seraphina* (1850), Julia Maitland wrote, in the doll's words: 'I am but a small doll, not one of those splendid specimens of wax modelled from the Princess Royal with distinct fingers and toes, eyes that shut and tongues that wag. I first opened my eyes to the light of the Pantheon Bazaar – a silver paper covering was removed from my face, and the world burst into my view.' The Pantheon Bazaar was one of the earliest in London. It closed down in

1867, by which time the more popular one was the Soho Bazaar, also situated in Oxford Street.

Pierotti claimed in his advertisement that 'Young Ladies by sending their own hair can have it implanted through the composition to form a wig. Likenesses modelled and Cast taken.' The last sentence is particularly interesting and it would be fascinating to find any record of a family who had taken advantage of the offer. Occasionally fine wax dolls are found which do seem to have a living likeness and human hair retains its colour and texture though it may be a hundred or more years old. In the Tunbridge Wells Museum, Kent, a doll dating from 1840 has a record attached which says the hair used for the doll was from Mary Anne Marriott after she had her hair cut short. But there is no clue to the maker of the doll.

The typical Montanari and Pierotti dolls resemble each other but have differences. Fundamentally, the making of them was the same: the moulded heads, arms and legs were sewn to a stitched stuffed body by thread or tapes through holes made in the wax and in larger sizes lined with a metal eyelet. The Montanari is characterized by a heavier type of face altogether, with little neck showing, full cheeks, low brow, a mouth with an expression which is sometimes almost sullen. The Pierotti 'child of the pure untroubled brow' has a more alert look and is sometimes so Italianate in looks that one wonders if it was modelled on some child in the family. Their baby dolls have short flaxen curls or hair almost Titian in colour, whereas the Montanaris usually have luxuriant long, dark locks. The limbs of the Montanaris are plumper and characterized by creases inside the elbow joint and at the wrist. It is, of course, impossible to generalize about such dolls, when we remember how long both families were in business. Besides being craftsmen, they were earning their living by doll-making and no doubt innovations were constantly introduced and new materials used.

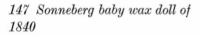
147 Sonneberg baby wax doll of 1840

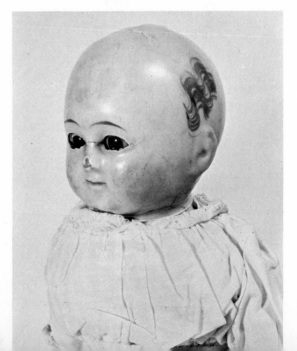

The Toy Museum at Rottingdean, Sussex, is fortunate in having been endowed with some of the tools and examples from the last years of the Pierotti firm – Mr J. C. Pierotti, grandson of Henry, continued in business until his retirement at the age of seventy-five in 1935. From this display [148] and the account of method which accompanies it, it is clear that the Pierottis were perfectionists. The best heads were made by three distinct pourings of wax: the first a very thin pale shell, the second a deeper pink colour and the last inner layer rather deeply hued to give the final flesh tint. A few existing Pierotti heads are marked with the name beneath the hair roots at the back, allegedly because of piracy. It was, of course, quite simple for anyone to take a cast from an existing doll head and make a replica, but to fake the careful finish of a master craftsman was a different matter.

Montanari dolls were also sometimes signed in ink across the torso, perhaps for the same reason. In addition to the fine poured wax models made by Madame Montanari, a cheaper version was marketed, invented by Richard Montanari, which was popularly known as a 'ragdoll'. Claire Mateux wrote in 1884 in *Wonderland of Toys*:

148 Display of Pierotti tools and doll parts showing blown and moulded types of glass eyes and hanks of hair

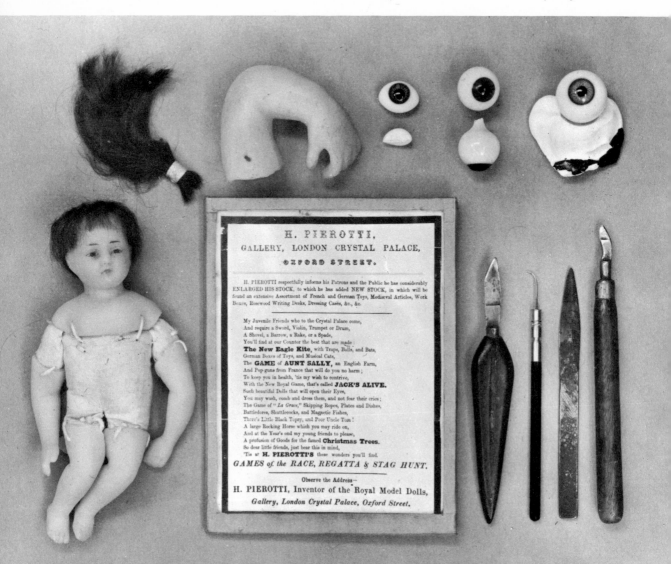

The rag doll is *not* made of rags. Its face is a kind of wax mask over which a piece of muslin has been stretched. It will very soon leak or melt if hugged too tightly. These faces have, as a rule, no back head belonging to them, but are fastened to a sort of skull, which is part and parcel of the body made of calico and stuffed with saw-dust just as that is. These limp blue-eyed babies are always arrayed in neat, tidy little night caps, the lace of which fits lightly around the soft features, and the bodies are in infant's robe and red merino hood to match the cap making altogether a suitable toy for a living baby.

Wax dolls are extremely difficult to date unless they survive with some positive family history, and the doll-researcher knows how often the most careful memory plays false. Some dolls bear the mark of a shop where they were bought, but most nineteenth-century toy-sellers had too long a record for even this to help very much in dating them. In London, Hamley's was founded in 1763, the Soho Bazaar opened in 1816, London Crystal Palace Bazaar 1858; the Corinthian Bazaar (1867) on the site of the old Pantheon and Cremer, in Bond Street, was selling both English and foreign dolls from the early 'sixties. Other well-known doll and toy shops in London were Pea-cock's in Oxford Street, Mrs Morell and Mrs Aldred of Burlington Arcade, Piccadilly, Aldis at Belgrave Mansions and E. Moody of the Soho Bazaar.

Some makers of wax dolls at this period have received more than their fair share of publicity, and others have lurked in obscurity because, even if we know their names, it is not possible to ascribe to them a single known example. It is an easier matter for the researcher in doll history – or in family trees – to track down Augusta and Napoléon Montanari or Enrico and Domenico Pierotti than, say, simple Charles Edwards or Herbert Meech. Yet Charles Edwards was listed as a dollmaker as early as 1853 and John Edwards, who is presumed to be his son, had established a factory in the Waterloo Road at which, according to an eyewitness report in the *Graphic* of 16 December 1871, he was manufacturing 20,000 wax dolls per week: 'We are not a great toy-making nation, but we admittedly beat the whole world in dolls, wax dolls. They are cast in moulds down to the feet with the delicacy of statuary art, the softly mottled and dimpled arms, the childish innocence of the faces, the eye swept with fine lashes and the hair real and elaborately arranged.'

These were not cheap dolls and the writer lists a superfine one as selling for £50. Just how skilful John Edwards was may be judged by the very beautiful figure which he exhibited at the 1871 Exhibition [157]. Completely Victorian in sentiment, with a certain resemblance to Millais's 'Bubbles', the doll represents a child at prayer. She is less a doll than a miniature waxwork. Yet the head, the arms to above the elbow and the legs to above the knees are made of poured wax and sewn to a stuffed cotton body through metal eyelet holes just as a doll would be. John Edwards was obviously keen to demonstrate how skilful the art of wax doll-making could be. The face and head is exceptionally expressive and the hair-rooting the finest I have ever seen; natural fair human hair has been inserted singly in the scalp and afterwards curled in tight ringlets all over with a distinct central parting. The lips are modelled, slightly parted with a tint of red, while the beautiful rayed forget-me-not blue eyes are set so that the eyelid droops a little over the pupil to give a dreamy, spiritual look. The linen entry form for the exhibition accompanies the model, which is listed as No. 100 in Class 10 'Girl at Prayers'. The twirly copperplate initial *E* written by John Edwards coincides with the imprinted *E* on the shoe sole of the Royal Baby Doll [146] and there are unmistakable similarities in the hand-made clothes which both dolls wear, which are rather simple garments of fine cotton with lace trimming.

Other dolls with a name or a shop address stamped on the linen fabric of their body have survived to bear witness to the sort of work carried out by some of the most important of the wax doll-makers of the nineteenth century. Charles Marsh, for instance, made some dolls which have a particularly Anglo-Saxon look, distinguished by fair flaxen hair, bright blue eyes and a well defined neck with the head held clear and erect from the shoulders. He is recorded in the London Trade Directory from 1878, but in an article in the *Strand Magazine* in 1895 about the Dolls' Hospital run by his wife after his death she says that they had been in existence for twenty years. This article even shows a sketch of the genial 'Dr Marsh' with some of her 'patients', besides publishing a photograph of one of her dolls. This appears to be almost as big as a child and has dark hair: 'she was born in this country and emigrated to America'.

Dolls made by Herbert John Meech are rare, and though it is recorded that he was 'Doll Maker to the Royal Family' and apparently a Royal Warrant Holder, the specimen of his work in the London Museum is unimpressive, and she has, in proportion to her size, very small hands and feet.

In most cases, wax modelling seems to have been the masculine side of the business, while the women dealt with the assembling and dressing. Mrs Lucy Peck, who was working at the turn of the century, made not only fine quality play-dolls [150], sometimes with movable eyes worked by a wire, but she also excelled at fine model dolls.

A report of 1893 in the children's magazine *Chatterbox* said: 'In London alone there are about forty manufacturers of such toys [wax dolls], mostly of better class. These superior articles are manufactured in large works where they go through many processes.'

But this was the last chapter for wax dolls. Fashions in dolls change, and the French and German bisque-headed dolls, cheaper, more finely made and more durable, had already begun to oust the luxury wax doll from its pinnacle. Most of the craftsmen had disappeared by the beginning of the twentieth century, though a few still advertised repairs and the last of the Pierottis was to continue until the 'thirties [152].

149 *Reproduction of a page from* The Strand Magazine *(1895):* '*Dr Marsh —mending dolls*'

150 Group of fine English
wax dolls with original clothing:
left, Montanari, 1863, 24 inches;
centre, Montanari, 1863, 25 inches;
and Mrs Peck, 1870, 27 inches.
Note the distinctive type of
Montanari costume

151 Late Pierotti doll bought at
Hamley's in London in 1916

152 French-made wax doll, one of
the first available in
England after the Siege
of Paris in 1872; 12 inches

12

....

Porcelain Dolls

153 and 154 Hochst figurines of about 1775 designed by Peter Melchior and showing doll types of the period

Dolls and doll-heads made of porcelain may be divided roughly into three categories: China, Parian and Bisque; but since these terms are not always understood and there has been much confusion in using them, it may be useful to give a little technical résumé.

The true difference between various types of porcelain and pottery is that of 'body' or ingredients on the one hand and method of making on the other. Just as in making a cake, the different materials, the proportions in which they are used and the way of mixing them together can produce entirely different results, though there the analogy must end, since though a cake may be a masterpiece, its life is at best temporary, while a precious vase, figurine or doll may, with care, last for ever. Nor is the production of fine porcelain the work of a single man, as its processes demand careful teamwork. In the first place there is the artist who fashions the original model from which the moulds are made. He *may* also be a potter or it may be left to a different artisan to carry out the actual skilled production and firing and finally to other men still to give the figure its painted details and glaze.

Although many attempts had been made to imitate the admired oriental wares brought from China, the country of its origin, true translucent, hard paste porcelain was not made in Europe until the Meißen manufactory in Germany discovered the secret of the necessary raw materials in about 1710. The fundamental ingredient is kaolin or china clay, but the addition and fusion under great heat of other materials determines the quality of the finished product, and glazing or 'enamelling' the matt surface of the baked clay still further alters its appearance.

The porcelain clay in its raw state ready for modelling may be kneaded and rolled out in sheets rather like a bread dough, cut into suitable pieces and pressed into moulds to take an impression. This was the method largely used for the fine bisque-headed dolls of the nineteenth century dealt with in chapters 13 and 14. Bisque or *biscuit* is merely the potter's name for the state of the cast when it has been fired once, before any colouring or glaze is applied. The porcelain is then hard, brittle, translucent and of dazzling whiteness. Colour and a light glaze or 'smear' may then be added and baked to make them fast.

For making small figures it was more convenient to use a different technique and the heavy clay mixture was watered down to form a rather liquid cream-like consistency which was called 'slip'. When slip was poured into a mould of plaster, or sulphur, the inside coating speedily dried out as the mould absorbed surplus moisture and the potter could pour back liquid slip before the cast was dried ready for firing, leaving a hollow interior. This method was adopted by some of the most famous German factories of the eighteenth century. Heads, bodies, legs, arms or any other piece of the model would be made separately, carefully joined together with liquid slip before the final firing and glazing operations. Figure 153/4 shows two comparatively simple but charming figures made in the Höchst factory in about 1775. Often the artist who first made the model from clay or wood or wax remains anonymous, but in this case it is known that the figures were designed by Peter Melchior. One little girl is shown holding up a swaddled doll of the wooden type popular in Germany in the eighteenth century; the companion piece shows a child with a jointed doll of a rather more sophisticated type. Note the high glaze, the careful modelling, the painted features, for the first 'China' doll probably evolved from these early figurines.

True 'Parian' ware was first produced by the English firm of Copeland and had a marble-like aspect as its name proclaims. It was never used for doll-making but most often for statuettes, classical-type busts and the figure groups particularly popular in Victorian times. The Parian type ware was, however, copied on the Continent of Europe and the name has now been extended to describe unglazed dolls with heads and limbs of this hard, matt texture which were made with poured slip in the same method as china dolls. The Parian body was particularly suitable for the portrayal of detail as it produced so clean-cut a line and it could also be effectively decorated with touches of glaze to highlight colours. Although true Parian was always completely white, colour was often incorporated in imitation Parian. Usually features were painted on. Larger model heads with inset glass eyes have been found, but they are uncommon. Parian was, in any case, not used very much before the eighteen-fifties and certainly the earliest type of porcelain doll-head was the highly glazed china one.

Where did these first doll-heads in porcelain originate and at what date? German ceramic experts tend to place them not very much earlier than the eighteen-thirties and certainly reference to them as playthings does not seem to appear before then. A contemporary report on a German trade exhibition of dolls in 1844 included wood, wax and papier mâché but it did not mention porcelain. The earliest made seem to have come from the fine porcelain factories and heads have been found with such famous marks as Meißen and Berlin and Nymphenburg, but a French report on the great London Exhibition of 1851 referring to 'the new porcelain heads made at Coburg and at Sonneberg' shows that by this date the vogue had reached the rich clay districts of Thuringia where the majority of dolls' heads were certainly produced. There is rarely any factory mark to help identify with certainty, but comparison of the surviving types does suggest the possibility that this art began at some factory where figurines were made, inspired perhaps by the idea of the separate head and limbs which had to be moulded and finally attached together. Maybe we shall never know for certain but all the evidence seems to indicate that they were in the first place fashioned for adults, a sort of 'dress your own figurine' novelty with a bust made with sew holes and arms and legs with an incised rim which could be attached to a made-up body.

The rare example pictured back and front [155] was brought to my notice by Frau Emmy Lehmann, custodian of the Sonneberg Museum. This head is thought to date from 1780–90 because of the hair style, which has a sickle shaped roll with the back hair held by a wide black

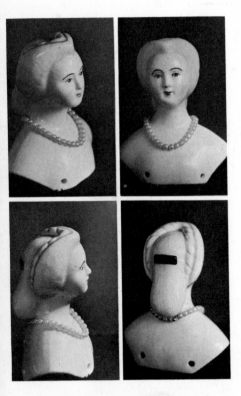

155 Early porcelain head from Sonneberg; late 18th century (?); 4½ inches

156 opposite: Wax over papier mâché doll with sleeping eyes worked by wire, German; 1850/60; 26 inches

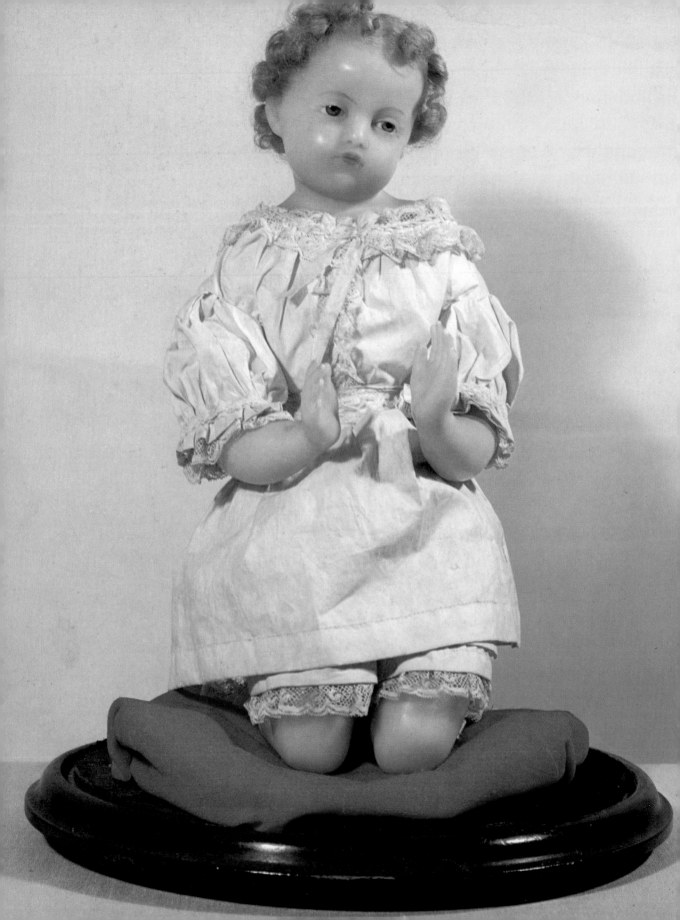

57 opposite: 'Child Praying':
a 1871 exhibition piece
signed by John Edwards
London; 16 inches

58 'Madame Enigma':
a puzzle of attribution;
made of Nymphenberg porcelain
for an exhibition in Munich in 1908
and dressed in period costume;
inches

159 China doll of 1830 with Berlin mark; 21 inches

clasp. It belonged to a family in Dessau and was treasured on account of its beauty. At one time it plainly belonged to a doll.

It is above all the fine quality of the porcelain itself and the individualistic modelling which identifies the earliest dolls. The hands posture with fingers separately moulded, the faces show expression, there is a delicate tinting of the cheek, the flesh colour is realistic and the limbs are remarkable for their long proportions and elegance. Mrs Severa, the Curator of Wisconsin State Historical Society Museum, christened one doll [158] Madame Enigma because of the problems she posed. Eighteen inches in height, she has been dressed in regal fashion over a wire supporting skirt and seems to depict some noble personage. Identical dolls, variously costumed and with different hair-styles, are in the Sonneberg collection and it has come to light that they were all part of an exhibit used in 1908 at the Munich Exhibition. The porcelain parts were supplied by the Nymphenberg factory on the model of a figure which originally dated from about 1750 and these were made up in the old style with leather bodies and clothed in historical clothes for the display. All of them have legs moulded to the knee with a roman sandal laced up the leg, painted in blue under the glaze.

Figure 159, from the Nuremberg Museum, shows a doll which bears the Berlin mark inside her shoulder. She is typically dressed in the colourful Bavarian national costume with dirndl skirt, embroidered blouse and bright headscarf tied in at the neck. She is twenty-one inches tall and is thought to date from the 1830s. Her hair is straight and painted brown beneath the glaze. She still has an adult

160 German Play-doll
of Biedermeier period with
contemporary clothing

161 right: Early nineteenth-
century
china-headed doll from
Thuringia

162 Rare German porcelain baby
head of Biedermeier period
mounted on 12 inch doll

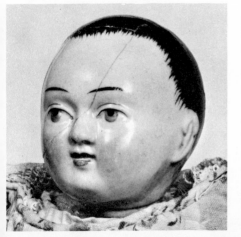

look, though it may be noticed here that the moulding of the fingers is less delicate.

The Biedermeier period in Germany, which extended roughly from 1805–1840, was one of affluence and comfort, typified by bourgeois respectability and domesticity which was reflected in the architecture, furnishing and clothing of the period. Two dolls from the Focke Museum, Bremen, show the accepted dress, with a lacy bonnet worn over ringlets or severely straight locks, a pretty full dress with loose or 'gigot' sleeves and snowy white apron [160 and 161]. These dolls begin to look more like true playthings and the porcelain face became progressively rounder and plumper and the arms and legs sturdier and more practical.

Figure 162 shows an unusual early baby doll-head with the fringe-painted hair-line which seems to have been the idiosyncracy of one Thuringian maker. The head is mounted on a twelve-inch stuffed body which is possibly handmade, for the dolls' heads made in various sizes were exported in bulk and sold ready to be sewn to a fabric or leather body or a movable wooden torso. This of course made them especially suitable for 'needlework' dolls (see chapter 7). One type of china head was in fact produced without a painted or moulded hair line; a round black painted disc indicated where a made-up wig might be secured, or it could be decently covered with a hat or bonnet. These heads seem to date from the Biedermeier period and the characteristic feet of the time have ankle boots without heels or little lace-fronted slippers and, sometimes, the fancy indication of a garter or sock.

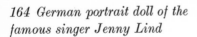

163 Patent specification for Petit doll heads, dated June 1843

In 1843, a famous Parisian potter, Jacob Petit, made a bid to contest the German doll-head market and occasional examples are found with his mark. The heads [163] were made from porcelain paste by exactly the same method as his other wares and he designed both a girl's head and a young boy. The girl resembles the portrait of young Queen Victoria at her coronation and indeed portrait model heads were popular with the makers of porcelain heads. Another favourite was the Swedish singer, Jenny Lind, about whom there was a great furore on each of her foreign visits. Often she was in Germany on tour and in 1846 she was entertained by the people of Munich,

164 German portrait doll of the famous singer Jenny Lind

166 Parian head doll with lustre glaze decoration and painted features

staying there privately with friends. Between October and December, she performed various Mozartian roles in the Hoftheater such as Donna Anna in *Don Giovanni* or Susanna in the *Marriage of Figaro*. The tall elegant figure with a winsome expression is a rare model which must date from just about this period [164].

Although high glaze might be suitable and attractive for figurines and ornaments, and of course provided a washable protective covering for the porcelain surface, it was not as realistic as the dull finish of Parian ware or bisque for a doll complexion. It was easier to convey detail with the chiselled Parian outline and a great range of different styles is found with fancy hats, ornamented hair with flowers or bandeaux, and even bust details of dress impressed from the mould as well as coloured.

Figure 165 has blonde hair groomed in a chocolate-coloured net snood which she exhibits for us as she gazes serenely into a little Georgian mirror. Her dress is of embroidered taffeta with an extremely elegant ground pattern of thin black lines on cream, set off by the blue bow and gold line of her embossed cravat, which show just above the neckline. The young lady in figure 166 bears an almost sisterly resemblance – and has the same rather poorly shaped stiff arms. She seems to be a shop-dressed doll with her simple flounced net dress and was no doubt a popular commercial line. I have found the same head used for *Autoperipatetikos* walking dolls (see chapter 10), which dates her certainly in the early 1860s. The gay hat is finished with pink lustre: an attractive touch used to ornament other similar dolls of the period. The term 'lustre' has sometimes been confused with glaze and used to describe the very high complexion colour used for certain china dolls. Lustre is, in fact, a metallic decoration derived chemically from gold or platinum in solution for use with porcelain. The gold lustre in particular is very translucent and when applied over a white ground provides an attractive pink or mauvish lustre after firing.

167 Boy doll with lustre boots, about 1870; 18 inches; German

From lustre hats to lustre boots brings us to an unusual pair of brother dolls in Worthing Museum [167]. There is no doubt at all that these are boys, for they wear their hair very neatly brushed in a quiff across the forehead in keeping with their very smart Sunday-best velvet suits. If velvet was *à la mode* in Victorian England, it was the kilt in Scotland, and plate 171 shows a Parian boy doll dressed in Highland Regalia (right down to red flannel underdrawers) in exactly the same manner as young Master Edwin Spencer Chalk whose photograph accompanies it. It is recorded that pieces of material from the child's dress were used for the doll. It is not known what Edwin thought of this project of his dressmaker, but the doll has never been played with.

Royal personages were especially popular as models for dolls in Parian. The Empress Eugénie, wife of Napoleon III, probably headed the list, after Victoria herself. She must have been a great beauty and a fascinating character. During the eighteen-fifties she was a European leader of fashion and her patronage made the Paris couturier Worth famous. In the porcelain dolls which have her style we need look no further for a likeness as there is nô doubt that she set the fashion for the roll of short hair off the forehead and coiled at the back. Her hair never seems to be reproduced in true colour: although of Spanish descent she had auburn hair. In a pencil sketch [168] made of the Empress when she was on a visit to the Isle of Wight in 1857, Queen Victoria, who was a fair artist, seems to have captured a good likeness. 'She is very pleasing, very graceful, and very unaffected, but very delicate,' wrote the Queen. When she bade Eugénie farewell, she was in tears and much grieved at her leaving. 'A dear, sweet, engaging and distinguished being, a fairy-like *Erscheinung* [appearance], unlike anyone I ever saw.' The Empress Eugénie was about thirty-one at this time and she lived to be ninety-four, so her 'delicate' appearance was deceptive!

A rare model pictures another Empress: Augusta Victoria of Germany, wife of the Kaiser Wilhelm II, grandson of Queen Victoria [169 and 170]. She is always found moulded with the Iron Cross on her bosom; she has pierced ears and wears a band of enamelled jewels in her hair. Both dark- and fair-haired versions are from the collection of Wisconsin Historical Society and must date from about 1881, the date of her marriage. In the second half of the nineteenth century the link between England and Germany was a strong one. Not only was Queen Victoria the daughter of a German, who was the widow of a Duke of Coburg, and herself married to a German husband, Prince Albert of Saxe Coburg, but in 1861 her eldest daughter, the Princess Royal, married a German prince and the Queen's first grandchild was destined to be the future Kaiser Wilhelm II. The Crown Princess was never popular in Germany, which perhaps explains the absence of dolls modelled in her image.

168 Pencil sketch by Queen Victoria, of the Empress Eugénie, 1857

169 and 170 Dark and light haired versions of Kaiserin Augusta Victoria: parian head doll with details of cross etc. moulded on bust

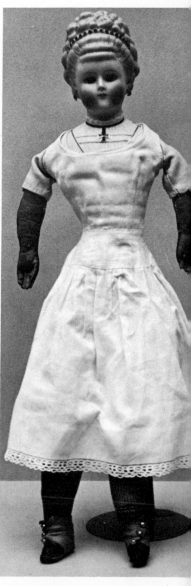

153

Many of the German porcelain factories were at that time geared to the English market because of these close royal connections. A great variety of ornaments and dolls were produced in Germany to appeal to this overseas market. Some carried on the making of dolls as a sideline in addition to other more valuable types of pottery and this was one reason why it was possible for German dolls to be produced so cheaply. Few of the manufacturers marked their dolls, so, although the records show that they made such wares, it is difficult to trace which pottery made which range of doll. Conta und Boehme, for instance, of Possneck in Saxony, a firm founded in 1790, had a long record of manufacturing all sorts of novelties as well as dolls in 'hard porcelain'. They are well-known to collectors through the series of 'Early to Bed' groups which bear comical captions in English and are stamped with the trademark of a shield with upraised arm. A trade advertisement of this firm (1907) listed: *'Fabrikation Hartporzellan: Luxus- u. Phantasieartikel für In- u. Ausland. – Spez. u. Export: Basarartikel in allen Preislagen, Kandelaber, Tafelaufsätze, Jardinieren, Uhrenständer, Spiegel, Gruppen, Pagoden u. sonstige Wackelfiguren, Spitzenfiguren, Figuren, Heiligenfiguren, Weihkessel, Tiere, Tabaksdosen, Zigarrenständer u. -schalen, Ascheständer, Streichfeuerzeuge, Menühalter, Senfmenagen, Schreibzeuge, Schmuck- u. Spiegeldosen, Vasen, Großartikel, Badekinder, Puppenköpfe, Zeugpuppen, Wandreliefs, Leuchter, Jardinieren zum Hängen. Ferner Fabrikation von feinstem Alabaster, Modell-, Form-, Stuck-, Bau- u. Düngegips.'* This list covers a very wide range, including 'Nodders', 'Holy figures', groups, people and animals, besides ornamental forms of ashtray, candlesticks, mirrors and porcelain 'boxes'. A box in my own collection which is typical shows a pretty fair-haired child in a flowered pinafore asleep in a high chair, with a little Polichinelle doll in a blue and white striped costume resting on the tray before her. This measures six and a half inches and has the trademark stamped inside the lid. The face is left only lightly glazed compared with the rest of the model and all the colour is underglaze apart from a few gilt details applied afterwards. The list including *Badekinder, Puppenköpfe* and *Zeugpuppen* shows a considerable entry in the toy market: separate doll-heads, dolls with a stuffed body and 'bathing boys'.

The bathing boys were a curious novelty [174] and their great attraction seems to have been that as they were made of hollow porcelain they could float and could be washed all over without spoiling their fabric. They were made in various sizes up to about sixteen inches and appeared with both fair and black hair. They look particularly Germanic in build and pose and for some reason seem to arouse strong feelings among collectors who find them either very attractive or completely repellent! A different type of bathing doll is shown in figure 175. Here the dolls are made entirely of unglazed porcelain or bisque, with coloured hair; a small bath tub completes the set. The bath is marked with the trefoil sign of the factory of Limbach, who also had a long history of dollmaking. Their factory was founded in the early 1770s by the Greiner family who are said to have owned seven porcelain factories in Thuringia in the eighteenth century.

171 The Scottish Parian doll of Master Edwin Spencer Chalk German; 1880; 17 inches

172 overleaf: The dolls pack their holiday trunks: Poupée Modèle *(1866)*

These are miniature dolls' house type dolls and by the end of the nineteenth century it was mostly this category of china dolls that was supplied. The doll which had been the rage in the 'fifties had become *démodée* by the 'seventies, when it was supplanted in popularity by the attractive wax and expensive bisque dolls. A trade announcement of 1873 which said that these last were far prettier than 'old-fashioned China dolls' was obviously trying to swing popular opinion. The dolls with soft stuffed body and head, arms and legs of highly glazed china were still the cheapest, but the shape of the heads became stereotyped, the expressions careless and monotonous. Numerous small potteries copied the famous factories. It was always possible to use an existing doll form as a model and take an impression. This no doubt explains the fact that late and crudely produced dolls sometimes exhibit earlier, pirated hair styles.

A French jury reporting on the Exhibition at Vienna in 1873 wrote that all the province of Thuringia, stretching from Gotha to Coburg, was involved in the doll-making industry and in producing porcelain dolls' heads and dolls which were supplied to the entire world. China dolls were also made in Copenhagen in the Royal Copenhagen Manufactory between 1843-80, according to Mrs Estrid Faurholt, but until the French began producing bisque-headed dolls of their own in the latter half of the nineteenth century, the Germans had little opposition.

By the early nineteenth century numerous small potworks in Staffordshire, England, were also producing what they advertised as 'toys' but this never included playthings intended for children. It covered a wide range of little ornamental figurines and trifles, often crudely modelled, gaily coloured to appeal to a public who might display them on a cottage mantleshelf; a poor man's imitation of the delicate Chelsea or Meißen 'toys' owned by the wealthy. A description of one such 'bank', as such small potteries were called, turning out these inferior wares in the 1850s at Longton, listed: 'all kinds of toys consisting of images in gold and colours of men and women and rustic groups and dogs and cats and Swiss cottages, and Bonapartes, Victorias, Great Moguls, Dukes of Wellington, Tom Thumbs, Shepherds, Dairymaids, Cows, John Bulls and John Wesleys and many other models too numerous to mention.' Children were allowed to work long hours for very little money under unhealthy conditions in such banks.

The only actual doll-making in the English potteries seems to have been occasioned, as it was in the United States, by the 1914–18 war, when German supplies were cut off. In a letter from Mr G. W. S. Sherratt, partner in the Mayer and Sherratt China Manufactory, he provides a marvellously authentic account of this period. He has kindly allowed me to use the letter, which I quote in full, with its circumstantial detail of Staffordshire doll-making:

We made dolls' heads at Mayer & Sherratt's China Manufacturers of Clifton Works, Stafford Street (now the Strand) Longton during the First World War. Manufacturing started at the instigation of

173 Early Jumeau 'poupée' or Parisienne type with kid body; F. G. head; 1870; 14 inches

the then Board-of-Trade, who were trying to replace the toys which were previously nearly all imported from Germany.

The heads were made of a pink felspar body – once fired – a few arms and legs were made but not many. I was away in the forces at this time, but on my return to the works in May 1920 we were still making a few, but were anxious to get out of the business, as Germany was already starting exporting and the making of dolls' heads was a chancy business, the margin of error in firing was very low. I expect the fireman was firing china ovens one day and felspar the next and although we had Buller's rings, we used to say the fireman decided if the oven was fired by 'spitting on the clammings'. Anyway I remember some very grotesque dolls being drawn from the oven (round ovens of course).

In 1915 we took over the small factory adjoining Clifton Works in King Street, Longton (now Kingscross St). This factory was previously worked by Bridgett, Bates and Beech (the busy bees). It was the only factory I remember that was entirely manual although I believe there were others in Longton. I remember the blunging was done in a large brick ark (trough) with a man working a huge wooden 'paddle', then handsieved into another ark, and hand-pumped into a press.

No pugs, all hand wedging, string throwers' wheels and hand turned flat jiggers. B. B. & B. made china tea ware.

The factory was suitable for dolls' head manufacture as we only required slip which was hand blunged in the brick troughs and carried in buckets to the castors. Both factories are now demolished and the site is the new shopping centre.

If we required hair or wigs for the dolls, we got them from a factory in Chancery Lane (Dark Entry) which is also demolished now, run by Enoch Tams. I don't know where he got them from. I don't think he manufactured them, he made crude pottery, nest eggs, jam jars and marbles. Our dolls' heads were impressed *Melba* on the back of the shoulders.

I remember our big headache was what we called 'liming' a white deposit which came on the dolls on firing. The same thing can be seen on new red brickwork. I believe we used a barium antidote, but it is nearly fifty years ago and as I say it was the end of our manufacturing I was concerned with.

174 Bathing boy in high glaze porcelain; German; 13 inches

175 Small bath dolls, bisque with coloured details, marked Limbach

To this account, Mrs M. A. Bryan, who was working at this factory in 1916, is able to add that there were 'different kinds of heads: baby dolls and heads that had to be cut out at the crown to have hair put on. Also dolls that had eyes that opened and shut with slits cut out for the eyes.'

Advertisement has so far failed to produce a single example of a Melba doll, but Mr A. R. Mountford, Director of the City Museum at Hanley, has sent me a photograph of a Goss doll exhibited in the museum [176] and also made during the Great War. In a history of the firm of W. H. Goss, Stoke-on-Trent (*Proceedings of the University of Newcastle-upon-Tyne Philosophical Society, Vol. 1*, No. 4 1965), Mr M. J. W. Willis-Fear wrote: 'Apparently these Goss china dolls were just beginning to successfully capture the English toy market, despite their relatively high price, when the war ended in November 1918 and the German toy industry promptly revived its former speciality, forcing the Goss factory to cease this line as the German dolls were considerably cheaper.' Any example of this short-lived English china-doll industry is rare and interesting and consequently a list is included separately of firms who have been recorded as producing china or pottery dolls during the First or Second World Wars (see below).

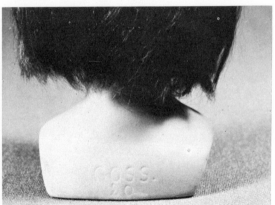

176 English doll head marked 'Goss'; from the 1914–18 period when Staffordshire potters were encouraged to replace the German imports

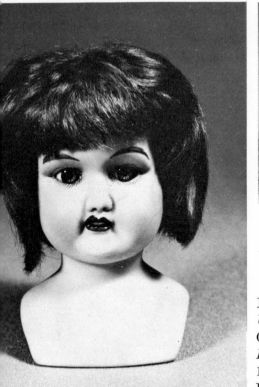

ENGLISH POTTERIES, WHO INCLUDED DOLLS IN THEIR MANUFACTURE (Staffordshire)

D. S. Baley and S. J. Baxter, *Longton, Staffs* · Blue John Factory *Union St, Hanley, Staffs* 1940 · Browne, Westhead, Moore & Co. · Cauldon Works (see Ridgway) · Diamond Tile Co Ltd. *Brook St, Hanley* 1942 · Thomas Dodd, Roxy Factory, *Lockett's Lane, Longton* 1914–18 · Doric China Co. *China St, Fenton (Parian) (Greens)* 1934 · Empire Porcelain Co, Pottery *Stoke-on-Trent* 1914–18 · W. H. Goss *Stoke-on-Trent (Marked Goss)* 1914–18 · Hewitt Bros, Willow Pottery, *Longton, Stoke-on-Trent* 1920 · Howard Pottery, *Norfolk St, Shelton* 1925 · Mayer & Sherratt *Clifton Works, Stafford St* (now the Strand) *Longton,* (impressed MELBA) · Ridgway, J. W. Cauldon Works, *Shelton* 1914–18

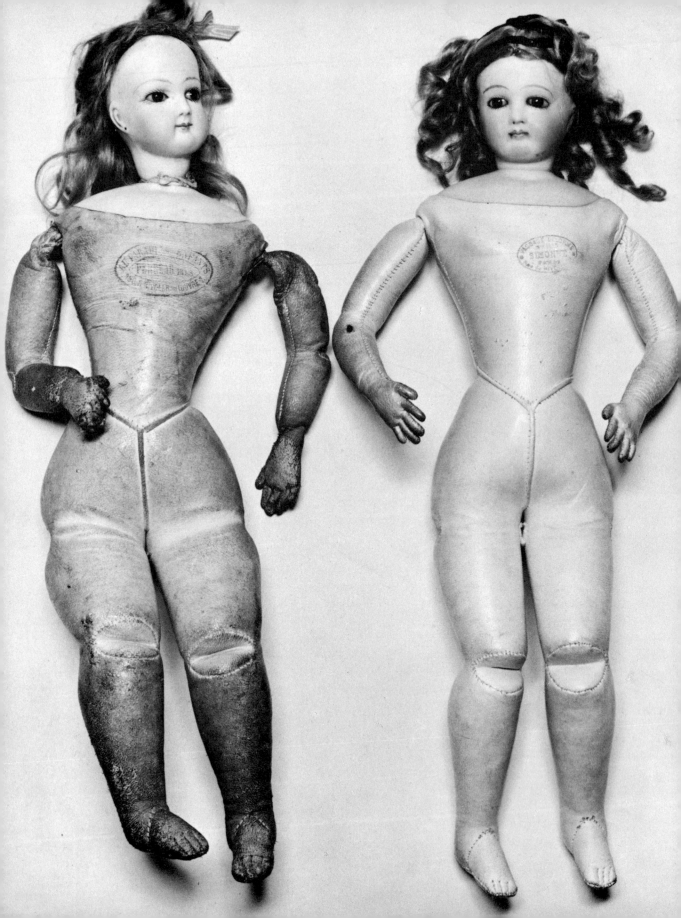

13

Parisian Bisque-headed Dolls and the Jumeau Story

The most popular form of Parisian doll in the 1860–70 period was the prettily modelled doll with bisque head and neatly tailored gusseted body of kid leather stuffed with hair or sawdust, or with an articulated kid-covered wooden body [177]. Such dolls were sold both clothed and unclothed, but since the accent was especially on the fashion of their clothes and the wealth of their accessories [207], representing all a wealthy lady might require, it is easy to understand why so many of the leading *Maisons* or doll-making concerns were run by women. Mademoiselle Calixte Huret, Mademoiselle Peronne, Madame Léontine Rohmer, Mademoiselle Bereux and Madame Simonne were among the foremost makers of such dolls and marked examples of their work attest to their high quality and artistry: they are among the most eagerly sought of all collected dolls.

177 opposite: Parisian dolls with gusseted kid bodies. Marked 'Simonne et Perreau fils'; c. 1860/70; 12 inches

178 Parisian poupée modèle *of the 90s, dressed in brown velvet and coffee-coloured silk; 13 inches*

For advertising purposes, some of these firms produced small magazines for children. Those that survive provide fascinating sidelights on the Parisian trade. *La Poupée Modèle* (1863–9) was associated with and perhaps edited by Mlle Peronne, who ran a shop called 'Poupée de Nuremberg', 21 rue de Choiseul. She seems to have married in 1865, from which time she appears in directories at the same address as Madame Lavallée Peronne. This charming publication aimed, as she wrote in the introduction to the first edition, to instruct little girls to look after their dolls just as well as their mothers looked after them. It included many patterns for making up clothes and hats and detailed instructions for sewing and embroidery, as well as a *causerie* about doll fashion written in imitation of the fashion gossip which appeared in contemporary adult periodicals such as *Journal des Demoiselles*, which was published from the same address as *Poupée Modèle*. Children were recommended to buy accessories at the shop of Mlle Bereux, 21 rue de Hanovre, and their dolls, naturally, from Mlle Peronne. On one occasion she describes her dolls as 'elegant as Parisiennes and as pretty as humming-birds', and as a fashion note adds that every well-dressed doll is wearing little gloves made of dog-skin *(peau de chien)! Poupée Modèle* was prettily produced with fold-up pattern sheets and hand-coloured fashion plates by acknowledged artists, such as Paul Lacourière and E. Preval (172, 208). A rare little illustrated paper for children called *Gazette de la Poupée* was produced on a rather more humble scale for a short time in 1865–6. This seems to have been promoted by another doll-maker, Mlle Huret (who was more famous at this time than Maison Jumeau). The editor purported to be a doll herself; and in one of her editorials 'petite Violette' commented very forcefully on the sort of children whom she had heard playing and asking one of their number: 'Have *you* got a Huret doll which costs eighty francs?' 'O, no, I haven't.' – 'Then you can't come and play with *us*!'

But much as little Violette appeared to dislike snobbery, it seems to have been pandered to by the sort of party which was reported in a later copy of the magazine. At the Salon Hertz, in the affluent, luxury quarter of Paris, rue de la Victoire, Maisons Huret and Bereux staged a *soirée* for little girls to attend with their dolls and partake of chocolate. The entrance fee was twenty-five *centimes* – 'A convenient price for the purse of our little Mothers'. Again in the following year, 1866, a really grand affair was arranged for 25 May. A garden party was held at Jardin Marbille, 87 Avenue Montaigne, off the Champs-Elysées. This was free for orphans but otherwise a charge of two francs was made. There was not only an exhibition of 'all the foremost makers', a performance by puppets of the Théâtre Guignol, a tombola and other sideshows, but the Grand Ball was capped by a parade of visiting dolls and a prize for the best was awarded in the 'Salon de Réception'. Present-day collectors will no doubt find such a spectacle mouthwatering and the winner must have been a very grand doll indeed. The account in *Gazette de la Poupée* tells us that little girls of twelve to fourteen years of age were responsible for the arranging and the judging. It is fascinating to picture such a scene, a nineteenth-century period piece with beautifully dressed children parading their expensive dolls, and all the pathos of an invited contingent of orphan children from some neighbouring institution, dressed in the simplest of uniforms and watching with covetous eyes a world they could never enter.

The writer of this magazine was anonymous: perhaps it was Mademoiselle Huret herself, as the editor seems to know so many details. There is a certain sense of irony detectable in a little serial story which threads through each number called *Mémoires d'une Poupée, racontés par elle-même* ('A Doll's Memoirs, told by herself'). A porcelain doll tells how she was 'born' in the Boulevard des Italiens (where the Huret establishment was first founded). As a preliminary to her adventures, she was taken to a room full of very young girls who 'showed no pleasure in me, so that the smile froze on my porcelain lips'. Instead, she was passed from hand to hand in this workroom, where the first one put on her a lace trimmed chemise and her neighbour added stockings and little grey shoes, then long drawers, crinoline and embroidered petticoat. Finally, a beautiful gown of blue silk with flounces and a low neckline completed her dress and made her feel *très coquette* as she was placed in her box for sale.

At the Paris Exhibition of 1867, both Mlle Huret and Mlle Bereux won awards for their dolls and it is interesting to find that in the official report it was said that the dolls' clothes made by outworkers in Paris gave occupation to several hundred women who earned less than fifty centimes a day doing the work in their own homes. They had, in fact, very little cause to smile at their task, however elegant the dolls they handled.

At this same Exhibition in 1867, the firm of Jumeau gained the Silver Medal for their entry of dolls, dolls' clothes and the heads of dolls, and though at this time he was no doubt producing rather similar dolls to the other makers such as Huret and Simonne, Jumeau was presently to leave some of his competitors far behind. The progress of the Jumeau family was, indeed, one of the success stories of nineteenth-century France. The first mention of this firm is found when the name of Pierre François Jumeau was coupled in the Paris directories of 1843 with that of M. Belton at an address 14 rue Salle-au-compte. Emile Jumeau himself said that the firm was founded in 1840. Together they were accorded a *Mention Honorable* at the Paris Exhibition of 1844, but two years later the men had parted company and at the 1849 Exhibition Jumeau alone was awarded the Bronze Medal. He was now in business on his own in a small unfashionable quarter in a mean narrow street which is still in existence called rue Mauconseil. Perhaps he had married and started up in a small way but he was there for over twenty years before he moved to larger premises at 8 rue Pastourelle in the very heart of the Marais dollmaking centre (see chapter 15).

A direct descendant, Mrs Hughes* tells me that Pierre François had two sons, Georges, the elder, and Emile. Georges died young and it was left to Emile to inherit and continue the doll business, although he had trained to be an architect. With many of the dollmakers their

* Mrs Hughes' grandmother was the daughter of the twin brother of P. F. Jumeau. Emile was her first cousin.

business seems to have fizzled out on the death or retirement of the first generation. With Jumeau the opposite was true. A Gold Medal was awarded to Pierre François in Paris in 1873 and in Philadelphia in 1876 but by this time it seems that his son was taking over the concern, now established at a new factory at Montreuil-sous-Bois which was eventually to become world famous.

Emile Jumeau prospered not merely because of the quality of his products or the ingenuity of his ideas, which were rivalled by other great Parisian dollmakers of the 'seventies such as Bru and Steiner, but also because he shouted the loudest about his wares. He was one of the first to recognize the advantages of sound, clever advertising as against the discreet name-dropping used by Mlle Peronne.

179 Doll dressed as Princess Alexandra in her robes as Dr of Music, Royal University of Ireland. Doll from the Jumeau factory with a bisque porcelain head impressed 'F. G.' about 1881; 24 inches

180 opposite: Two bisque-headed dolls used to demonstrate fashion at Debenham & Freebody in 1891 'New Season Harris tweeds and sailor suits for children'

Before the factory was built at Montreuil in 1873 with kilns for porcelain firing, it was necessary for the heads to be obtained from an outside source. Some Jumeau dolls are found with heads with 'F. G.' imprinted in bisque. M. Girard and M. Moynot, the last proprietors of the factory before it finally gave up doll-making, considered that this was the mark of Ferdinand Gautier who had been making porcelain heads at a factory at Charenton since the early 'sixties in competition with imported German ones. Figure 179 shows a very fine doll with swivel-neck, impressed 'F.G.' on the shoulder plate. The doll, measuring twenty-four inches from top to toe, displays a statuesque type of beauty that may have been responsible for her owner electing to dress her as the Princess of Wales in her robes as Doctor of Music of the Royal University of Ireland. Princess Alexandra was photographed when the honour was conferred in 1885 and the black silk gown with primrose-

WORK-TABLE COMPANION

Expressly designed for the
Englishwoman's Domestic Magazine.
1850 · 1860

yellow lining is authentic down to the little lyre-shaped clasp at her throat. The bisque is a completely matt surface, almost powdery in quality and delicately tinted. She wears real hair, carefully plaited and coiled, and, in her pierced ears, earrings of pearl and topaz in a claw setting. Thin eyebrows arch over the blue-grey eyes and her nose is very pointed and aquiline. The deep bust with sew holes back and front has 'F. G.' marked at the very edge of the bottom of the shoulder. The body is machine-stitched material and is made to sit down perfectly with an inserted flat seat piece. She measures seven inches from head to bust. The six-inch arms are of delicately modelled porcelain, but the leg is of sewn stuffed material with a joint at the knee and measures twelve inches from sole of foot to body. The doll was originally sold in a *Jumeau Bébé* box, but it was labelled *Mousquetaire* in hand-written ink and was obviously a dressed costume model.

The Jumeau factory at Montreuil, on the long straight road connecting the town with the capital and in easy reach of Paris, was built on modern lines, not large by present-day standards but advanced and forward looking in 1873. Perhaps Emile was able to incorporate some of his architectural ideas in its design. A postcard showing the factory in 1878 shows its main features with two large wings running at right angles to the main building enclosing a fine courtyard with trees and an ornamental fountain and ample space for loading goods [183]. The main fabric still remains to the present day though the factory is given over to a plastics concern. The left wing has been replaced by the entrance to a Métro station, Robespierre, and a heavy steel gate has replaced the ornamental wrought iron between the brick walls. The proudly displayed *BÉBÉ JUMEAU* in high letters has also vanished and in the adjacent quiet streets, which have replaced the open country, the people are employed mostly in motor-making instead of the doll-trade.

Up-to-date methods also prevailed inside the factory, which was heated by hot water pipes and was even connected by telephone to the showroom in rue Pastourelle in Paris. Although part of the factory continued to be used for the production of the early type dolls called *Parisiennes* or *Poupées Modèles*, it was geared principally to the production of the famous *bébés* – a more childlike doll in appearance with jointed limbs and 'carton' body. Large numbers of women were employed as outworkers for the process of moulding hands and feet and were given moulds which they could operate at home after being taught the method.

The heads were made of the very finest quality kaolin paste, moulded in plaster casts in two halves for back and front. In the larger sizes it was necessary for the ear to be applied after moulding but, of course, before firing. The finished heads with open crown and holes cut for the insertion of eyes were placed on fireclay trays and baked for twenty-four hours at a very high temperature. After coming from the kiln the startling dead whiteness was relieved by two coats of pale pink paint. When this skin tint was air-dried and features were painted on the heads they were finally refired for a short period at a lower temperature to set fast the colours.

181 A needlework companion doll of 1865 with china head and limbs; 8½ inches high. Here it is shown with a page of the Englishwoman's Magazine *of approximately the same date* *(see p. 86)*

182 *Jumeau* bébés:
left, 14 inches, 1884, marked
'E.J.' right, 26 inches, 1885
marked 'Jumeau'.
Swivel neck and composition
bodies and original clothes

The beautiful naturalistic eyes, which were so much a feature of the French dolls and for which Jumeau in particular was famous, required special skill. Girls served several years' apprenticeship before they were proficient. Each one sat at a bench equipped with a strong gas jet for melting the coloured glass rods with which she worked. In one hand she held a glassmaker's rod about ten inches long and, using coloured rods in turn, she made first a black pupil then a circle round it of blue or brown and finally when pupil and iris were formed on the tip of her tool, she took a stick of white opaque enamel, heated it and filled the correct size mould for the iris. A centre was gouged out and the coloured pupil set into it and finally a thin coating of melted clear glass gave the eye luminosity. The eyes were all passed finally to an annealing oven to cool off slowly. Glass must cool gradually or it is spoilt. The eyes were fixed within the hollow heads by plaster and their lifelike quality did much to give the Jumeau dolls their special appeal.

Finally all parts of the dolls passed to an assembly shop where limbs could be added to bodies and the head finished with its coiffeured wig. A solid piece of wood within the hollow body held the hooks to which the swivel head was fastened and the elastic cord threaded through the legs and hooked on from beneath. Arms and legs were jointed at the knee and elbow by the use of hollowed-out wooden balls. Calmettes, visiting the doll factory (the Jumeau factory after it had become SFBJ), commented that the assembly room bore a resemblance to an ogre's larder with huge racks on the walls holding every sort of size of little pink limb. It is interesting to find that by this later date the eyes were made by a far simpler and less skilful

183 *The Jumeau factory at Montreuil in 1878*

process, by dropping a blob of colour into the pre-made white. He added that a skilled worker could produce four to five hundred pairs a day, and one hundred and twenty five pairs of '*yeux fibres*' – eyes with a white-rayed iris. At this period the bodies and limbs were also sprayed with paint instead of being hand-painted.

From the Jumeau factory at Montreuil dolls were taken by road to the showrooms in rue Pastourelle, where Madame Jumeau handled the dressing side of the business and employed many outworkers who submitted designs and would receive an order for so many outfits in different sizes. They were displayed with the usual Parisian *élan* in showrooms set up with little scenes and included both historical, fashion and play-dolls. The growing business was handled by Emile Jumeau himself and he organized exhibitions of his dolls as far away as Australia and the United States, so that a doll issued in 1880 was proudly able to boast of Gold Medals won in Paris, London, Vienna, Philadelphia, Sydney and Melbourne, of which he had reproduced replicas all along the skirting wall of this factory.

Dolls were sent out in stout cardboard boxes with an advertisement which read:

Every doll sent from the factory carried the name of Jumeau and customers were warned to refuse any *bébé* which did not carry this guarantee, acknowledging the competition with which the foremost dollmaker in Paris was faced. The *bébé* or childlike doll, as opposed to the ladylike fashion *poupée*, was marketed by many firms, each of which extolled the virtues, the beauty, the unbreakable quality and the novelty of their dolls; but the interesting thing in studying these bisque-headed dolls is not how they differed, but how closely they eventually resembled each other. Their features and materials might vary in detail from maker to maker, and, as outlined in chapter 15, novelty functions were introduced in their 'behaviour', but they were still 'sisters under the skin' and in spite of registered patents any new advantage was likely to be copied or emulated by other makers.

In 1886 Jumeau's service to his country was recognized and he was made Chevalier de la Légion d'Honneur; the Paris press extolled his virtues both as dollmaker and philanthropist, for he had made a practice of employing orphan girls at his factory, keeping them in food and clothing throughout their apprenticeship. In addition to giving these poor girls a chance to learn a trade and earn an honest living, it no doubt proved a cheap form of labour. Another Frenchman, Leo Claretie, who was interested in the economics as well as the aesthetics of doll-making, tabled the amounts paid in a special tariff for convicts at some of the Parisian prisons during the 1914–18 war. Piece-work was taken to the prisons from the doll factories and the prisoners were paid so much for rubbing down the rough edges of moulded pieces, so much for colouring, and for painting features they were paid item by item. It is odd to look at one of these Parisian beauties and remember that some poor prisoner may once have earned himself a pittance helping in her production!

In 1889, when the Eiffel Tower was built to demonstrate the potential power of steel construction at the Centenary Exhibition in Paris, Jumeau marketed some dolls to America which were wrapped in a sort of propaganda game sheet (see *Doll Collectors of America*, 1964). The printed game was dedicated to Young Americans and represented a race up the Eiffel Tower. At the left-hand side a Jumeau doll mounted on a pedestal held the tricolour and on the right, her German counterpart flaunted the German flag in opposition. By this time his German rivals were more of a menace than his home competition.

In '*Renaissance de la Poupée Française*' (*Gazette des Beaux Arts*, 1916) Jean Doin wrote:

> The German doll reigned supreme. This was the result of a patient and carefully planned contest. The Germans acted in the doll industry as they did in other things: they offered goods at reduced prices, with easy payments and exemption of duties...
>
> After a few years they had ruined our doll industry. Several firms such as Rabery, Bru, Pintel and Eden Bébé (produced by Fleischmann & Bloedel – a German firm centred in Paris) gave up the struggle and about 1,900 were absorbed in the Jumeau firm: the only one that manufactured entire dolls. All the other houses had bought their porcelain heads and glass eyes from Germany.

The writer, it seems, had absorbed some of Jumeau's powerful propaganda, since this account was not strictly true. Although many of the smaller makers had continued to rely on German stock for dollmaking, others of Jumeau's Parisian rivals had potted their own heads or had relied on French makers such as Gaultier. Jumeau himself supplied some of the dolls used for making up mechanical and musical toys made by men such as Decamps, including types of Mulatto and Negro mould for conjuring models.

Jumeau must initially have employed the services of a specialist potter when his *bébé* was planned. The moulding and construction of a doll-head out of finest bisque porcelain called both for skill and experience, not only in the actual making but in planning the work-rooms and organizing materials. Calmettes mentions that 'in our time, excellent artists were set to fashion faces, both smiling and serious, for fashionable dolls. One sculptor, M. Lejeune, specialized in this type of work, and the Maison Lanternier at Limoges is renowned for the heads of *bébés*.' On the evidence of the very beautiful quality head [185] which seems to have so Jumeau-esque a cast of features, I wonder if M. Lejeune was one of the people who originally helped Jumeau. This doll is marked on her neck '*Fabrication Française A.L.C. Limoges 10*'. She has wooden arms and legs jointed with wooden spheres, a strong carton body and fixed blue eyes of fine quality. Her height is twenty-four inches. The Lanternier factory was recorded as early as 1871 and was producing dolls' heads in the early nineteen-hundreds.

The coalition of French makers mentioned by Doin resulted in the formation of the *Société Française de la Fabrication des Bébés et Jouets* which continued at the Jumeau factory at Montreuil and did in fact use some of the individual early moulds. When Queen Elizabeth and King George VI of England made a state visit to Paris in 1938, some model dolls of Jumeau bisque were made by order of the French Government in the likeness of Princess Elizabeth and Princess Margaret Rose for the royal parents to take home to the children. They were thirty-two inches high with real eyelashes and hair and flirting eyes; a splendid trousseau packed in fifteen little blue leather dolls' trunks, mounted in silver, accompanied them – a royal finale which Jumeau himself would surely have relished!

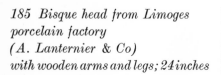

185 Bisque head from Limoges porcelain factory (A. Lanternier & Co) with wooden arms and legs; 24 inches

14

German Bisque and the Trend to Realism

186 A German bisque head of fine Early quality with fixed glass eyes, unmarked

It was no accident that the porcelain factories of Thuringia in Germany became the dangerous rivals of the Parisian dollmakers at the end of the nineteenth century. A district which the omniscient Baedeker described in 1897 as 'mountainous and wooded and full of interest to the pedestrian' had all the natural advantages for such an industry: a plentiful local supply of fine quality china clay, of wood, both for doll-limbs and for kiln firing, and water power provided by the fast streams which laced the district were coupled with an effective railroad system for transport and a plentiful population which could be absorbed as a cheap labour force. Even more important, there was a tradition here of skilled workmanship. Old established potteries producing ornamental ware for export and domestic goods for the home market had existed since the beginning of the nineteenth century. Men versed in the one skill were available for specialist doll factories, apart from those concerns where doll-making was carried on as a sideline (see chapter 10).

It has never been established who first originated the idea of a more child-like head to replace the *poupée modèle* style with its grown-up 'ladylike' cast of feature [186] shows an interesting early example, dated 1860, of a fine quality German bisque head with details of moulded hair and blue ribbon bow embellished by a slight glaze or 'smear', the technical term for the thin coating added for the second firing. She has beautiful fixed blue glass eyes, 'fibres' or 'threaded', and well defined painted features. Her ears are pierced through the head to receive earrings and the head is mounted on a stuffed body with leather arms and legs. Heads of a similar type have been found with an imprint 'SH', which is thought to stand for the firm of Simon & Halbig who became famous for the production of bisque doll-heads at their factory at Ohrdruf, Thuringia.

The production of porcelain dolls which, as we have seen, had first begun in Germany, and was then adapted by the French and brought to full eminence by such famous makers as Jumeau and other specialist Parisian dollmakers, now swung back again to the German firms, who copied the principle of the *bébé* with its beautifully moulded head, jointed limbs and body of wood or composition. By the end of the nineteenth century thousands were sent over the border to France to be dressed and they were much cheaper than any which could be produced by the French themselves. Doin referred to the French dollmakers who used German components as 'tributaries of the great German river'.

Simon & Halbig were probably one of the earliest and most experienced firms in leading this 'great German river' to concentrate on emulating the special type of *bébé* head, but there were several other major firms, such as Kestner of Waltershausen, Handwerck, and Kammer & Reinhardt of Waltershausen, Armand Marseille and Heubach of Koppelsdorf, Cuno & Otto Dressel of Sonneberg who followed suit, besides numerous smaller concerns.

Simon & Halbig were specialist makers of dolls' heads by the 1890s. They supplied dollmakers with heads of their own sculpting but also made heads to order for other firms. This is why heads are often

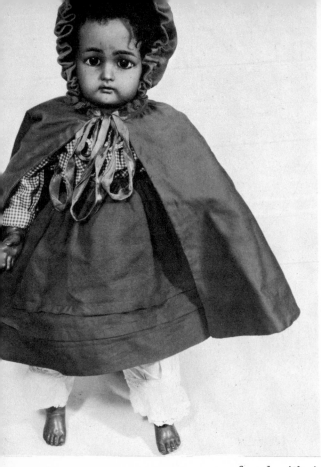

*187 Negro model doll marked
'Simon & Halbig KR 53'; 22 inches*

*188 right: Burmese model doll,
marked 'S. H. 1129 Germany
Dep. 4'. It has a composition body
and bisque head and is made by
Simon & Halbig*

found with initials of two concerns: 'SH' and 'KR' or 'SH' and 'JUTTA' (a registered name for the *bébé* made by Cuno & Otto Dressel). Small heads were produced for mechanical dolls and were also used for *marottes* or *folies* – carnival dolls with a stick handle joined to the head and decorated with gay trimmings and bells and sometimes containing a musical fitment which worked when the dolls were twirled round.

Novelty dolls were produced, such as the three-faced doll with changing expression [203]; another popular line was the double-headed doll, sometimes called Topsy-Eva, with a fair blonde child at one end and a little coloured piccaninny at the opposite end, joined together at the waist so that a reversible skirt always hid one face. This idea has been copied in modern times for a Mary Poppins transformation (see page 247). Simon & Halbig seem to have been at the forefront with new ideas and they were one of the first firms to use coloured bisque to represent dolls of other than European type: they made chocolate-coloured Negro heads with authentic modelling and Burmese children with slanted eye holes, coffee complexion and sultry eyes [188]. These were no doubt made especially for a foreign market. By 1895 an American magazine was carrying an advertisement for a set of four different types called 'Dolls of Four Races' – European, Negro, Chinese and Red Indian. Nine inches high with jointed limbs and wearing national dress, they were described as 'typical beauties of their race'.

Fleischmann & Bloedel of Fürth were probably connected with that famous firm of Fleischmann in Sonneberg mentioned by Cremer in 1873 as one of the foremost manufacturers, employing 32,000 people in the district – on outside as well as factory work. They made all sorts of dolls and registered the name of the 'Eden Bébé' in 1870 and 'Bébé Triomphe' in 1898. Their output included walking dolls, kiss-throwing dolls and mechanical walking dolls. Figure 189 shows a type patented in 1895 which was driven along by revolving chains which moved little wheels in her feet. Apart from the fact that her legs are made in one piece and stiff instead of jointed, she is a walking *Eden Bébé*. Fleischmann had a branch in Paris and became one of the principal shareholders in the SFJB coalition – a share he had to relinquish on the outbreak of the First World War when he was expelled as an alien.

189 Fleischmann & Bloedel walking and talking Eden bébé *doll with chain drive in legs; 18 inches*

The dolls of Simon & Halbig and of Fleischmann followed the Parisian *bébé* pattern. The Germans, however, never specialized in the dressing of such dolls, though in making them they were extremely proficient. The bisque examples of the Kestner firm of Waltershausen probably represent some of the finest ever made. J. D. Kestner was followed by his son, J. D. Kestner junior, who established a porcelain pottery at Ohrdruf. He not only sold whole made-up dolls but also doll parts and even kits with changeable parts so that a doll could be altered from a blonde to a brunette or to a baby head. Kestner took out various patents connected with doll joints and the simplification of assemblage. It was to his firm also that many of the later American dolls made in fine bisque, such as Kewpies and Bye-lo, were entrusted [223].

An international tariff law passed in 1890 made it necessary to mark products with the name of their country of origin. The imprint on these bisque doll-heads, which is usually at the back of their neck – a maker's name, initial, trademark, size – has been a course of constant satisfaction to the latter-day doll collector who can hope to trace in such hieroglyphics the original source from which the doll was issued, the country, maker, series and sometimes even date. What is more valuable, it has been possible with painstaking research and the cooperation of collectors either working together, or supplying information to a common club, to assess the range of work covered by a particular maker, the variations and improvements as his output increased. Rarities are discovered – perhaps a doll was produced over a very short period or in a pattern that proved either unpopular or impractical. With a thoroughness at which the original makers might stand amazed, collections and records have been assembled which reconstruct the complete 'lines' produced by certain famous makers and a clear view of their characteristics emerges.

The rule of marking is not an infallible guide for dating a doll: some manufacturers used marks before the law made it compulsory – either as a guide to assembly or for advertising their own work, just as in other forms of pottery and porcelain, where it was customary to add the mark or name of the factory. A few factories had produced dolls with an ornamental name in relief moulded on them. Names such as Agnes, Daisy, Florence, Mabel, etc. were used by such well-established firms as Hertwig & Co. of Katzhütte and Porzellan Fabrik Co. of Veilsdorf. Dolls also exist which were made later than 1890 but which have no identification stamped on them; possibly they carried a label or were boxed with the necessary 'country of origin' printed on the lid. It has also been said that the rule was relaxed when, for instance, German parts were assembled in England.

The firm of Armand Marseille went one step further in the commercial war and flirted with the French market by producing dolls indisputably Parisian in appearance [190] with heavy eyebrows and lustrous brown eyes. The factory at Koppelsdorf, established in the 'nineties, under what was presumably an assumed name, was near to that of Heubach, to whom Marseille was related, according to Geneviève Angione in *Spinning Wheel* (March, 1966). Armand Marseille made many

190 Dolls by Armand Marseille, marked 'Armand Marseille Germany 390 A 3/0 M and 1894 A M 7 dep'; 12 inches, 21 inches

191 Armand Marseille babies marked A. M. Germany 351/4, and 351/3½ A M, 19 inches and 16 inches

types of doll for the export market and was responsible for the Queen Louise doll registered in the United States in 1910 for the Louis Wolf Co., but made in Germany for assembly in America. Armand Marseille died in the nineteen-twenties and the firm continued a little after his death. His baby dolls [191] were particularly popular at this late date.

The Heubach family were an old-established firm of potters with records reaching back to the eighteen-twenties. Janet Johl, author of *Still More about Dolls* (1951), was told by Margaret Heubach, a grand-daughter of Jean Paul Heubach, that there was a family connection with the Dressels, as it was his mother's maiden name. J. P. Heubach, born in 1808, went to America from Sonneberg in 1871 and died there three years later. Just as among the prominent potters of the Staffordshire region in England, the German doll-makers of Thuringia were often connected by marriage as well as associated in business. The names of Greiner, Dressel, Heubach appear sufficiently often in association for us to assume family relationships and in the early years of the twentieth century the Heubach factory was managed by a Dressel.

Heubach were one of the first firms to produce 'character' dolls – with smiling, puzzled or even tearful expressions. 'Little Boy Blue,' figure 192, is made of a different type of porcelain called in German *Mattlack*, as it has a rather rough powdery surface as opposed to the usual smooth bisque. The eyes in this doll, and in many Heubach examples, are painted in a curious and individual manner as they are inset: a hollow made for the socket receives the paint and a touch of glaze for realism which gives rather an intense searching expression.

Heinrich Handwerck was also a large-scale producer of dolls in Germany. His factory was founded at Waltershausen and was housed in a large building where his speciality was wooden bodies and limbs for dolls. When he died in 1902 the factory was taken over by the firm of Kammer & Reinhardt who were established in the same town. Max Handwerck, the son, seems to have continued to be concerned in the business as doll heads stamped with his name can be found, usually with very poor carton bodies. The Heinrich Handwerck registration of *Bébé Cosmopolite* was succeeded by Max Handwerck's *Bébé Élite* in 1901.

Curiously the large, Heinrich Handwerck doll [193] must have been one of the last made before the 1914–18 war; it was not in fact bought until 1919, when its present owner, Mrs Doyle, found it in a large London store. The doll bears the impressed mark: 'Heinrich Handwerck/Simon & Halbig' and presumably moulds continued to be used for the *Bébé Cosmopolite* long after Heinrich had died. Although the box of strong card bears the trademark of *Bébé Cosmopolite* it was actually sold by the Kringle Society doll firm, as an additional label proves.

During the period just before the First World War there was a vogue for these very large models of almost childlike proportions, with enormous heads, rather gross in feature, however perfect technically.

192 Little Scottish lad, marked 'l Halbig K R', 10 inches, and Little Boy Blue, marked 'Germany', with Heubach trademark; 11 inches

193 right: Heinrich Handwerck doll called Bébé Cosmopolite; *marked 'H: H. Simon & Halbig'; 6½ inches*

194 Kammer & Reinhardt baby,
1910, Marked 100, size 88;
11 inches

195 Kammer & Reinhardt
character doll: a rare model
marked 107, size 55; 22 inches

It was as a reaction against such soulless dolls that the move towards realism took place. At an exhibition in Munich in 1908 an artist called Marion Kaulitz showed some 'artist-made dolls' which she had designed herself and dressed in a childishly naturalistic manner. The heads were made for her in bisque by a sculptor, Paul Vogelsanger, and they wore Bavarian national costume which has always figured so predominantly in Munich fashion. The idea occurred to Reinhardt of the Kammer & Reinhardt firm that play-dolls made up in similar style might prove a popular commercial line and, in a refreshing reaction against some of the insipid and vacuously pretty doll faces, he began to introduce 'character' dolls. His baby [194] really looks a little puny and fretful against the plump Teutonic idealized babes marketed by Armand Marseille [191] but the doll-children who followed in its wake are delightful and were so successful that their image was 'borrowed' by other makers.

'Baby' was the first of the realistic dolls based on legitimate human features. He appeared in 1910 and curious legends have since arisen about him: that he was the Kaiser as a baby, or the Kaiser's baby son with a withered arm, and even, in one version, that the Kaiser did not approve the finished model and had its issue suppressed, which accounts for its rarity! In truth, the doll's head was based on a live baby only six weeks old, the son of the sculptor. The body to which it is attached is more mature and the doll was in fact shown in contemporary advertisements as a crawling baby, which would suggest an age nearer one year old.

'Baby' was followed by Peter, Marie, Gretchen, Hans, Elsa, Carl, Elise and Walter. A little boy, Reinhardt's nephew, acted as model for Hans and it is his sweet expression that is perpetuated in this beautiful doll [195]. The eyes are painted and look slightly to the right. The manufacturer thought that they might have had a more instant success if the eyes had moved, as did the eyes of many dolls made for export.

After the First World War, realistic dolls became an increasingly popular trend. The use of plastic materials made it technically simpler to reproduce detail exactly and dolls were mass-produced in a more life-like image of children, sometimes using famous living children as their model, such as Shirley Temple and Christopher Robin. Prettiness was not enough. The character face developed a twentieth-century expression: 'pert' and 'cheeky' are words which come to mind. Children who had customarily been kept under and in the background were produced, held the stage and encouraged to be precocious. Many dolls followed suit.

It is interesting to find that Reinhardt put on the market models of both boys and girls in his 'little playmates' series. Boy dolls have always been much rarer than girl dolls, principally because they were intended as playthings for girls only. The liking which some little boys have shown for playing with dolls has usually been frowned upon and thought unmanly, even considered slightly sinister. It scarcely seems logical that a sensitive or artistic boy should find such treasures any less attractive than his sisters, and nowadays, with a general interest in fashion led by top-line couturiers, perhaps even Anatole France's poor little Sylvestre Bonnard would be encouraged. In this story, written in 1910, he told of a little boy no more than eight years old, who fell in love with a doll in a shop in the rue de Seine: 'a poor thing with a dab of scarlet on each cheek, short flabby arms, and ugly hands made of wood, and long gangling legs. Her flowered skirt was pinned up to her waist with two tacks. It was a doll in the worst taste of provincialism.' His Uncle Victor thought the child's request for this trumpery doll preposterous: 'Good Heavens! Buy a doll for a boy! You just want to disgrace yourself. You longing for this common little doll! Really my lad, I am surprised at you. Ask me for a sword or a gun and I'll pay up willingly – but to buy a doll! Upon my word, you should be ashamed. Never in my life will I do such a thing.'

One of the earliest-known photographs of Queen Victoria shows her holding her eldest son Edward, who is clutching a long-legged doll. As they grew up, the little princes were decisive trend-setters in boys' attire and this is amusingly reflected in dolls' clothing of the period. The royal children were painted in Highland dress by Winterhalter in 1849 and a fashion newspaper of 1852 wrote: 'The costume worn by the Prince of Wales, when at Balmoral, has set the fashion of adopting the complete Highland costume.' Even German dolls without a trace of Scottish ancestry were not ashamed to flaunt the tartan and assume with the dashing uniform a masculine character that at once lent to the pretty face with its mop of hair [192] a boyish mischievousness, an air of devil-may-care.

The strong naval tradition in the English and German royal families also introduced a vogue for children's 'sailor suits'. When Edward was five years old, another painting by Winterhalter showed him on the occasion of a royal visit to the fleet in naval dress and the style persisted through the nineteenth century. A fashion note of 1879 reads: 'Sailor suits are always popular and ever since the Prince of Wales' two sons have adopted the naval uniform the preference has increased.' By the 'eighties it had been recognized as a useful all-the-year-round outfit, and *Woman's World* pronounced in 1888: 'This is a very sensible dress. The woollen underwear, the blue blouse for winter, the white one for summer and blue serge trousers form a very good dress for a boy.' As may be seen, it also presented a very charming doll style [180].

The Fauntleroy suit was not apparently so popular with boys, however sweet the hero of Mrs Hodgson Burnett's book, written in 1886, looked in it. Sir Compton Mackenzie, looking back to the time in 1889 when he was six years old, wrote in *My Life and Times*, 1963:

That confounded Little Lord Fauntleroy craze which led to my being given as a party dress the Little Lord Fauntleroy costume of black velvet and Vandyke collar was a curse. The other boys at the dancing class were all in 'white tops'. Does this require explanation, as a white top to one's sailor suit instead of the blue of daily use or the pale blue of summer?

The fashion was not actually invented by the book illustrations, however, but merely popularized an existing style, which curiously enjoyed a second innings when Freddie Bartholomew starred in the film in the 'twenties. A description included in *The Lady* of 1885 mentioned 'A little fellow of seven... tunic and knickerbockers of sapphire blue velvet and sash of pale pink. Vandyke collar and cuffs, if not of old point lace, should be of Irish guipure.' Dolls dressed in velvet, with long hair imitating the period, date from just this time and indeed the fashion was a great deal more suitable for a doll than a young boy. Another favourite style of hair cut was the 'Titus', after Rembrandt's portraits of his son – an even page-boy style which enabled a doll to become a girl or a boy.

German dolls, unlike their Parisian sisters, were not usually supplied with fine clothes and were more often sold with a mere trimmed slip; but with the popular Victorian accomplishments of needlework, knitting and crocheting this was often an advantage: a cheap doll could be transformed by beautiful hand-made clothes. It would be difficult, for instance, to find a prettier ensemble than the two miniature German dolls in figure 196.

196 Small German dolls: Simon Halbig and K. R. Baby miniature in decorative workbox with crochet work

15

Functional Dolls and Doll-Play

It is not difficult to instance throughout the history of doll-making individual examples of fine workmanship: even as early as the first century AD, for instance, some unknown Roman maker could provide a beautifully jointed doll, well-proportioned and with a handsome face [14]. But this chapter is not concerned with unique specimens made for special children, or even with makers who produced a few fine dolls of a specific type, handmade from wood or wax. It is rather an attempt to trace the sequence which led from the quite poorly made playthings of the beginning of the nineteenth century to the splendid and sumptuous *bébés* of the last years: dolls which were completely articulated in their joints, could walk and talk, blow kisses with both hands, had fine natural hair wigs over their delicate porcelain brows, eyes with real lashes which both slept and 'flirted', pearly teeth in their half-open mouths and which were dressed in a rich selection of pretty, professionally made costumes (184).

Up to the beginning of the nineteenth century, dolls for little children had been for the most part unpretentious. The swaddled doll, *enfant au maillot*, made of pressed papier mâché and merely a head on a shaped cylinder, was one type of doll popular as a customary new year's gift in Europe. This seems to have been manufactured in one form or another in both France and Germany. The French writer Claretie disparagingly likened it to a 'mummy in a cocoon' without legs or arms. 'Its head painted, the hair a spot of wax, the eyebrows in parenthesis, a heart-shaped mouth, flaming cheeks, blue eyes and three pebbles in the stomach.' (The pebbles meant that it was also a rattle.) Contemporary engravings show such dolls being sold by pedlars from large baskets, and Claretie said that they were made outside Paris at Villers Cotteret (a small town to the north-east). The 'grey dolls of glue and pasteboard' were sent into Paris to be decorated and dressed. The German variety had a pointed base and its shape was compared to a carrot, but the principle was the same whether it was fashioned from wood or from papier mâché.

During the *Empire* period in France the customary dressed dolls for cheap sale were no more than a head supported on a rudimentary framework, with two sticks as legs or even a single central support holding up a doll complete with legs and arms. We can have some idea of how they looked from pages reproduced in colour from a toy-maker's catalogue of the period. This almost legendary catalogue belonged to M. Arthur Maury, the Parisian collector and puppeteer. It had fifty double pages with life-size pictures of dolls and toys – some of which were reproduced in *Les Jouets* by Henry d'Allemagne (1908) – but it has since disappeared. Plate 197 shows some of the more *de luxe* examples, dressed as a Mameluke or slave, as the Duc de Reichstadt and a dancing Polichinelle. The date must have been about 1815 as the Duc de Reichstadt, the son of Napoleon, called also *l'Aiglon* or 'little eagle', was born in 1811. They are charming, gay-looking toys, but with such a flimsy construction beneath the clothes, it is not surprising that actual examples have not survived.

Characterization in dolls seems to have been popular in France as a novelty, and the report of the Paris Exhibition of 1849 stated not only

197 Dolls of the Empire *period from an early toy catalogue*

LE DUC DE REICHSTADT EN POUPÉE

that about ninety dollmakers (comprising eight hundred and five workers in all) were engaged in constructing little dolls of 'leather and cardboard', but that it was possible to follow the day-to-day history of Europe in the products of these makers. Not only were tin soldiers and wooden Hussars made, but little 'Victorias', Quakeresses and Chinese people. Kossuth, the Hungarian patriot, was a popular model. This strange mixture is an interesting pointer to the relative 'news values' of the period.

The pattern of doll-making in Germany and France was quite different at this time. In Germany the industry spread over a wide area according to the location of raw materials: the clay districts of Thuringia and the fine forest timber of Saxony and Bavaria gave rise to local crafts which contributed to central marketing centres such as Nuremberg and Sonneberg. In France, Paris itself was always the centre of doll-making and it was only later in the nineteenth century that firms who had become pre-eminent found it necessary to have their own kilns and factories in the provinces or in the outskirts of the city.

In a serious study of the trade and working conditions of the Paris doll-makers, Calmettes said that these artisans mostly lived in the Marais district of Paris since it was preferable for makers of the same sort of goods to be grouped close together. Trade directories of the first half of the nineteenth century prove how correct he was, for many of the doll-makers lived within the district round the Temple, the third *arrondissement*, one of the most picturesque and oldest parts of Paris. The district is little changed after a hundred years: long narrow streets criss-cross each other lined with tall houses with jalousied windows. This is one of the workshops of Paris, where craftsmen still carry on metal work, glass work and jewelry-making; much of the wholesale commerce is in toys and novelties, buttons and all sorts of trinkets which will later find a place in the luxury shops of Paris along the boulevards further west. Day-long traffic snarls up the streets, but between small shop fronts, narrow doors lead off into large quiet courtyards where there are many entrances, the blocks of rooms being divided among many owners and trades: a positive warren of industry.

M. de Maroussem in *La Question Ouvrière* (Vol. iii, 1894) painted a graphic picture of these little artisans 'in a small way' of business, who had very few worldly possessions: an eating table upon which they also worked, a few chairs, a stove and sometimes many beds, for children 'were more plentiful here than banknotes'. The routine of their work must have been similar in many cases: making up dolls with imported porcelain heads from Germany which the women of the house could dress prettily. The body of the doll would be made of tightly stuffed leather and then dressed *à la mode*. This was the type of doll which was gradually improved upon in various ways and this was the district which saw the birth of many of the most famous Parisian doll-making firms, possibly from quite small family concerns.

The competition must have been keen between the makers and in the attempt to produce a doll in some way outstanding, many patents

198 Bru Musical doll

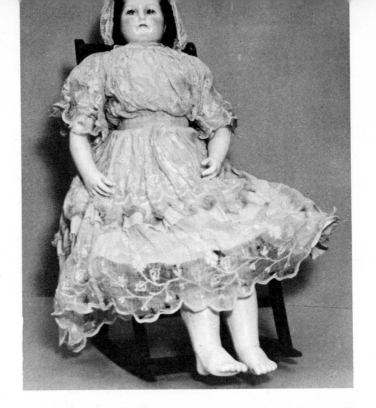

199 *China-headed doll made by Mme Rohmer of Paris c. 1860; 20 inches*

200 *Mme Huret patent for a doll's head which 'could move all ways', 1861*

201 *Bru patent for a fully articulated doll, 1869*

202 *right: Musical doll, unmarked but probably the 'Surprise' doll of Mme Bru, 1873*

were taken out in France to register a new design. Some of these patents were eccentric and probably short-lived in production. Very many dealt with improved forms of jointing or methods of using new types of materials, substituting strong linen for kid for the body fabric, or using the newly processed rubber and gutta-percha substances for unbreakable limbs and bodies. A few of the patents were sufficiently original to alter the whole future development of doll-making and set manufacturers on the way to the fully articulated unbreakable Parisian *bébé* which was to be the furore of the eighteen-seventies.

The earliest porcelain heads from Germany had been made in one piece with the shaped bust joined to the head by an immovable neck. The idea of a head which could change its position on a movable or swivel neck seems first to have been pursued during the middle years

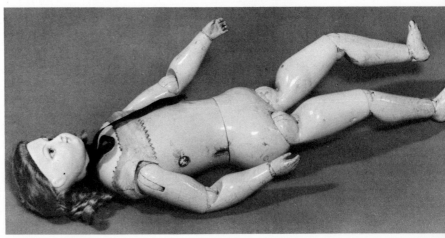

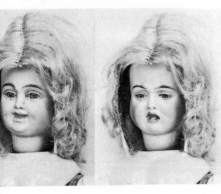

203 Three-faced doll, bisque head; German

of the nineteenth century, when various makers were working on a more complicated form of articulated doll. In Paris, Mlle Rohmer took out several patents during the years 1857–8 for improved doll bodies, including a new type of swivel head held in place by a cord attached inside the crown and passing down through the neck to a crossbar holding the arms in place [199]. The head, which was made of porcelain or composition, had a wide neck which actually rested over the neck of the body and could turn merely from side to side.

Mlle Huret (see page 164) was also a considerable innovator. In a patent she took out in 1850 she claimed a new method of making an articulated jointed doll which would produce something more realistic for a child than carved wooden models. The material she chose for moulding was gutta-percha, with a coating intended 'to simulate ivory'. A contemporary report on her products said that the number of dolls made each year was limited to about 1,500, as the raw material shipped from Ceylon was expensive owing to the amount of waste material it included. According to her specification the first heads which she used were porcelain, carton or any other material (Huret dolls have also been found with metal heads and hands). From the extension of the patent which she took out in 1861 it is clear that all the heads had originally been in one piece with the bust, for she now added an improvement for a porcelain head with a spherical base which socketed into the neck unit so that the head 'could move all ways' [200]. She also perfected an arm joint which allowed the arm to move from side to side as well as up and down.

By the eighteen-sixties the inventors began to turn their minds to novelty dolls. Casimir Bru of Paris, who was responsible for various ingenious working dolls, took out a patent in 1867 for a two-faced doll, one face sleeping and one waking, which was worked by a little lever at the shoulder. He called this his 'surprise doll' and later the idea was copied in Germany where three-expression and even five-faced dolls were produced with a simplified mechanism turning the head by a metal ring on the crown [203].

Two years later, in registering a patent for a fully articulated doll made of moulded rubber, Bru explained that doll-making had become so important in France that it was difficult to suggest improvements, but that this material would be more durable and sturdy. The specification showed a doll jointed at wrist, elbow, shoulder, hip, knee, ankle and midriff [201].

Later, the French makers were quick to realize the possibilities of a hollow body of carton (laminated layers of paper) and its advantages over other types of doll body. It meant that variation could be produced with an interior working part – for a mechanical or musical doll for instance – and it enabled simpler systems to be adopted for jointing arms, legs and head. Primarily it was a step towards mass-production. This was the century in which the beautiful doll of expensive construction became, as it were, a status symbol of the wealthy family. It was another direct result of the industrial revolution in Europe which could provide revolutionary tools and factory methods side by side with an increasing demand for such luxury goods.

204 Three types of joining dolls' heads and bodies used by German makers

The great International Trade Exhibitions of the nineteenth century did a great deal to promote commercial competition between countries and accounts of them are also a very good source of information about the types of toys exhibited at a given period and trends in their manufacture. In the French report of 1873, it was said that though France had previously excelled mainly in dressing dolls, since the Franco-Prussian war (1870–1) the country was freeing itself of the need to buy its doll heads from Germany and was becoming self-sufficient. Jumeau (who was awarded a Paris Gold Medal and was quoted as the first and foremost doll-making house) was said to be the maker who had freed the French from using German porcelain heads.

Jumeau seems to have recognized the value of giving vivacity to dolls' eyes. He concentrated on supplying his dolls with natural, life-like eyes and finally perfected a special process which made his *bébés* outstanding for their beauty in this respect. He also experimented with more realistic methods of closing and sleeping eyes. In 1885 he took out a patent whereby the actual eyeball would remain rigid but an upper eyelid would slide over it and simulate sleep (worked by a lever at the rear of the head), and the following year presented an improved form which could make the eye move as well. The patent seems to have been little used, so perhaps it was either found too difficult technically or too expensive to produce.

Jumeau and other Parisian makers such as Bru, Steiner and Schmitt found it necessary to take factory premises on the outskirts of Paris for the actual manufacture of their dolls, relying on showrooms in the city for their sale. From the 'seventies, the competition began more and more to involve providing attractive heads with improved details. In most cases the modellers of these beautiful doll faces remain unknown, though it does seem likely that some of the professional modellers from Limoges must have been attracted to the doll trade when so much artistry was represented in their work.

Great rivalry obviously existed between such firms as Bru, Steiner, Schmitt and Jumeau (see chapter 13). In 1879 Bru patented a drinking doll *(bébé têteur)* who sucked liquid from a bottle by means of a long tube joined through a teat in the mouth to a reservoir inside the head. Slight pressure on an ivory button at the back of the crown worked the doll. This doll enjoyed a huge Christmas success and the following year he echoed his triumph with an 'eating' doll. In 1872 he had produced a 'surprise' musical doll fitted with an apparatus with a key for winding it up and a lever to change the tunes [198 and 202].

The 'breathing' Bru (patent 1892) must have been positively eerie, with its musical clockwork mechanism to accompany a little apparatus in the chest which pumped up and down to simulate breathing! Such novelty dolls were of doubtful interest for children. Though they enjoyed a seasonal popularity and a few hours of fascination, they were given as an expensive present rather than becoming a family favourite. From those preserved in immaculate condition it is clear that they were often kept as a novelty and never given to children to play with.

With the invention of the phonograph by Edison in 1877 the age of

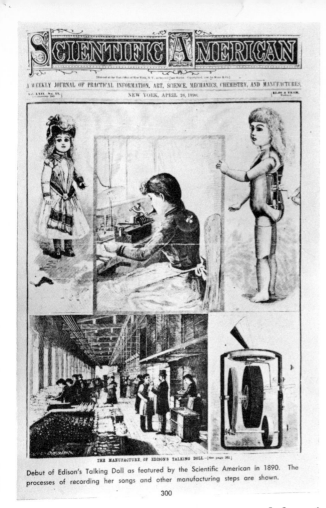

Debut of Edison's Talking Doll as featured by the Scientific American in 1890. The processes of recording her songs and other manufacturing steps are shown.

300

205 Advertisement for the Edison Phonograph doll showing how records were made

206 right: Jumeau phonograph doll: 'Records entitled 'Polichinelle' and 'Le Réve d'Enfant': 4 francs each'

recorded music and voice had begun and the novelty was soon to be incorporated in a doll. The front page of the *Scientific American* in New York for 26 April 1890 carried a full feature on the Edison Talking Doll, though it was not so much a talking doll as a doll with a phonograph inside it [205]. She appears, from an example still preserved by the Edison company, to have been a very pretty bisque-headed doll with jointed arms and legs, but her body was made of thin strong steel capable of carrying the mechanism. She was exhibited among the 'Wonders of Electricity' at the Lennox Lyceum in New York and sold at ten dollars. The *Scientific American* stated that the factory produced about five hundred dolls a day, and in the engravings, the workroom is shown with girls hard at work fitting up piles of dolls, while separate illustrations show the machine itself, the complete doll, dressed and undressed, and – most intriguing of all – a young woman recording songs and nursery rhymes from the doll's repertoire; simply dressed, with her hair in a plait and a pinafore about her waist, she makes a new chapter of doll history!

Jumeau provided his version of a phonograph doll with a slightly different mechanism and changeable records [206]. His 1895 advertisement mentioned three new models of indestructible jointed *bébés*: dressed and undressed; without the Jumeau mark with a difference of 40% to 60%; *New Créations Bébé Phonographe; Bébé Marcheur.*

191

By the 'nineties patents were taken out for a fully articulated doll which could walk, talk, throw kisses and turn its head from side to side. There were rival claims as to who had first created the *bébé*, but it was in fact a collective achievement originating with the French, contributed to and improved upon by many inventors and swiftly imitated by the German factories. The initiative which had swung to Paris in the 'sixties was re-echoed by German makers and brought to its peak in the years before the 1914–18 war. The war and the depression years afterwards put an end to the luxury doll. The demand was then for cheaper toys for the masses.

The image of the sweet, prettily dressed little girl gently at play with her dolls was one the nineteenth century liked, to match the 'angel in the house': the fully domesticated and in all ways perfect lady who was her Mamma.

It was, of course, very much in the interest of the dollmaker and toy-seller that this propaganda should be spread. W. H. Cremer, who had a famous toy shop in Bond Street, London, wrote in his *Toys for Little Folks*: 'A new life dawns upon that infant, if it be a girl, the moment she becomes a possessor of a doll. Always the subject of good works, the doll becomes the instructor of the mistress in several useful arts. For example the mere clothing of the doll teaches her how to use her needle – acquirements than which there are none more serviceable to womankind in everyday life, whatever may be said to the contrary in the drawing room and at meetings of the British Association.' Cremer was an astute business man, and without being unduly cynical, it is easy to see that another effect of providing dolls for the daughter of the house would be to keep the Cremers of London and his counterparts in France and Germany in business.

As well as dolls, all their accoutrements were part of this thriving trade. In 1867 an account of the Paris Exhibition said that a number of the dolls' trousseaux showed so much taste and elegance that they were even used by dress and bonnet makers as models. Cremer wrote that one such French doll presented by an American lady to a little Marchesa of Rome cost about 2,000 francs (equivalent to £100 or $240 at the contemporary rate).

Such aristocratic little personages may have been expensive but there seems to have been a ready market for them. 'Marie', of the Essex Institute Historical Collection, Salem, Massachusetts [207] has a double claim to historical fame and must have been a much-travelled

207 Marie: French doll of about 1870 with her travelling trunk (see pages 156–7)

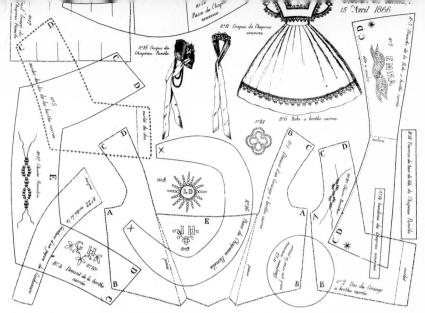

doll. She was brought originally from Paris in the eighteen-seventies for Mary Crowninshield Endicott, who was destined to be the wife of Joseph Chamberlain, English Prime Minister, who described her as 'a Gainsborough walking free of its frame'. After his death she married William Carnegie and returned once more to the United States.

The well-dressed doll of the period was not content with what she stood up in, but must be equipped with a finely turned out small trunk with a tray and a real lock to contain her possessions when she travelled. By the end of the century doll-dressing had deteriorated and there was an accepted style of doll fashion, over-trimmed with highly decorated beribboned bonnets and hats which matched the rather stereotyped doll face, which was pretty but vacuous and unrealistic.

The art of 'doll-play' was fostered as a suitable occupation for well-bred little girls in the nineteenth century, and a few copies of little books issued as a sort of primer to the pattern of such play exist. As early as 1806, *Les Jeux de la Poupée* was printed in Paris with very dainty engravings by A. Noel. The seven plates were each accompanied by a moralizing verse and the doll portrayed looked just like its mistress in miniature, with curly hair and loose fitting low-cut gown tied with a sash. Her adventures were of the simplest: she is shown finding the doll as a 'New Year's Present,' showing it to her sister, taking it for a walk, putting it to sleep and arranging its breakfast with a delicate little coffee-pot and dishes.

A fuller account of doll-play in a much later and less artistic colour-printed book of 1881, *Le Jeu de la Poupée* by Adrien Marie, includes undressing and giving a bath to the doll and even 'vaccination' by a small boy acting the part of the doctor. This French doll is seen progressing from a diet of milk, fed from a long tubed baby bottle, to gruel cooked in a tiny saucepan and, finally, on her 'mother's' knee she takes a sip of sweet wine and a biscuit. (*Gateaux* are said to be bad for dolls, and presumably for small girls also.)

The doll which in 1806 was pictured taking an airing on 'leading strings' has by 1881 acquired a cute little three-wheeled baby carriage in wicker work and she is put to rest at night in a beribboned cradle, since it is 'very unsuitable for a doll to sleep with her mother'.

From country to country, the diet and behaviour of dolls varied and this is reflected in both the books and the equipment of the period. The English dolls sat down to afternoon tea and a great variety of fine tea-sets was available for the purpose, some in quite cheap pottery and others of the very finest porcelain of Sèvres or Nevers, Worcester, Leeds and Beleek. Figure 209 shows a charming Kate Greenaway design made in 1890 by the Atlas China Company, Stoke-on-Trent, Staffordshire.

209 A tea service made by the
Atlas China Co.
of Stoke-on-Trent with
Kate Greenaway designs, 1890

Doll-dressing and undressing was one of the favourite games for girls in the last century and this is also very prettily illustrated in books. From 1875–82, the Parisian publishing firm Hachette were issuing a series of cut-out paper books for children entitled *Magasin des Petits Enfants*. The books were illustrated by brightly coloured pictures in chromolithograph and had an easy-to-read story in large print. Some of the plates represented little cut-out pieces which could be stuck in gaps on the corresponding missing section of a picture (210 and 211). This is a type of doll-dressing book which has never diminished in popularity and it furnishes a wonderful guide to the ornaments and fashions of the time. Note particularly the variety of fancy hats and gloves and the old-fashioned 'towel horse' in the bottom right-hand corner for airing and warming clothes before the open range.

Although similar play books persist in a modern idiom, doll-play generally is rather out of fashion in the twentieth century, except among very young children. There is a great contrast between the dolls of today and those of a hundred years ago, but an even greater difference is evident in their young owners. The lapse from popularity of the doll in the twentieth century is not merely the result of a change in dolls but of a change in children and in their upbringing.

*210 and 211 Cut-out pages
from* Magasin des Petits Entfants,
1875

16

American Dolls

The dolls of America form a cosmopolitan family sharing a lineage that stretches back to that first over-publicized Elizabethan doll put into the hands of a naked Indian child when Sir Richard Grenville led a colonizing expedition to Roanoke in 1585. It is difficult to imagine the impact of such a miniature ambassadress of peace from these exotic visitors from 'outer space', but obviously the gesture was recognized and the historian to the expedition wrote: 'wee offered them of our wares, as glasses, knives, babies (dolls) and other trifles, which wee thought they delighted in. Soe they stood still, and percevinge our Good Will and courtesie came fawninge uppon us, and bade us welcome.' Miraculously, the little doll was pictured by the artist who accompanied the expedition, John White [215].

With the later pioneer parties who came to colonize America, European dolls were gradually introduced and a few rare examples have survived such as 'Letitia Penn', proudly cherished by the Pennsylvania Historical Society, dating from about 1699 and twin sister to similar examples which have been preserved in England and France [212]. But in America, the position was different from any other country as the manufactured dolls were newcomers, pioneers and emigrants without a native tradition; they came in fact to establish their own pattern on their new home, like the people who brought them.

Consignments of dolls from England are recorded as being sold during the eighteenth century and papers in Pennsylvania and Philadelphia carried advertisements from time to time for dolls and toys and little articles of china or pewter for doll-play, which had been shipped across and were offered for sale at various stores. By the beginning of the nineteenth century German dolls were also imported and an advertisement of 1822 in Poulson's *American Daily Advertiser* mentioned 'Philadelphia Leather Dolls with composition hands' and 'Children's German Toys', as though German heads were being made up in America with leather bodies.

By the nineteenth century there was an increasing flow of European imports, American buyers began to explore European markets and bring back goods, and, more important, immigrants arrived who set up manufacturing methods in America based on their own traditionally acquired skills.

In doll-making the influence was predominantly German. The American makers never sought to reproduce the fine luxury-style English wax dolls and no factory was ever established for large-scale production of porcelain dolls. There were of course many hybrids with doll-heads of European manufacture fitted to American-made bodies – some professional, many homemade.

One of the first and most famous of American-made dolls was the Greiner papier mâché. Ludwig Greiner was a German who had come from Lauscha in Thuringia: a centre famous for doll-making and also for the production of fine glass eyes. He had no doubt learnt the art in his native land before arriving in Philadelphia, for the doll which he put on the market was to all intents and purposes a German doll made in America. The recipe for the material of which the head was

212 Letitia Penn, one of the early American 'immigrant dolls' of 1699; 20 inches

made was essentially a German one, constituted of boiled white paper, whiting, rye flour and glue, and the patent he took out in 1858 did not in fact claim more than that it was an 'improved' method and that the important difference between a Greiner head and others preceding the patent lay in the reinforcement. When the two halves of each head were joined, back and front, the interior was strengthened at 'the seams and projecting or exposed parts by cementing or pasting on those parts muslin, linen, silk etc.'. Greiner had been in business for twenty years before he took out this patent and had produced doll heads at an earlier date. 'His first labelled heads are thought to be those reading "Greiner Everlasting Doll Heads" in three lines. The second label was evidently the same as the first, with the addition of a line reading "Patent Applied For",' according to Mrs Jo Gerken. Heads were sold both with a commercially made-up body of stuffed cloth with leather arms, or separately for those who wished to make the body themselves.

Greiner's close friend and business associate Jacob Lacmann, who came from the same part of Germany, seems to have cooperated with him, as Greiner heads are found with Lacmann bodies. Indeed as Lacmann simply advertised a Manufactory of Doll Bodies, it seems likely that he relied on Greiner and other makers for the supply of heads. The Greiner patent was renewed in 1872 and the founder of the firm died two years later, though his sons carried on the business until 1883. Sweet and homely in appearance, the Greiner doll made no pretensions to grandness: it is reminiscent of the placid Biedermeier type of German porcelain head with black or blond hair centre-parted and tidily arranged. Greiner himself did not claim that he was making something new, only something better. The structure was his own idea and the quality finish was no doubt responsible for so many fine examples of his dolls surviving in good condition [216].

In at least two instances, nineteenth-century chemists were responsible for providing quite new substances for use in doll-making: rubber and celluloid, both of which have been used with variants and improvements right up to the present day.

The use of raw rubber long pre-dates its commercial use and it was known to the Aztecs in its natural state before the arrival of the Spanish in South America. Its elastic properties were recognized by the natives both for making balls and for soling shoes. It was not until the American Charles Goodyear devised, in 1839, the process of vulcanization – softening rubber by heating it with sulphur – that it assumed its commerical value. He licensed its use for making doll heads to Benjamin Lee of New York City, as he recorded in his book *Gum Elastic* (1855). Rubber dolls were advertised in the *Daily Mercury* for December 1850 in addition to rubber animals and balls; these may have referred to articles made by the India Rubber Comb Co. of New York, who were licensed to use a formula for hard rubber, applied for by Nelson Goodyear, brother of Charles, and finally patented in 1851. They must have been pretty enough when new and painted with features and hair after the fashion of papier mâché models, but time ravaged them, the rubber perished and the paint flaked away, leaving

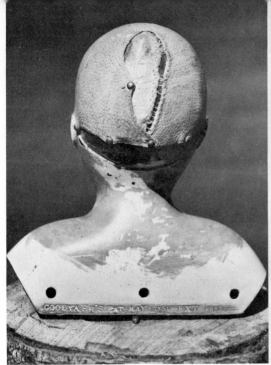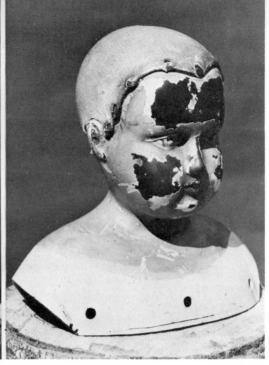

213 A rubber doll head with the Goodyear patent mark dated; 1885 note the leather scalp for wig attachment

sombre patches, so that very few of the earliest prototypes have survived. The doll heads were made with holes in the yoke for attaching the stuffed body. An interesting head in the possession of Mrs John Scripture (*Doll Collectors' Manual*, 1964) shows the later version of 1865 – the patent was renewed fifteen years later – with finely modelled features and a leather cap fastened over the crown for a wig attachment [213].

Unlike rubber, which is a raw material, celluloid is a man-made plastic and the forerunner of a long line of synthetic substances used for making doll bodies, eventually to usurp almost every other type. Alexander Parkes of England first processed celluloid in 1855 by means of the action of nitric and sulphuric acid on cotton with camphor and alcohol, which made it highly inflammable. In 1865, two brothers of Albany, New York, John Wesley and Isaiah Hyatt, won a competition by using celluloid as a substitute for ivory in billiard balls! Later they experimented with its use for making doll heads. It is intriguing to find how doll-making, which was not an old tradition in the United States, was often introduced there as a sideline or development from other types of trade. From industrial and mechanical inventions arose the composition, pressed wood and plastic dolls, from the homemade cottage dolls came eventually the commercial rag and stuffed dolls.

The Hyatts had established the Embossing Company of New York in 1870. They used machinery to make toy bricks with a raised pattern and during the 'eighties and 'nineties they manufactured celluloid dolls at Hyatts Celluloid Manufacturing Co., New Jersey, using special patents taken out in 1880 and 1881 by W. B. Carpenter for methods of colouring the eyebrows and finishing off the head which gave 'a most beautiful natural look'.

Another original method of manufacture was instanced in a patent taken out by Franklin Darrow of Bristol, Connecticut, in 1865 for raw-hide dolls – dolls made before the leather was tanned – and an improved patent followed the next year. Darrow was principally a manufacturer of leather belts for machinery and the dolls' heads were made by pressing material into the required shape and attaching the finished head to a stuffed body. If the material was not the most suitable to make a pretty doll, at least it was very tough and durable and the finished result, with a coat of paint and added features, was not unattractive, resembling some of the cruder papier mâché masks [216]. The dolls bore a label on their front printed in black on green paper 'F. E. DARROW Patent May 1st. 1866', and it is said that the fondness of rats for this type of meal deprived a good many collectors of the Darrow doll which they would have liked to own!

The speed with which America was settled during the nineteenth century is one of the most dramatic episodes of her history. Emigrants from Europe who, for one reason or another, set sail for a new land and a new life brought their old skills and trades with them. A census in 1790 counted nearly four million people but after one hundred years this figure had risen to over fifty million, and toys and dolls were needed to meet the demands of the army of new children being reared on American soil. There was both opportunity for a new home toy trade and the labour to man it.

It must often have occurred to the retailers of imported dolls that if they could market a homemade version they would score on the profit side, though they did not always find that they could produce cheaply enough to compete with imported goods. One such store-keeper turned dollmaker was Philip Goldsmith, who ran a retail store in Covington, Kentucky, in the eighteen-seventies handling sports-goods and dolls. With Wolf Flechter, who was probably of German origin, he experimented with a papier mâché doll head, which is distinctly Germanic. It was made of flour, glue and paper pulp. 'This mixture was kneaded by human feet in a big tub as wine is pressed from grapes.' The dough was rolled out like a pie-crust, cut in proper sizes, and put in a three-part mould, one for the back of the head and two for the face. After being dried in a hot room the pieces were removed from the moulds and glued together, and then they were dried again. Rough joins were trimmed off and sandpapered, the head was dipped into flesh-coloured paint and the cheeks coloured. Then it was given two coats of varnish. The bodies were made of cloth stuffed with hair and sawdust and in a typically German manner hair was added at the joints to prevent the sawdust seeping out.

Having parted company with Flechter, Goldsmith established a large factory in 1880, which he called the American Toy Company; five years later he patented an amusing doll body incorporating a fancy corset, decorated with braid, which simplified the stuffing method as the seams hid the joins. The doll was made of kid and cloth with an imported head, and Goldsmith actually intended to bring German workers from Sonneberg to his factory to provide wax heads. Unfortunately he was drowned in an accident in 1894, the doll-making lost its impetus and the factory was carried on by his sons purely for sports equipment, such as baseballs.

Certainly, in the first half of the nineteenth century, the home-made doll must have been far more customary as a plaything than any bought toy. If father, with his carpentry, could shape the wooden bed or cradle, mother with her needle and scrap bag would fashion the baby and its clothes and wrappings. The Bucks Historical Society, Doylestown, Pennsylvania, retains a little doll coffin which dates from about 1804, when it was made by her grandfather for a small girl called Ella Good. He was a cabinet-maker by profession and the child was able to imitate a scene which was probably all too familiar at that time, though in her case it was always possible to soften the sadness of the occasion by a 'resurrection'.

Mrs Alice Trimpey recalling her childhood days with a beloved china-headed doll in *Becky – My First Love* wrote: 'for entertainment, religious services seemed to be the preference. Funerals were especially popular, with Becky ever the willing victim. I used to wonder whether any other doll in the world had caused so much grief. Without complaint she merged from one sickness into another – died at the proper time – entertained the mourners and then started all over again.'

One of the first to think of producing rag dolls on a commercial scale was Mrs Izannah Walker of Central Falls. She used a method of stiffening the face fabric with glue and reinforcing it with layers of stuffing and webbing. She is said to have been using this method for some years before she took out a patent in 1873. This shows how a simple hand-worked press was used to give the head shape on the moulds; the front and back pieces were pressed separately but simultaneously and then joined together. The dolls had painted features; some represented boys but little girls with two curls in front of the ears were more usual. Many must have been destroyed or discarded, but the Izannah Walker dolls are considered among the most 'collectable' American dolls extant.

It was in fact one of these 'primitives' owned in childhood which gave another famous maker the first idea of making up some rag dolls for her children. Mrs Chase, who was born near Central Falls, started making rag dolls in about 1889 and after a Boston store had become interested in them and encouraged her to make some up professionally, she found a thriving business on her hands. The dolls were made of stockinet and cotton cloth with cotton stuffing. The face had hard raised features on which hair, eyes, nose and mouth could be over-painted. Much of the popularity of the Chase dolls lay in their proportions, for they had large heads and pudgy childlike bodies [214]. Like those later dolls made by Käthe Kruse in Germany, they had a realism that made them genuine little playmates. Mrs Chase also made some dolls dressed as Dickens's characters and others such as George Washington or Black Mammy. The child rag doll was improved by substituting oiled cloth for stockinet and painting the doll with waterproof paint, so that it could be bathed and washed. It was this quality which led to an order being placed in 1910 for a life-sized

214 Chase stockinet doll;
20 inches

215 opposite: Roanoke Indian
child holding an Elizabethan doll
brought over by English
colonists to the New
World in 1585

'infant' for nurses training at Hartford Hospital. From then on the making of hospital-training dolls represented a considerable proportion of the Chase Stockinet Factory output. To assist medical training they were made with internal tanks at nose, ear and abdomen. Different sizes represented a new-born baby, a baby of two months, four months, a year old, four years old and an 'adult manikin', which was life-size. Such was the firm's pride in the workmanship of this doll, which was guaranteed to be entirely handmade, that it advertised 'If Stradivarius had made dolls he would have made the Chase Stockinet!'

The Arnold Print Works of Massachusetts were founded in 1876 and specialized in the production of material for doll-making. Printed dolls could be bought by the yard, ready for cutting out, sewing together and stuffing. One of the most popular lines produced by this firm was the Brownies, patented by Palmer Cox in 1892 [217]. 'Brownies like fairies and goblins are imaginary little sprites who are supposed to delight in harmless pranks and helpful deeds. They work and sport while weary households sleep and never allow themselves to be seen by mortal eyes.' So the writer Palmer Cox explained his creation in the frontispiece to his first book, *The Brownies: Their Book* (1888). The 'wee folk' were traditional in his native Scotland, but to them Palmer Cox brought a vividly illustrative pen which gave them modern dress, individuality and personality; the Scotsman with his tam o'shanter, the Dude with top hat and monocle (an English milord?), a Chinaman with pigtail, a policeman, Bell-hop, Jockey, Uncle Sam were just a few of the recognizable disguises which made these costume Brownies different.

By the eighteen-seventies many fine toy-making concerns were established in the United States and not least among them for versatility and originality of output must be listed the Crandall family. The toy historians Marshall and Inez McClintock have been able to trace eleven members of this family associated with toy-making between 1830 and 1929, foremost among them being two cousins,

205

Jesse A. Crandall and Charles M. Crandall, who worked separately (see *Toys in America*). The family came from around Hopkinton, Rhode Island, and although their chief concern was a progressive output of velocipedes, rocking horses, hobby horses, carriages, sleds and various types of building blocks and games, Jesse patented a jointed doll in 1874 and Charles took out a patent for doll joints in 1876. The Crandalls were exceptional for their inventive ideas. Games such as the District School produced by Charles [218] retain a 'homemade' look and the figures are of flat cut-out wood, coloured and featured, with rivetted movable limbs, and little slotted stands to hold them erect. This game was sold in London by H. Jewett and Son, who acted as the London agents for Crandall toys. In finish it can scarcely compare with European toys of the period, but it scores in having an individual and quaint look and is a delicious reminder of a time when sober *domini* held law absolute and little boys really wore a dunce cap when they misbehaved.

Springfield, Vermont, has been called the 'cradle of invention', an allusion to the wealth of mechanical talent established there during the nineteenth century. Certainly it was the cradle of a very famous group of dolls. Joel A. H. Ellis, who came to Springfield as a young man, founded a company in 1858 called Ellis, Britton and Eaton; its output included splint baskets, toy carriages, furniture and pianos for children, as well as wooden cases for guitars and violins. After 1869, when floods washed away part of the factory, the Vermont Novelty works were refounded; a year or so later, Ellis extended his activities to doll-making and the Co-operative Manufacturing Co. was formed for their production. It is not known what prompted the new venture; perhaps he employed German workmen who influenced or assisted him in the design, but the doll for which he took out a patent in 1873

218 The District School Game with jointed dolls made by Charles Crandall and marketed in London in 1876

219 Two Joel Ellis jointed dolls; 12 inches

had an obviously German inspiration [219]. It was rather like a sophisticated and *de luxe* 'Dutch' doll, with head and body turned in one piece, and splint joints at shoulder, elbow, thigh and knee fastened with screws. It is amusing that an advertisement issued by the firm a little later actually gave it the name of 'Patent Manikin', like that of the early German artists' figures.

The dolls, made of rock maple, were produced in three sizes, twelve, fifteen and eighteen inches high with hands and feet of metal. The roughly shaped head was finished off under a steam pressure mould, dipped in paint and finally given detailed features and blond or brunette hair by hand painting. Some of the dolls seem to have been made to represent negroes by a dark coat of paint, and all these tough little creatures were capable of assuming various positions. A son of Joel Ellis, reminiscing in *Memories of Boyhood at Springfield, Vermont*, could well remember the original 'Stone Shop' of the works, built beside a dam on the Black River which provided the plant with the equivalent of two hundred horse-power. He recalled also a 'tumbling barrel' turned slowly by a leather belt worked from a power pulley which could act as a sanding machine for small pieces of wood which needed smoothing. This, he thought, was his father's invention, but in fact it was a method known in Germany from much earlier times.

The Joel Ellis dolls were made only for one year and he was perhaps discouraged by their not being a great success. He seems to have been one of those inventive geniuses who are happiest whilst new plans are afoot, and when he left Springfield in 1878 after the Vermont Novelty works had been destroyed by fire, it was left to others to continue the tradition of doll-making which he had established. Mrs Enid Crawford Pierce, in *Antiques* (1942), said that local historians in Springfield recorded that after the fire Henry Mason, Luke Taylor, George Sanders, C. C. Johnson and Frank Martin met to see whether the works could be started up again. It is not known how far they had cooperated in producing jointed dolls, but they had all worked with or known Ellis. That they were interested either in producing dolls or the machinery and materials involved in doll-making is evident, as over the next few years all five were concerned in patents for improving or adapting the type of jointed doll which Joel Ellis had first produced.

In 1879, Martin secured a patent for improved doll joints which claimed that the 'upper part of the arms that fits into the socket of the shoulder is held in position by means of an elastic or spiral spring'. The next year a patent by Sanders introduced true ball and socket mortised joints in place of the less manoeuvrable splint joints. The jointed doll patented by Mason and Taylor in 1881 was made of poplar instead of hard maple. The arms and legs alone were made of maple and attached by dowel pins. The patent described the doll as having a 'composition head that revolves and a modern cylindrical device unites the head, with no added outside neck or collar, through the shoulders fixed with a pin so that it revolves'. The head, made of a sort of composition sawdust paste, enclosed a hub which revolved on a spindle embedded in the wooden body.

About this same time a 'witch' or 'wizard' doll was produced with this type of composition head, but without joints at knee or elbow. A unique neck-joint contraption of metal, with a three-point catch, engaged and disengaged as a knife was sliced through the neck, giving the illusion of decapitation. The doll was ten inches tall and was dressed in a kimono, with flat slippers with turned-up toes and a painted Japanese face with slanting eyes and mop hair. The principle was not an original one; at the Great Exhibition in London in 1851, an Englishman, J. V. Albert, showed amongst his 'philosophical apparatus' and dolls, the 'Moor's Head conjuring toy which admits of a knife traversing the neck without severing the head'. The mechanism was said to be simple but 'could not be made clear without a diagram'.

A patent was taken out by Colonel C. C. Johnson in 1882 for a further improvement in dolls' heads, constructed on a wooden foundation and covered with material from which facial features could be moulded and painted.

An advertisement displayed in 1884 for the 'Jointed Doll Company' (then under the proprietorship of J. N. Patton and William Slack, to whom Sanders had assigned his patent) showed a jointed doll with a Johnson-type head, measuring twelve inches and costing seven dollars per dozen. The advertisement claimed: 'We also furnish an improved jointed doll with an elastic body so designed to fit all heads of American Manufacture.'

Mrs Pierce, relying on local reports and on the evidence of surviving doll forms, thought that there was an amalgamation of ideas and work, and that it is possible to find the different parts and patented ideas incorporated. She had even heard of an Ellis body without a head and a Mason head made in one piece with a body.

A novelty doll which was all the rage during the Christmas season of 1882 was the singing doll patented by William Webber of Boston. An ingenious bellows device, working a sort of miniature body organ in the doll's chest, could play a tune of twenty-five notes of various pitches and the little 'Prima Donna in every home' had a varied repertoire (though each doll could only 'sing' one tune) including such tunes as 'Yankee Doodle', 'Home Sweet Home', the *Marseillaise* and '*Frohe Botschaft*'. Webber used a musical part made by the Massachusetts Organ Co., but unlike the Goodwin mechanical dolls (see chapter 10) he used foreign heads. The doll was produced in sizes of twenty-two or thirty inches, with a *de luxe* edition of each with sleeping eyes, wax head and real hair, advertised as a 'First Class French Doll'.

Another American-made wooden doll which became even more famous than the Springfield dolls was that made by Albert Schoenhut. Schoenhut, descended from a line of German toy-makers, arrived in America in the 'sixties and seems to have had a musical bent, as he specialized at first in children's musical toys: elegant little pianos, zylophones and glockenspiels. Although he made a moderate living, his real success did not come until he patented a 'Humpty Dumpty' circus set in 1903. The items were sold separately and with them a child could enact the scenes of one of the travelling shows so popular at that time, with animals, clowns and all the personnel of a circus troupe [220]. They were sturdily made of wood and cheerfully coloured with slots in the hands and feet so that they could pose on apparatus or hold things like ladders and chairs whilst special elastic joints enabled them to hold a set pose. The equestrienne was made with a German bisque head.

Schoenhut flourished and by 1911 was able to describe his factory in Philadelphia as the 'largest in the world devoted exclusively to the manufacture of toys'. This was the year in which he took out a patent for a large play-doll, entirely made of wood. It is said that he did not invent the elastic-jointed circus figures but was sold the idea by an unknown visitor to his factory. The Schoenhut 'All Wood Perfection Art Doll', however, incorporated his own improvements on the idea and had articulated joints with a device comprising steel springs and swivels. The hands and feet were made of enamelled hardwood, and two holes drilled in the soles of the feet were intended to receive pegs of a metal stand which held the doll erect.

The dolls' faces were not carved by hand but on a multiple cutting machine following a master mould which could skilfully reproduce fine lifelike expressions [221]. Some dolls had moulded hair and others wigs; eyes were painted or inserted wooden 'sleeping' type.

220 Schoenhut circus doll equestrienne *with china head from Humpty Dumpty Circus 1905(?)*

221 Jointed wooden Schoenhut doll; 21 inches — according to a 1911 patent he articulated them with steel springs so that the limbs could hold any position

Patricia Schoonmaker in *Research on Kammer and Reinhardt Dolls* says that he borrowed the idea of character faces from other makers – notably the beautiful types modelled by the KR factory – but pirating of dolls' faces occurred on quite a wide scale all through the nineteenth century. The Schoenhut dolls were large and rather heavy, but they were also attractive and durable. After Albert Schoenhut's death in 1912, the toy-making firm was continued by his sons until 1935, but the dolls were discontinued in the 'twenties.

Although E. I. Horsman has been called the 'Father of the American Doll Industry' he was yet another manufacturer who began in quite a different line. His record shows him always to have been a busy and enthusiastic man with an eye to commercial success, following the vogue for any popular new line with considerable financial flair.

From about 1864, when he set up in business, he made games and sold imported dolls as a sideline. He followed the fashions of baseball, croquet, tennis, and archery, making equipment and dealing in any lines which were profitable. His first entry into doll-making, in about 1901, was with stuffed rag dolls, but it was after he had acquired the Aetna Doll and Toy Co. in 1909 that he achieved a large-scale success. He was one of the first to realize the possibilities of dolls allied to advertising and the potential of clever selling propaganda by slogan and catchword. A patent taken out in 1892 by Sol D. Hoffman for a hard composition head made of a mask dipped in a melted mixture of glue, glycerine, zinc oxide and Japanese wax had proved so successful that salesmen were able to prove its efficacy as a really unbreakable material by banging dolls' heads on the floor or driving nails into them. The formula for these 'Can't Break'em' dolls passed to Horsman, who scored various continuing successes, first with 'Billiken', a grotesque mascot doll, then with the 'Campbell kids', in cooperation with the soup company, and various character dolls. Mass-production was under way. 'The Multitude became Visible' and voluble also in its demand for a share of the good things of life. With increased production and lower competitive prices there was a gradual end to handmade toys and dolls on the mass market.

There were exceptions, of course, in which individual artists scored spectacular success and one of the most impressive was in the famous Kewpie doll. Often a new type of doll has emerged and taken shape in the first place on a drawing board intended for some quite different purpose than the design of a doll. Such a history lies behind the emergence of the Kewpie.

In 1909, an enterprising editor who had envisaged a popular children's strip cartoon using some of the drawings of Miss Rose O'Neill, encouraged her to adapt the little baby faces, which up to that time she had drawn for decoration and magazine illustration, and use them to illustrate a story. In reply to this suggestion she wrote: 'for such a

222 Section of letter from Rose O'Neill concerning her 'kewpies'

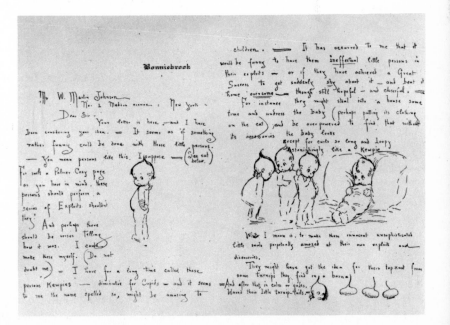

Palmer-Coxy page as you have in mind these persons should perform a series of Exploits shouldn't they? ...I have for a long time called these persons "kewpies", diminutive for Cupids, and it seems to me the name spelled so might be amusing to children.' Indeed these 'persons' and other characters following in their train conjured up by her ready imagination were to be popular with more than children: they constituted a craze which swept the whole world. 'I had never had the faintest idea there was going to be a Kewpie explosion that would girdle the earth,' Rose O'Neill wrote, many years later, but from their first appearance as a children's feature in *Ladies Home Journal* in December 1909 to the present day, they have maintained popularity [223].

Rose O'Neill herself was a curious and romantic personality. From childhood she showed great talent for sketching and seems never to have had any other ambition than to be an artist. Her success came early when she won a competition for drawing among Nebraska schoolchildren. At fourteen years of age she was already submitting both poems and drawings to local papers. Her serious art training was carried out at the Convent of the Sisters of St Regis in New York and she was able to pay her way for the three years' study by contributions to such periodicals as *Truth, Collins Weekly* and *Harper's*. Her personal life, apart from the success of her art and the fame which she later won through Kewpie dolls, was not altogether a happy one. She suffered two broken marriages and her greatest consolation in later life seems to have been the beautiful family home,' Bonniebrook', in the Ozark mountains of the Missouri, where she could enjoy 'the ragged rascal beauty' of the remote forest land and hills with her mother and devoted sister.

The Kewpies, which had been born in the pages of the *Ladies Home Journal*, progressed into book form and appeared in October 1912 as 'Kewpie Kutouts' issued with copies of the *Woman's Home Companion*. Some extra characters emerged, such as Wag, the Kewpie Chief who wore a little 'K' flag on his head, Dotty Darling and Dotty Darling's baby brother. Dotty Darling seems to have first expressed the author's intention of modelling Kewpies as dolls when she said:

> *I wish that every single child*
> *Could have a Kewpie for its own*
> *To stay with it and play with it*
> *And just belong to it alone.*

The first copyright for a Kewpie doll was filed by Rose O'Neill (at that time Mrs Wilson) on 17 December 1912 and patented on 4 March 1913. The first models were manufactured by J. D. Kestner in Germany and their importation to America was sponsored by George Borgfeldt and Co. of New York. Recollecting this exciting first production, the artist wrote:

The drawings and verses began in 1909. By 1913, the dolls were all over the world. First many children began to write to me, asking if I couldn't make them a Kewpie they could hold in their hands.

Just for fun I moulded a little statue of a Kewpie. Then the doll factories got the idea. I selected a factory and the whole thing was done. These first bisque Kewpies were manufactured in Germany. I went over there, molded nine statues of different sizes, saw that they came out right and before the World War began there were about thirty factories turning them out as fast as they could pull them out of the oven.

Sufficiently doll-like for a child's toy, impish enough for an adult mascot, Kewpies invaded thousands of homes and even made their debut as figurines on the radiator caps of cars. After the First World War, their design was familiar on all sorts of printed fabrics, as a decoration for nursery china and on wallpaper. Indeed the Kewpie must carry the distinction of having been made up in the largest range of plastic materials imaginable, from finest bisque to fairground plaster (they were commonly used on the shooting range, both as target and prize). They were made up into lamps, inkwells, spoon-handles and brooches, notepaper, sweetmeats, toilet soaps and for children as cut-out dressing sets. The familiar image was commercialized through all the variations of rubber, celluloid, wood, metal and confection, right down to the present-day unbreakable vinyl Kewpies produced by Cameo Products.

In a definitive biography of Rose O'Neill by Mrs Rowena Godding Ruggles, well illustrated from many collections, a variety of the 'action' Kewpies appear who are caught in some of the many activities depicted in Rose O'Neill's verses: playing instruments or accompanied by the 'Kewpiepoodle' dog – a plump, cheerful little animal which was founded on the recollection of a bull-terrier pup given to her in 1905 by the author Booth Tarkington.

In 1925, a further character joined the page which continued to appear in *Ladies Home Journal*: a baby doll called 'Scootles' because, as was explained in her first introduction in 'Kewpieville' in April, 'she was always scooting away to find adventure'. For this same reason she was also sometimes called 'The Baby Tourist'. When Scootles appeared in doll form she never became as popular as the ever-present Kewpie. In the same year, Rose O'Neill, with her sister's help, produced a rag doll, known as Kudly Kewpie, with face made of pressed moulded cloth and painted features.

In 1940, Rose O'Neill's last attempt at doll-making was presented in the form of a little laughing Buddha called 'Ho-Ho', but with Pearl Harbor just around the corner it was not the most auspicious moment for launching an oriental character, and in any case this doll lacked the whimsical appeal which delighted children.

The secret of Rose O'Neill's success was no doubt her great love of children, coupled with sound business acumen. In later years, speaking to her niece in an interview published in the *Kansas City Star* in May 1938, she said: 'I dreamed them... They were bouncing about all over the coverlet chirping their little newborn name. One perched in my hand like a bird. It's little sit-down wasn't warm like a human baby's, it was oddly cool. So I knew they were elves but of a new kind.

223 Kewpie of finest quality bisque with glass eyes, wings moulded on the neck, and jointed at shoulders hips and knees, made by J. D. Kestner of Germany; 13½ inches

I had a strange impression that their intentions were of the best. In fact I knew at once they were bursting with kindness, that their hearts were as well rounded as their tummies. I meditated on them for days afterwards, and bit by bit, I saw they had philosophy.'

In fact one wonders how near Rose O'Neill's dream would have come to reality had it not been for the discerning editor who saw the possibility of transforming the little face with winsome eyes and brushed up topknot into a story character, or later the German porcelain manufacturers who were able to reproduce the little sit-upons literally in cold china!

At the School of Ozarks, Shepherd of the Hills Memorial Lodge Museum in Branson, Missouri, personal relics of the artist are preserved, together with costumes that she liked to wear when she was at work.

Another famous 'American' doll which owed its production to skilful German porcelain manufacture was the 'Bye-Lo Baby'. The sculptress Grace Storey Putnam was by no means the first to envisage how popular a lifelike new-born baby doll might prove: Horsman had put Baby Bumps and Negro Baby Bumps on the market with 'Can't Break 'Em' composition heads and this seemed to be a copy of the rather wizened character of 'Baby' produced by Kammer and Reinhardt in 1910. The Armand Marseille works in Germany had produced pretty, if idealized, baby heads [191] and the Amberg New Born Babe, produced in 1914, preceded the Great War. But the Bye-lo Baby, or 'Million Dollar Baby', surpassed the success of all of these, coming at a time when high-class dolls were in short supply. It sold on the merit of its modelling and was originally based on a tiny illegitimate waif, a baby girl only a few days old, modelled by Grace Storey Putnam in a Salvation Army home in 1919. The sculptress did not at first find a taker for her model, which was even thought by some toy-makers to be too realistic. Eventually when Borgfeldt of New York had patented the doll under its trade name in 1923 there was some long delay before the bisque heads were satisfactorily finished by the German manufacturers who undertook the work, and none was sold until 1927. A small number of life-size copies of the first model were made in wax and sold at high prices and it is said that men bought them as a novelty for their wives.

Ceramic dolls were never manufactured in American factories on a large scale, but just as in England the Staffordshire potteries sought to perfect a home-produced doll when the 1914–18 war halted the import of German dolls (see page 159), there was a parallel attempt in the United States. The Fulper Pottery of Flemington, New Jersey, successfully produced dolls with an attractive bisque head which had tongue, teeth and glass sleeping eyes [224]. The Rookwood pottery of Cincinnati produced a beautiful baby head, using a basically pink slip. The Giebeler Falk Corporation manufactured an unbreakable doll during the latter years of the war using heavy gauge aluminium of the sort used for saucepans. Metal sleeping eyes were fastened inside the forehead with an arrangement of fibre washers stacked and secured with a nut and bolt to adjust the swing of the eye weight. The

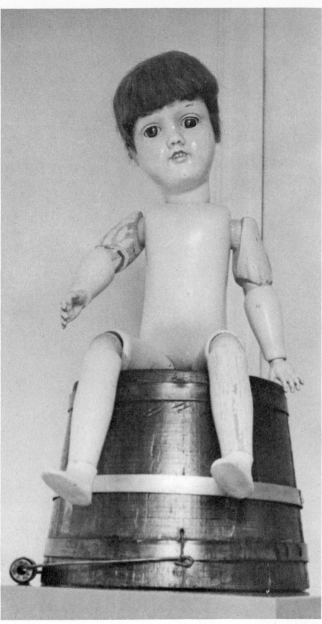

224 Fulper doll of 1917–20 with a kid jointed body; open mouth with two bisque teeth and celluloid tongue which is slightly movable and blue sleeping eyes; 22 inches

225 right: Unbreakable aluminium doll from the Giebeler Falk Corporation, 1918–20; 19 inches

head was baked on enamel and this helped to make it nearly indestructible. The hands and feet were metal but the body with ball-jointed limbs was of lathe-turned wood [225].

After the war there was a rearrangement of toy markets. The fine English wax dolls were virtually finished, the SFBJ in Paris had a monopoly of French bisque-headed dolls which also lapsed and the German china factories were eventually to be superseded by concerns which produced dolls in more durable materials. Celluloid and plastic models gave them a death blow. Advertising in America gave added impetus to a home-based doll trade, which had to satisfy one of the biggest demands in the world, and set the pattern for a manufacture which was eventually to challenge the former German monopoly of doll- and toy-making.

17

....

Japanese Dolls

There is a history of doll-making in Japan which probably stretches back in a continuous tradition further than that of any other race in the world. Just as in the West, various factors contributed to the evolution of dolls, but the fact that Japan was isolated from the West and used quite different materials indigenous to the country and independent techniques ensured that its dolls remained at all times highly national in type. Not until the end of the nineteenth century, when Japan began to contend with the commercial producers of the West, were dolls made in imitation of their western sisters.

The Japanese doll-expert, Koba Tsutomu, in his introduction to a catalogue of the Japanese Fine Arts Exhibition *(Jidai Nishiki Tenrankei)* in 1935, where antique dolls were displayed alongside historic brocades and lacquer work, explained that the art of doll-making had evolved along two distinct lines of descent. One was of ritual origin and the other was purely decorative and allied to a tradition of making and admiring beautiful things and a preoccupation with artistic design. On the one hand the belief in very early times that the 'dirt' or 'natural sin' of a person could be transferred like a physical disease and 'rubbed off' on a doll by close personal contact led to the use of primitive *hitogata* (little man-shaped things) – effigies which could be thrown into a river and float away for ever, bearing their owner's load of sorrow. At a much later period, a more sophisticated form of evolution was thought by Koba Tsutomu to have produced the purely decorative dolls which portrayed the everyday life and characters, real or mythological, of the time. But there was a great deal more to it than that, and the magnificence of the feudal Japanese court circle with its accompanying luxury was a background which readily gave rise to the custom of giving expensive presents, so that the art of beautiful doll-making flourished among the kindred arts of lacquering boxes, weaving precious brocades and silks and producing rare pottery.

One type of doll in particular, the *gosho ningyo* (court or palace doll), owes its name to its popularity as a present among the noblemen and court ladies of the Edo period (1615–1867). These dolls were not only prized as artistic objects but seem also to have been considered as good-luck symbols. Perhaps this stemmed from the fact that the baby boy is highly esteemed throughout Japan, for the *gosho ningyo* was made to represent a chubby baby, with a rather large head, in various positions. Even in recent times the doll is sometimes given to the parents of a new-born child to bring luck. Figure 226 shows a typical example, very fine in quality, dating from the early eighteenth century. Age has rubbed away some of his expression and almost completely removed the thin red lines painted on his crown, representing *mizuhiki*, threads used for tying the hair. But his face is typically subtle and reminds one of the saying: 'The Japanese is born grown-up and remains a child all his life.' *Gosho ningyo* were originally carved from wood and this one could have been from a block measuring five inches square; the doll was then smoothed and polished and coatings of *gofun* (a paste made of powdered oyster shell and glue) were applied to give the typical shining skin tone. The hands at one time held something, as was usual in this type of doll:

226 Gosho ningyo; *18th century; 11 inches*

217

227 Saga Ningyo *1744; Edo; 10¼ inches*

a fan with a dangling sash, a rattle with a stick, a flute or drum, or even some toy such as a ball or hobbyhorse. Traditionally naked, he has only a little piece of red brocade worn as an apron, called *haragake* or 'belly-cloth.'

Models of this sort were sometimes called *O-miyage* or 'souvenir dolls', because a Daimyo or feudal lord might buy them to take home with him after the compulsory period spent at the Royal Court. Some of the most famous even perpetuated the shop where they were bought in eighteenth-century Osaka and were called *Izagura ningyo* after Izagura-ya, a shop near the Yotsu bridge. Although the finest were always made of wood, replicas were sometimes made of clay or papier mâché or a moulded sawdust composition called *neri-mono*.

Among decorative dolls of the eighteenth century, the early *Saga* dolls are the most prized and are aesthetically the most exciting. The word derives from the place on the west boundary of Kyoto where they were first made and tradition honours as their founder Sumino Ryoi, a skilled craftsman during the *Kanei* period (1625–43). These dolls were carved entirely of wood and their beauty lay partly in the skilful lines, partly in the richness of their decoration. As in the *gosho ningyo*, a thick layer of *gofun* was applied over the finished carving, and colouring and gold leaf were then used to represent clothing and ornament [227]. The dolls were usually small, under twelve inches, because of the intricacy of the workmanship and they represented a great variety of subjects: warriors, actors, people in various trades such as monkey showmen or puppeteers, characters from mythology such as the Gods of Good Fortune, Hotei and Daikoku. Occasionally, a novelty *saga ningyo* was produced with a nodding head loose in the neck socket and a tongue that poked from his mouth – the forerunners of some of those porcelain 'nodders' made in Germany and so popular last century.

A different technique was used for *kimekomi ningyo*, which also date from the Edo period and seem to have progressed from the *saga ningyo* as they rely for their charm on real material applied to represent clothing over the wooden carved body. The word *kimekomi* (fitting in grooves) actually describes the method by which such dolls were clothed. The head, hands and feet were finely carved and coloured, but the body was clothed by making a series of cuts into which the end of a strip of material could be attached with glue, folded, pleated or draped in naturalistic style and fastened by sticking the other end into a different groove. In this way the silk or brocade was given fullness and simulated the draping of a costume without making the doll clumsy.

An alternative method of dealing with this same difficulty was used by the makers of the *ukiyo ningyo* who, when dressing carved wooden doll figures with material, cut away the underneath surplus. Under-garments could be represented by many folds at the neckline and the hem of the outer kimono, but had no actual substance. With the same intention of preserving an elegant body line, the body itself was often of very slight structure and the doll was virtually all clothing, modelled over a shaped stick or straw base [228, 229].

228 Ukiyo-e Ningyo: *a young girl entertainer; 1715; 13 inches*

229 *right:* Ukiyo-e Ningyo: *a young kabuki actor; 1730; 9½ inches*

Ukiyo, as will be apparent to all who have met the word describing beautiful *genre* colour prints or paintings, stands for the mundane or the everyday thing, literally 'the world as it passes'. *Ukiyo* dolls are elegant three-dimensional models of the characters who inhabit these colour print scenes depicting actor and courtesan, splendidly dressed and coiffeured [229]. Sometimes the name *oyama ningyo* underlines the fact that beautiful women on the Kabuki stage were impersonated by male actors who specialized in such parts and were called *oyama*.

Clockwork was not introduced into Japan until the entry of the Dutch and Portuguese in the sixteenth century, but the Japanese had their own mechanical dolls and toys before that time, and beautiful examples of working dolls were made as early as the Fujiwara period (1086–1185). They were called *karakuri*, literally 'worked by a handle', and were mounted on a wooden box with a handle in the side which worked threads to make the doll's limbs move like those of a puppet. Favourite subjects were children playing drums or cymbals, dancing with a fan or juggling with balls and parasols.

The *gosho, saga, kimekomi, ukiyo ningyo* and mechanical *karakuri* may be looked upon largely as historical dolls; modern versions, — where they exist — imitate the old dolls with as ubtle difference. A collector who comes upon an old example may consider himself really

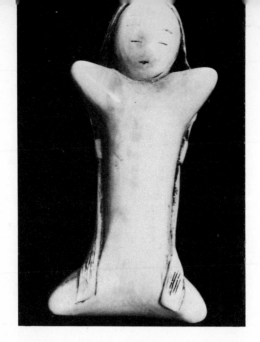

230 Amagatsu *or primitive doll
carved as an ivory netsuke
by Masanao; 18th century;
2¾ inches*

231 Saru ningyo: *traditional
monkey doll represented in
a wooden netsuke by the famous
carver, Miwa; 18th century;
1⁹/₁₆ inches*

232 *opposite: modern* Sakura *doll:
beautiful girl in traditional
Japanese costume; 15 inches*

fortunate, for the Japanese honour their dolls and do not readily part with such treasures.

Sometimes the shapes of these early dolls and the technique of making them is echoed in those miniature works of art called *netsuke*. A fashion which seems first to have become popular in the seventeenth century, the *netsuke* was worn at the belt as a sort of toggle so that the Japanese man could carry such things as pouch, purse and *inro* (a little fitted box for medicines). It became an ornamental accessory and miniature figures were an ideal subject. Ivory versions of the *gosho ningyo*, lacquer and inlay representations of costumed figures were popular and *Nara ningyo* were a speciality made at Nara by a special cutting technique. Most of them were made from the wood of the cypress, which was first soaked in water to bring out the fine grain and then cut with a single knife in a deep and dramatic style and coloured afterwards with pigments that did not have the usual *gofun* base. Some *netsuke* even depicted ancient dolls which have disappeared. The *amagatsu* [230] was a stylized primitive doll which used to be placed near the head of a new-born child in supplication to the gods to protect him and grant him good health. The little carving here is no more than $2^3/_4$ inches high and is made from ivory by Masanao in the late eighteenth century. Earlier still, the work of Miwa, a master carver among *netsuke* artists, is the wooden monkey doll or *Saruningyo* [231], a simplified simian form suggesting the rag dolls which were good-luck symbols in early times. The carver has cleverly made the little creature into an almost abstract design.

Early books which depicted artisans at work sometimes included Japanese dollmakers among their pages, showing how recognized a trade it was. Two pictures from *Jinrin Kimmo Zuye*, a sort of encyclopedia of the times and dated 1690, show different types of craftsmen [234 and 235]. It is always stressed that techniques were not interchangeable; one man would make only one type of doll and his craft would sometimes be handed down from father to son for generations. Figure 234 shows a workman stripped to the waist and viewing with evident satisfaction the dressed figure which he has just completed. There are other finished characters in the front of the scene, a standing woman and a little man with a fan, whilst neatly arranged before them are the tools of his trade: knives, chisels and mallet. The second dollmaker [235], who is also holding up a completed figure for our admiration, is a maker of *dairi hina*: dolls for the 'Girls' Festival'. On a shelf behind him are arranged some other finished dolls, including a little wadded *amagatsu*, in the same traditional shape as the *netsuke* version [230]. He is holding up an Emperor whilst the Empress is on the working block before him, with scalpel, tweezers and awl and a separate little stand which perhaps holds glue.

The Japanese Doll Festival *(Hina Matsuri)*, which seems to have had its origin in the ancient purification ritual which was held on that day, is still celebrated on 3 March. Modern stores sell the dolls and furniture in complete sets for erecting on the day at varying prices depending on how large and pretentious they are. However much their owners esteem them, they come nowhere near in beauty

233 Dolls were made by hand by Madame Paderewski and her compatriots to raise funds to help the 1914–18 war effort

or workmanship to the individual handmade pieces of the past, many of which could stand in their own right as works of art. Uniformity has replaced the variety of earlier periods and there is an orthodox method of setting out the dolls and their belongings. The occasion holds a special place in the heart of the people; Japanese friends have explained how much it meant to them as little girls, for the day is not only a national and traditional festival but is also celebrated as a family occasion and remembered in much the same way that a European child has nostalgic memories of her birthday parties.

Usually fifteen dolls make up the set and these are arranged on five or seven shelves (lucky numbers in Japan) in tiers one above the other and draped with a red cloth. At the top, seated in front of a folding golden screen, are the *Dairi-hina*, the figures of the emperor and the empress to the left and right of the 'ceremonial tree' in their middle. Below them are placed three decorative dolls who represent the court ladies-in-waiting *(kanjo)*. On the third shelf down are seated five musicians *(goninhayashi)* playing the flute or the hand-drum and one 'vocalist'. A pair of *zuishin* or armed guards stands on the fourth shelf and lowest of all are three *shicho* or menials, humbly dressed as befits their station. If there are seven shelves the last two are arranged with various articles of furniture: tables set with food, gift boxes tied with a ceremonial knot of red cord, kimono stands and 'dowry' chests, the large carrying chest full of her possessions which might follow a bride when she married and moved to a new home.

234 Doll-maker from Jinrin Kimmo Zuye *a Japanese Encyclopaedia of 1690*

235 A doll-festival craftsman from Jinrin Kimmo Zuye *of 1690*

236 *Miniature wedding carriage drawn by bullock for ceremonial wedding procession; lacquer; 6 inches*

The Dolls' Festival represents in fact a curious combination of ideas and its significance and performance have gradually changed. There is the old ritual significance, the purification ceremony with the dedication of a child to its national duties; historic and legendary figures often appear in early versions of the scene. There is the spectacle of a feast for the Emperor and Empress, the court splendour which seems to have been traditionally 'arranged' in the late eighteenth century when Shogun Yoshimune, eighth of the Tokugawa family, made much of the custom for the benefit of his own children. On the day little trays of *mochi*, green rice cakes, and lozenge-shaped sweets are prepared by the girls and served with tiny cups of *shirozake*, a sweetened white rice wine. Miniature chopsticks, rice bowls and soup bowls are laid out on the tables before the dolls. Originally such cakes and wine were the accompaniment to a simpler form of the ceremony in rural districts when humble clay images of the *Dairi-hina* were displayed and the company themselves ate and drank.

Finally the sets often include representations of a bride's outfit, in the hope that the daughter of the house will enjoy a successful and happy marriage. There are such items as a chest of drawers for clothes, a mirror on a stand, tiers of boxes, cupboards for china, picnic sets and *hokai*, circular boxes tied with tasselled cord for carrying sweetmeats. Peach blossom, which symbolizes happiness in marriage, is usually arranged in vases as decoration and many marriages take place on 3 March.

My own set [237] contains various pieces of different periods and workmanship. It was collected in Japan many years ago and its variety may be explained by the fact that dolls and dolls' furniture were treated as family heirlooms and added to with each new girl member of a family. When a girl married she would take with her her own set, which probably contained older pieces which had belonged to her mother and her grandmother, and to these would be added in time new things made for her own children. In this way one set may represent several generations, for they were always carefully stored away after the occasion in the family 'treasure house' until the following March.

When gay carp 'wind-socks' of cloth or paper are hoisted on long bamboo rods over Japanese houses it is a sign that the Boys' Festival of 5 May is being celebrated and that the family has a son. The carp stands for endeavour and fearlessness – it is traditionally believed that a carp laid on the carving board and touched with a knife ceases to move, as though 'resigned to death' – virtues particularly admired by the old Samurai class of Japan. The dolls used in the display for the Boys' Day include famous warrior heroes and gods such as Shoki, the queller of demons. The Empress Jingu, famed in history for her exploits against the Koreans, is a curious feminine exception, and always appears dressed in full armour and attended by her minister Takenouchi-no-Sukune who is renowned for his longevity – he is reputed to have lived three hundred years. Together they represent a long life and a brave one. Nowadays the most popular model of all is Kintoki, the wonder boy of Japan, the legendary strong child who

237 Emperor and Empress: Dolls' Festival figures and furniture of the 18th century in fine black lacquer with metal details; 3 inches

238 Miniature articles for the Dolls' Festival including musical instruments, books, painted scrolls, brush set, netsuke and geta (wooden sandals)

could uproot trees and wrestle with bears: a sort of infant Hercules. All the dolls of the Boys' Festival stress the attributes of strength, bravery, manliness and patriotism which the Japanese wish to instil into their sons. There is less ceremony than in the Girls' Festival, but feasting and outdoor games make it memorable; in some families an antique model from the past is treasured, a warrior standing or astride an accoutred horse and fully clothed in handmade armour by all the skill of the metalworker. More often the symbols of a warrior – a general's fan, a sword, drum or miniature helmet – have to suffice, and these are placed on display rather as in the Girl's Festival.

239 Hana Musubi Nishiki-e Awase, *illustrated by Sukenobu 1739: a pattern book for composing brocade dolls from cut-out scraps of material stuck over a printed figure*

Figure 239 is from a rare book of 1739, *Hana Musubi Nishiki-e Awase*, illustrated by Sukenobu, which demonstrates fully the tools and methods used in making *Nishiki-e* or 'brocade pictures' in which small cut-out pieces of material are assembled over the background figure of a Japanese woodcut print. The designs were quite complicated and the rare surviving examples show them to have been skilfully made and pretty. Rather in the fashion of the Protean figure (page 47), numbered pieces were cut out and laid down one by one, the shaded area representing in each case the section covered by the next piece.

A shelf of Japanese folk-toys has a fascination all its own and is difficult to surpass in interest and gaiety, but it is impossible to touch here on more than a few types from the infinite variety available. Like *netsuke*, Japanese folk-toys, apart from the beauty and quaintness which make them so popular with foreign collectors, either tell a story or are connected with some ancient custom of the place in which they were made. In this way, Japanese children learn of the heroes and gods of their country. The folk-toys reflect past tradition and are often a poor man's version of the rich man's luxury dolls. Not all of them can be said to be well made: some are very frail and are constructed of scraps of wood and paper, straw, bamboo sections, beans or destructible material such as clay and papier mâché.

240 Kokeshi *dolls: modern figures made in traditional pattern.*

Most famous among the folk-toys are the *kokeshi* dolls [240], which exist in a bewildering variety of shapes and sizes according to where they are made. There has always been doubt about their original derivation. Some connect them with the *kinakina*, a plain stick doll with a movable head which squeaks when rotated – hence the name, which imitates the sound – and is used as a baby pacifier; but a far older significance is thought to lie in their resemblance to phallic symbols with early religious ceremonies. Whatever its source, the *kokeshi* with its gay painted face and traditionally patterned body is highly ornamental. These armless, turned hardwood dolls usually have rounded heads which are made separately and attached by a knob into a hole made by the lathe while it is still hot, so that it is automatically held when the wood cools.

Folk dolls often have no body other than a framework clothed in a decorative paper kimono. The so-called 'elder sister' doll, *anesoma*, made in a variety of styles, was originally intended to teach little girls traditional styles of coiffure and cosmetics. Making them used to be a popular pastime with court ladies of the old regime, but with Westernization, the little girls are now probably looking in other directions and thinking of perms or 'Beatle' cuts.

Clay dolls were sometimes trifles turned out as a sideline in districts where pottery or tile-making was the major industry. Especially famous is the Fushimi district of Kyoto. Kazuya Sakamoto (author of *Japanese Toys*) said that in about the middle of the nineteenth century approximately three thousand different themes were included in the Fushimi repertoire, but today this has been reduced to less than six hundred. Fortunately the modern popularity of folk-toys has inspired some of the country districts to enter into production once again along traditional lines.

The wife of a missionary who had spent most of her life with her husband in Japan told me that once when they were living up country in a part where few Europeans were encountered, they had with them their infant daughter, a pretty child with fair skin, golden hair and blue eyes. This was so alien to the Japanese ideal of beauty that the village people politely averted their eyes from such a 'monstrosity' to save the mother embarrassment. The Japanese may now have learnt to tolerate Western looks and even American dolls are popular in Tokyo, but there has certainly never been any doubt in Western eyes about the attractiveness of the Japanese child, or the play-dolls which so closely resemble them.

The earliest Japanese dolls to be introduced into Europe towards the end of the nineteenth century were an instant success. With their ivory complexion, slanting dark eyes, brush-like mop of black hair and gay clothes, they shared a measure of popularity in the nursery with other late comers such as the bisque-headed *bébé*, the gollywog and the teddy bear.

The *yamato ningyo* (*yamato* is the ancient name for Japan) had a carved wooden head, jointed legs and arms fastened by a supple socket of material from the shoulder (giving the typical sloping shoulder of the Japanese). Sometimes the *mitsu-ore* technique, literally 'three-bend', used a waist joint which gave them the additional refinement of being able to bow forward from the waist, a very necessary accomplishment for a Japanese doll! Figure 241 shows a charming example, which is curiously lifelike when handled. It is said that early dollmakers in Japan had in mind the helplessness of an infant and the feeling one experiences when holding a baby in one's arms.

241 Mitsuore or 'three-bend' doll: loose-jointed to simulate the helplessness of an infant; early 20th century; 10 inches

242 Yamato ningyo: Japanese play dolls c. 1900; 13 and 15 inches

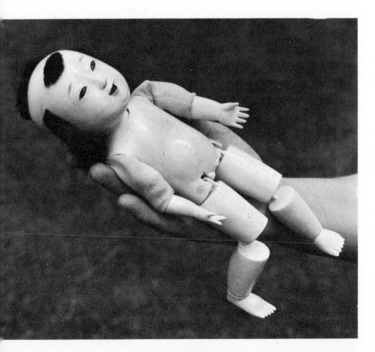

Kyoto was a great doll-making centre and heads made there were distributed to other parts of the country: an interesting parallel to the huge quantities of doll heads made in the toy-making districts of Germany and fitted to a body elsewhere in Europe and in the United States of America. Sometimes the 'alien' body was poor by comparison and such dolls were called *gatten kubi* – 'head that fits' – for when the maker added the head he might cry out '*gatten-da*': 'it fits!'

Yamato ningyo [242] are made rather similarly to the Western style *bébés* or jointed dolls as far as the separate heads, bodies and limbs are concerned. A master model of the doll is carved from wood, and moulds are made from hardened resin which can produce hollow copies pressed out of a composition made of kiri-wood sawdust and wheat starch. The secret of their oriental look lies in the process of finishing off the component parts. Dark glass eyes are fitted into rectangular recessed eye sockets moulded in the composition mask and then a thick coating of *gofun* is applied and allowed to dry. The whole surface of the doll is smoothed and polished, the eye is revealed by scraping away the paste which covers it and other features are marked in; then a top dressing of *gofun* of a special texture is applied.

When cheeks and lips have been coloured and eyebrows and eyelashes painted in, a final coating of chemical fixative ensures that the face will be 'kiss-proof'. Sometimes the hair is also painted on, but more usually a long tuft of human or synthetic hair is applied right in the centre of the doll's crown with glue and then allowed to hang in all directions. For a girl it is cut in a fringe, but a boy wears his hair trimmed short all round like a little mop. Dolls of this quality made by hand by an experienced dollmaker would take several days to complete.

A common criticism is that the mask-like Japanese face is always the same, but it is worth studying a selection of *yamata ningyo* with this in mind and finding out the wonderful variations of expression and character of which the Japanese maker is capable. Long before the European 'character' dolls, these little charmers assumed gay, winsome, stoic or pugnacious personalities.

Historical dolls are little made in Japan nowadays, but there are craftsmen who still like to experiment with the ancient methods and there are many amateurs who turn their hand to doll-making as a hobby. It is possible to buy in the stores the equipment for making a complete model of a doll and her clothes.

Far more popular and remunerative than the old styles are the *sakura* or 'cherry' dolls, which are purely decorative and owe their charm much more to the beauty of their costumes and grace of their pose than to clever carving [232]. These dolls, with their pretty faces and intricate coiffure, often have no more than a rather slight framework or rudimentary body for the rich clothing. Artificial flowers, fans, parasols give the authentic Japanese touch and they are particularly popular with visitors to Japan who wish to carry away a souvenir in the form of one of these highly decorative fashion dolls mounted on a stand for display.

18

....

Rag Dolls and Emergent Dolls

243 'Peace in our time' hand-made model doll depicting Neville Chamberlain after his historic meeting with Hitler in 1938

The rag doll has many advantages, and the fact that little, simply made cloth dolls have been found in early Egyptian and Roman tombs shows how far back it may trace its ancestry. As a plaything, it is comforting and cuddly, as a model it can be quite inexhaustible in its variety. It may be made up for virtually nothing from waste scrap, or expensively from luxury fabrics and ornaments; its form can be as naive as a child's pencil drawing, or as sophisticated as a political cartoon [243].

'Emergent' or 'emergency' dolls seems to have been an expression coined by Mr Edward Lovett (who as a member of the Folk-Lore Society of Great Britain spent many years in amassing a fine collection of dolls with the object of illustrating a scientific history from the standpoint of ethnography). He was perhaps one of the first to explore the importance of this facet of collecting and he left some interesting examples to illustrate his researches (see chapter 2).

The emergency doll was merely one contrived for a child from any raw material at hand, and probably in circumstances where the parents were too poor to buy a doll, or where it was left to the initiative of the child to make its own toys. Clothes pegs or brushes, wooden spoons or even an old large bone were among those objects collected by Lovett from which a doll had been created and dressed in scraps of rags and lace. The 'champing tree', a skittle-shaped wooden implement for mashing vegetables, was sometimes actually called a 'dolly'; and there is an example of one sold in a shop in the remote Falkland Islands with a face already drawn upon the 'head'. From a manufacturing town in Lancashire comes a wooden clog sole such as those used by workers in the mills. The features are represented by hammered-in brads and the doll is finished off with a padded velvet bonnet, colourful shawl over a print frock and four gay bright petticoats which make it a really comfortable bundle.

Some of the rag dolls are very primitive and roughly clad, but there are others on which every care has been lavished and which, in spite of simple materials, are dressed with great neatness and skill. The three shown here are very different in style and workmanship [244]. The left-hand example is carefully shaped and made with beautiful needlework stitching, though the features are practically rubbed out, whilst the one on the right is made entirely of firmly stuffed pink calico and wears a handsome stiff bonnet of velvet with a ribbon and a flounce of black satin over her frilly lace cap. Her face is not stitched but is painted in water-colours. Long lace-edged drawers and three petticoats are hidden beneath her stiff skirt of flowered damask and the same material is used to trim the cuffs and collar of her brown blouse. The tall doll in the centre could have been made by an older girl for her little sister. She is of very simple design, a long thick cylinder of fine calico, firmly but softly stuffed with rag. Embroidery silks are used for her hair and features and at the base of the cylinder her legs and feet are also indicated by stitching. The long tubular frock has dangling sleeves with stitched hands, but they have never been stuffed. A frilly bonnet finishes this rather graceless but decidedly characterful creature. She could almost be

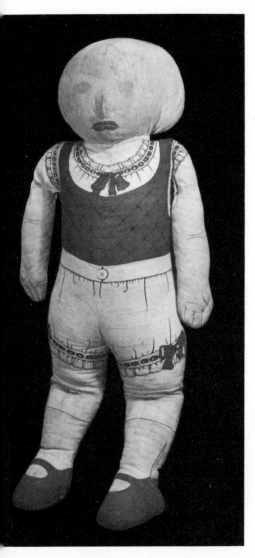

a 'portrait doll' made to represent mama or a favourite aunt. Miniature rag dolls were popular for dolls' house inhabitants and made to represent mother, father, children, servants and visitors.

Dean's Rag Dolls were more or less an extension of such simple handmade efforts, but they were on strong printed material with pieces of a doll, ready to cut out and designed with features and clothes, which could be stitched together and stuffed. Although Henry Samuel Dean had previously made soft toys, he first became famous when he put his rag-books for children on the market in 1903: a success still enjoyed today. In a short history issued in 1953 to mark the firm's jubilee, an old portrait of Dean shows him as a rather dashing young man in military uniform with well-curled moustachios; it is not explained how or why he hit on the brainwave of providing an indestructible nursery book. Obviously he had sound experience of young children, as he described the books as being provided for those who 'wear their food and eat their clothes'. The first books were modestly produced and were printed in one colour on unbleached calico by a handblock process, folded down the centre and tied with green silk ribbon. Anyone possessing an example has a great rarity. Success with the books and improved methods of production led him to patent the doll sheets in 1908 and these also carried the famous trademark of two dogs, a terrier and a bulldog having a tug o' war with a book: 'Wear Ever – Tear Never' ran the slogan.

The made-up doll of 1908 labelled 'Dean's Rag Knockabout Toy Sheets. Washable and hygienic', had ribbon-trimmed drawers and vest with bodice printed in red and black [245]. Separate sheets were also issued for garments for the dolls and these sold very cheaply. A row of stitches in the doll's knee made it bend. Later Dean's produced rag-dolls to a similar pattern, but made up and stuffed with 'Tru-to-Life' faces, 'Tru-Shu' feet (patented in profile relief) and wigs. Methods and materials have changed, but Dean's enjoy a high reputation for soft toys and animals to this day.

By the beginning of the twentieth century soft toys were being turned out in Germany in vast numbers – machine stitching and improved industrial methods had encouraged a new venture in toy-making. Beatrix Potter, authoress of *Peter Rabbit* and other nursery classics, had had ideas of starting something similar in England with her verve for animal design. She had actually made a 'Peter Rabbit' for one of the Warne children (Warne was her publisher) and she thought perhaps she might take up their manufacture as a sideline. None of the London toy factories, however, was willing to compete against the cheap German toys.

The German soft dolls of the pre-war period are sought after by collectors because they were the product of skilful and original design. The names of two women who established manufacturing concerns famous to this day stand out particularly: Fräulein Margarete Steiff and Frau Käthe Kruse.

Margarete Steiff (1847–1909) was a polio cripple who in the first place made up stuffed animals as a hobby to please children, but eventually excited so much interest that she formed a small business with extra help to make up models from her own designs. By 1900 she was so successful that she was exporting all over the world with the help of her brother and nephews. In 1905 she registered her famous trademark of '*Knopf im Ohr*' (button in the ear), and each animal or doll literally left the factory with a metal button in its ear stamped with the Steiff name; soon she added jointed dolls to her repertoire. A French writer, Jean Doin (see page 173) remarked acidly: 'We know that Mme. (*sic*) Steiff, the promoter of this genre, afflicted her dolls with a hideous squint, for such is the German idea of humour! By an unheard of aberration of taste, mothers in France were also infatuated with these little horrors. The result was disastrous: their children imitated the dolls!'

The French had reason to fear the threat of German competition and the fact remains that children everywhere adored the Steiff dolls and animals. Controversy has raged in modern times as to whether Margarethe Steiff or Michtom, founder of what eventually became the Ideal Toy Corporation (see page 243), had the prior claim as the inventor of the teddy bear. The truth may be that there were jointed bears in Germany before the famous Roosevelt cartoon provided in 1902 a name which has stuck ever since. There were certainly other jointed animals such as lions, elephants, dogs, cats and monkeys.

Where Margarete Steiff introduced a note of fantasy in her creations, like characters from a Disney cartoon, Käthe Kruse strove after reality and revolted against the vapid 'doll face'. She was originally an actress and the wife of a sculptor who assisted her in design. The toys she made were also in the first place a private invention for her children. She explained her own success in an article in 1912:

246 Dutch dolls and golliwog representing the characters from Florence Upton's illustrations for Golliwogg books; 16 inch golliwog

There was an exhibition of home-made toys in Berlin to which I was invited to send my children's dolls. From that day on the triumphal march began and neither the dolls nor I know how it happened for they were thought out only for my children and were made only for them. They were a success because I had simply made a doll that was unbreakable and washable and yet was a pretty doll. Each doll carries my name and number on the side of the left foot.

Today, requests for my dolls come to me from every country in the world. I have now assistants in my work. Every doll we make is a little different. The human hand cannot make exactly the same thing twice and everything on and about the dolls is handwork. How the little head is set on – this way or that – whether the hair or the eyes are painted light or dark, the rounding of the face and body, how the tiny feet stand – everything makes a different character and yet they have something in common. *Each doll goes through my hands at least twenty times!*

Her very first dolls were made of towelling. Those she described as lovingly handmade were always expensive to produce, and eventually they were reproduced by the Rheinische Gummi Celluloid Fabrik in plastic. These plastic dolls were first shown at the Toy Fair in Nuremberg in 1955, and Frau Kruse is still alive today to witness the progress made during a lifetime of doll-making.

The teddy bear, possibly the most universally popular toy ever invented, was also 'permissible' as a toy for little boys, as was the golliwog doll, who should perhaps also be acknowledged as of American derivation. This gay character, with his red smiling mouth, shock of fuzzy black hair and staring white eyes, first appeared in a book produced by Miss Florence Upton and published in 1895: *The Adventures of Two Dutch Dolls and a Golliwogg*. The characters were said to be based on some toys the author had as a child in the United States and the story was the beginning of a friendship lasting through yearly escapades until 1912, which incidentally introduced various innovations of the period: the bicycle, airship and 'auto' go-cart.

Florence Upton was born in New York in 1873, but her parents were English. After her father died when she was only sixteen, it was necessary for her to find work as a designer and illustrator, and when she and her mother finally returned to England in 1893, she had made up her mind to become an illustrator of children's books, as she especially liked drawing toys and animals. Her mother, Bertha Upton, not only encouraged her in the project but was able to cooperate in producing the verse stories which she illustrated. It was not immediately easy to find a market for the Golliwogg saga, but finally Mr Allen of Longman's Green & Co. backed this potential winner because his own children were delighted with it. Obviously they were sound critics, because although adults sometimes thought the golliwog a frightening character for nursery consumption (and recently there has been a move to provide a *white* golliwog – see page 246), most children loved him and the artist himself said 'he had a good heart'.

Florence must have a 'good heart' too, as it is recorded that in 1917 she auctioned 350 original drawings for her book illustrations in aid of the Red Cross (some of which went to the London Museum) and a case holding the original dolls: Golliwogg and Sarah Jane, Peggy, Meg, Weg and the Midget. The amount realized was enough to equip a complete ambulance for the Front and it was inscribed: 'Florence Upton and the Golliwogg gave this ambulance'.

The set of dolls shown in figure 246 is typical of the earliest which were inspired by the original Florence Upton drawings. The golliwog, unlike many other later versions, who have flat faces, has a real nose and stitched-on shirt and boot buttons for eyes. Sarah Jane and Peggy, clothed in portions of the Stars and Stripes, as the story relates, are fine up-standing examples of Dutch dolldom. Meg and Weg measure ten inches and nine inches, while little Midget is no more than four inches high and wears a shabby lace frock stiffened with a scrap of newspaper which bears a date in 1905. This was early on in Golliwogg's career, when he was fast becoming a popular motif for all sorts of nursery wear, fabrics, china and even advertising material. Like the teddy bear, he also achieved musical fame, as Debussy wrote a 'Golliwog-Symphony'. He even had the lasting distinction of becoming a new word in the dictionary, since 'like a golliwog' immediately summons up a picture of this black, rough-haired, smiling zany.

The fabric doll has often been useful for portraying historical character and costume. In 1890 Mlle Marie Koenig dressed nearly five hundred dolls to illustrate fashions of the past which created quite a sensation when they were exhibited at the Musée Pédagogique in Paris. The dolls made in Poland by Madame Paderewski and some of her compatriots in 1914 are historic in themselves and very beautiful in workmanship [233]. Wife of the world-famous pianist and statesman Jan Paderewski, she organized working parties among some of the Polish people exiled in Paris to make dolls to sell in aid of the war effort. Many of them were sold through the National American Committee of the Polish Victims' Relief Fund in New York and through other charity sales in England and France. Two of the most popular represented little Polish children called Jan and Hanska, known as the 'Waifs of Cracow', but others were dressed in picturesque regional costume and decorated with sequins.

The period after the 1914–18 war saw a realignment of toy-making throughout the world. Patriotic feeling encouraged the development of home-based industries in England and the United States where to many people the residue of bitter feeling against Germany made German toys unacceptable. There was a curious vogue for mascot dolls: perhaps people badly felt the need of some good-luck token in the disturbed years of depression and slump. In the gay 'twenties, exaggerated and fashionably grotesque dolls caught on as room decoration, but these were sophisticated toys for grown-ups, typical of the brittle façade of the period and never intended for children.

At about the same time as Rose O'Neill was dressing her 'Kewpies' (page 212), another lady artist had invented a delightful tribe of

"DIDDUMS."

247 top: Diddums: the most famous Mabel Lucie Attwell character

248 Little Happy: celluloid model by the Cascelluloid Co. of London in 1939

little children which in their turn were transformed into dolls and enjoyed tremendous world-wide popularity. Mabel Lucie Attwell was born in London in 1879 and remained a Londoner in spirit all her life, although she made her home in Cornwall, the land of her ancestors, for many years after the Second World War. Like Rose O'Neill she cared only for art from childhood and after a first success at the age of sixteen managed to keep herself and pay her art school fees until she became well established as a magazine illustrator and designer of postcards. Mr Ranald Valentine, managing director of the firm of that name in Dundee in Scotland, said: 'Mabel Lucie Attwell's drawings were an immediate hit from the moment they were sent up in the middle of the First World War and they have remained so ever since.'

Mabel Lucie Attwell herself maintained that she drew for an adult public and the appeal of her cards was the association of humorous caption with cherubic children. A best-selling card, dated 1923, during one of the post-war economy campaigns, depicts two children gazing disapprovingly at a new baby in its crib: 'Stravagance!' frowns one of the bairns. 'I wonder where Mother bought it.' The artist explained: 'I can't start a drawing until I've finally decided upon the title.' She would tear up twenty to thirty titles before she found the few words to satisfy her.

The children of Mabel Lucie Attwell were, like their creator, unsentimental and full of fun. The typical model was sturdy, roguish, innocent with a scrubbed shining look on his chubby cheeks, very wholesome as though he had been freshly tubbed and had put on clean clothes. They lent themselves ideally to modelling and doll-shape and enjoyed an instant success. Messrs Chad Valley produced the first during the 'twenties. They were made of hand-painted felt and velvet to 'faithfully reproduce the inimitable features of her well-known drawings'. Their clothing, with little cloche hats and flapper bows for the girls and Jackie Coogan bulky caps and romper suits for the boys, is typical of 'twenties fashions.

A patent was taken out by Chad Valley in 1924 for a doll's head made partially or wholly of textiles or felt suitably stiffened with shellac or starch and provided with openings into which glass eyes are inserted from within; by this method their products were virtually indestructible.

'Diddums' [247], the most popular character of all, who has served as a trademark to the series, has a plump defiant look as he stares with round blue eyes and places podgy hands on his rompers. He was produced both in rubber and celluloid by the Cascelloid Company of London and was a bestseller, though not many examples seem to survive either of this doll or of little 'Happy' [248].

As far back as 1871, in a report on the London International Exhibition, George Bartley wrote:

The so-called 'rag' dolls made by Mr. Montanari are very nice, though their name is somewhat of a misnomer. They are stronger than wax or composition and certainly retain all the beauty of

CHAD VALLEY BRAND

Made in 3 sizes, "0" Approximately 14½ ins. high
"1" " 16 ins. "
"2" " 18⅜ ins. "

Personally designed by Miss Mabel Lucie-Attwell, these delightful hand-painted Felt and Velvet Dolls faithfully reproduce the inimitable features of her well-known drawings of children

"MABEL LUCIE-ATTWELL" DOLLS

(Exclusive Registered and Patented Unbreakable Models)

An exquisite Range of Models in assorted Art shades

No. 715   No. 718   No. 720   No. 721

No. 722   No. 723   No. 724   No. 725

Each Doll packed in patent "Bye-Bye" Bed-Box (see Page 29)

HYGIENIC TOYS

249 Chad Valley catalogue showing Mabel Lucie Attwell dolls in the 1920s

both these materials, but they can hardly claim the indestructible properties which a rag doll should have. The adaptation of some materials combining the beauty of Mr. Montanari's rag dolls with the indestructible nature of gutta-percha would be a great boon to children and parents. In these days of progress, such an invention should not be beyond the power of some enterprising toy manufacturer...

This was surely a prophecy of the age of plastic, which was eventually to supplant most of the other methods of producing children's dolls by industrial means, though happily there remain many skilled amateurs (and a few famous professionals) who still practise the ancient art of the true 'rag doll'.

250 opposite: Faerie Glen Tina doll and her wardrobe

19

The Modern Doll

252 *Engraving by Arthur Boyd Houghton for* Our Mutual Friend *by Charles Dickens (1868 edition) showing a crippled child making dolls and her drunken father who has spent all her earnings*

251 *opposite: Jamaican character dolls: one selling fruit; 1915; 12 inches; one molasses, c. 1900; 14 inches*

There could hardly be a more ironical commentary on the enormous social inequalities of the nineteenth century than the contrast between the wealthy and cosseted child who received as a present some luxury doll of the day, and her poorer equivalent who worked somewhere behind the scenes making it. In 1891, a report in Volume I of the *Strand Magazine* on some of these child workers in London commented especially on the lot of some of the little girls who 'assist their mothers at home in tailoring and dolls' clothes making':

> The united work of mother and child yields only a wretched pittance and carried on as it is in a room where sleeping, eating and living go on, is of all forms of labour the saddest and most unhealthy. Meals consist of bread and tea, and work is prolonged till midnight by the light of one candle with the consequence that the children are prematurely aged and diseased. This is the most painful kind of child-labour that I have come across, and would be unbearable, if it were not ennobled by the touching affection that almost invariably exists between the worn-out mother and her old-woman-wise little daughter.

But already, at the end of the century, the social conscience of the nation was pricked by such reports and reforms began to make this type of sweated labour impossible. Changes in the English law made schooling compulsory for children and by 1890 some form of free education was available for most children between five and thirteen. A widespread increase in personal incomes made it easier for most families to allow their children to start work at a later age and reduced the number of married women who found it essential to work for their living.

It is useful to consider the social climate of the period, for it had a big influence both on toys and on the children who played with them. Women generally were awakening to the fact that other things in life counted besides idleness, domesticity or drudgery – according to the social stratum in which they were born. Beatrice Webb, a leader of the Fabian Socialist movement in England, and champion of women's suffrage, wrote in 1913: 'The whole of the thinking British public is today the arena of a battle of words, of thoughts and of temperaments.' Shortly there was to be added to this the 'battle of nations' in the holocaust of the 1914–18 war. Things could never be the same again, either economically, intellectually or morally. Change would inevitably have come, but the war accelerated it and the 'new woman' battened instinctively onto the progressive methods of education in which the principle of learning through play was in the forefront. Toys began to be thought of as an essential rather than a luxury and the 'character' doll as dealt with in chapter 14 was caught up in the move to provide a more suitable image, a more realistic toy.

From the 'character' doll developed the 'personality' doll, modelled on a well-known child either in real life or fiction. Germany and France lost their domination and the new-found industries of Britain, the United States and Japan began to supplant the previous exports of foreign toys with dolls which were to some measure national. Käthe

Kruse had represented the German ideal by modelling dolls after her own children; Lenci produced dolls with an Italian charm; Dean supplied Mabel Lucie Attwell dolls of a decidedly English character. The sculptress Dewees Cochran worked out six basic types of face recognizable among American children and in 1939 the Eff-An-Bee

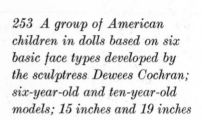

253 A group of American children in dolls based on six basic face types developed by the sculptress Dewees Cochran; six-year-old and ten-year-old models; 15 inches and 19 inches

firm used these as models for the 'Look-Alikes' [253], which enjoyed a success continued after the Second World War by the 'Grow-Ups', first produced in 1952.

When, on 28 May 1934, the world press covered the story of a hitherto unknown doctor who had successfully delivered quintuplet daughters to a woman in Callender, Ontario, Canada, the Dionne Quins became public property and were popularly produced as pretty dark-haired identical dolls at various stages of their progress through a sadly exploited childhood [254].

The 'Shirley Temple' doll, modelled on the child film star at the height of her fame, came near to the ideal of American childhood: cute and precocious, pretty and healthy. Produced by the Ideal Toy

254 The Dionne quintuplets: Annette, Emilie, Marie, Yvonne and Cecilie; 1938; 7 inches; made by the Alexander Doll Co.

Corporation in 1934, the doll was said to have gained over $200,000 in royalties for Miss Temple and 1,500,000 copies were sold, many of them now represented in collections of dolls [256]. This could be the measure of success for a really popular doll – the sort every child wanted. A firm started as a small concern in the beginning of the century could snowball during the next half-century to a giant business. Benjamin Michtom, whose father created and popularized the 'Teddy Bear' in the United States, likes to be called the 'Doll Father of America', and under his ambitious guidance Ideal has enjoyed many huge successes [255]. Like Emile Jumeau, he realized the enormous possibilities of advertisement. 'All we've got to do is show the kids something they want: after that they do the selling for us.' Twentieth-century advertising had a potential undreamt of by Emile Jumeau, and the doll became something not merely seasonal, as a Christmas or New Year gift, but an all-the-year-round seller. Learning through play made the doll seem a necessity. One of Michtom's selling lines is to provide a doll with something to do: a 'purpose' doll. The Toni doll of 1950 had hair which could be shampooed and set; the Miss Curity doll of 1951 taught health and hygiene and first aid; the Betsy McCall doll of 1952 made a child fashion-conscious and taught the elements of needlework, whilst the Harriet Hubbard Ayer doll arrived complete with vanity kit, harmless vegetable-coloured doll cosmetics and instructions on make-up. The dolls themselves carried an advertising line a step further into the home, since each was allied with a famous firm. A junior home perm from Toni, Bauer and Black medical products, McCall paper patterns or Harriet Hubbard Ayer cosmetic cream were coupled with them in a nation-wide publicity scheme. Since the Second World War dolls and advertising have often joined hands and parents have been blackmailed into buying a product to obtain the toy associated with it.

Achieving a novelty success is always something of a gamble. Many of the doll types made by Michtom have gone over the million mark in sales. One of the cleverest was 'Sparkle Plenty', who had a ready-made market awaiting her before she was even born. Sparkle was the daughter of two little characters drawn in the popular Dick Tracy strip cartoons by Chester Gould. When Gravel Gertie and B.O. Plenty had their child she was blessed like some princess in a fairy story with long golden hair and the doll version made up by Michtom in 1947 (with the added attraction of 'magic skin') was an instant success. The strip cartoon baby 'Bonny Braids' was born to Dick Tracy and Tess Trueheart in 1951 and another winner to these 'come alive' dolls was Saralee, based on an authentic Negro baby.

One of the most successful modern dolls both commercially and in its appeal to children might well be called the 'wishful-chinking' doll, for she represents the aim of every little girl with her heart desperately set on growing up [257]. 'It is not surprising that a seven-year-old asked Barbie's age will say "twelve", while a twelve-year-old will probably say "seventeen" or "eighteen",' says the advertisement for 'Barbie', who was called after the twenty-four-year-old daughter of the doll's creators, Elliott and Ruth Handler and marketed by Mettel Inc. of California. These long-limbed shapely girls are dolls in the modern style and their acceptance is assured. Perhaps they have been 'suggested' to children as a profitable commercial proposition – a doll who once bought retains an insatiable desire for new outfits and continues to need an ample dress allowance. In each country similar dolls have appeared, assuming a subtly different nationality, although they are 'sisters under the skin' and depict a similar modern miss. Their Christian names vary: in France 'Silvie' is slightly seductive *à la* Bardot, in England 'Sindy' represents the wholesome outdoor type and has acquired a mischievous kid sister, Patch; Barbie herself is going steady with a boy-friend, Ken, even longer in the leg than she herself (and who needs just as many new outfits to bolster his ego). She has a little sister called Skipper and a girl-friend called Midge who has a boy-friend called Allan and almost endless variations are possible in this little pantomime. Barbie has been perhaps unjustly labelled a 'sex-kitten' (it is possible to buy her a bridal outfit and put her romance on a really legal basis by marrying her off). Public opinion in one English village was scandalized by the display of Sindy in bed with her boy-friend in a toy-shop window. Whatever morals are attributed to them – and they reflect the sophistication of modern children – they are all the same part of the competitive search for new accessories, and present perhaps the most profitable doll thought up since the Parisian *poupée* of a hundred years ago with her 'Saratoga' trunk.

The mass-output doll is usually provided with dresses and accessories which are factory made, but there remain a few original manufacturers in England who depend entirely on outworkers. The stress nowadays is on the fashion-conscious little girl who is concerned more with keeping her doll's clothes up-to-date than with playing with her in the old-fashioned sense. Over a hundred years ago an exhibition

257 *An advertisement for Barbie and her accessories from Mattel Inc.*

jury commented, when awarding a prize medal to Jumeau (father of the Jumeau who later enjoyed such fame): 'The dolls on which these models are displayed present no point worthy of commendation, but the dresses themselves are very beautiful productions. Not only are the outer robes accurate representations of the prevailing fashions in ladies' dresses but the under garments are also in many cases facsimiles of those articles of wearing apparel.' A modern jury might pronounce similar judgement (though not so pompously) on some present-day dolls and their wardrobes.

It is very good to see that individual craftmanship (as distinct from the vast and intricate technical skill employed in a modern factory) can still exist and be commercially successful. Sometimes, as in the firm of faerie Glen, a one-man initiative provided the organizing genius which eventually expanded into a much larger professional venture. Peggy Franks, former table-tennis champion, and now Mrs Hook, aided by her mother and a team of outside piece workers, has been responsible for creating the little world of 'Tina' [250] – an unremarkable doll, twelve inches tall with vinyl head and arms and rooted hair, made in Singapore. In twenty years they have made her one of the fashion queens of the modern doll world and each item of her wardrobe is planned and executed by Mrs Hook and then made up to her patterns. It is not always easy to find the skilful needlewomen capable of the expert finish demanded for these miniature clothes. Outside piecework is still the answer, just as it was a hundred years ago in the sewing rooms of Paris. Little boots and shoes are designed by Mrs Hook and the work is carried out by a single male specialist in leather-craft. Although the sewing machine has to some extent replaced hand work, the skill is still exacting and needs special flair. What a difference there is between the outfits of one hundred years ago and the 'gear' of this modern miss! What would great-grandmama or her milliner have thought of the abbreviated sun-suits and bikinis, dice-patterned plastic 'macs', the 'skid-lids' and leather jackets or the scanty underwear and 'roll-on' belts which have replaced stuffy nineteenth-century garments and corsetry. Where Rose or Amelia had folded white kid gloves and posed with her parasol to avoid the disfigurement of freckles, Tina yearns for nylon stockings and ski-pants and woos the sun with fancy specs and tan lotion. The materials of her clothes are vastly different from the flannel and tulle, the velvet and lace of the dolls Dickens described in 'Our Mutual Friend' (1865): '...in a brilliantly lighted toy shop window in Bond Street [probably Cremer's], a dazzling semi-circle of dolls in all the colours of the rainbow, who were dressed for presentation to Court, for going to balls, for going out driving, for going out on horseback, for going out to walk, for all the gay events of life, for going to be married, and for going to help other dolls to get married.'

Emphasis on hygiene and safety is something which has also had its influence on modern dolls. Plastic and vinyl are ideal materials in this sense for they are washable and the colour can be bright and completely 'fast' and 'kiss-proof', nor does it deteriorate as rubber does or burn as celluloid does.

245

Soft toys have been brought into line and many of them are completely washable with nylon fur or hair and body fabric and foam-rubber stuffing. They come complete with their certificate of washability like the Wendy Boston Playsafe toys [258] and look forward to their weekly spin in the washing machine. Patent bolted-on eyes cannot be detached. Teddy veterans of the future will have become thin not so much from lack of sawdust as from over-laundering!

Sometimes, the old favourites reappear in a new version, in the modern idiom as it were. Golliwog assumes a white face and is introduced by Messrs Dean as 'Mr Smith'! With fresh zoological persuasion, Teddy Bear changes species and becomes a Panda Bear called after the Chinese Li-Li, complete with baby replica in her paws and the blessing of Mr Peter Scott on behalf of the World Wildlife Fund. Such novelties might be a useful beginning to a forward-looking toy collection for the future. In fifty years' time they will carry all the interest of historical relics.

History – and geography – take a hand in the production of some of those little hand-dressed character dolls which often form the nucleus of the tourist's collection. In the past colourful dolls from a foreign country were often brought home as a souvenir of a happy holiday or a picturesque place [251 and 259]. The modern enthusiasm for travel and 'tourism' has enlarged the collecting field. Famous characters from the past or dolls dressed in native costume are equally popular and form a colourful display full of interest and memories. Peggy Nisbet of Weston-super-Mare in Somerset, England, is one famous name among those who specialize in such miniature works of art. She is the brain behind the designing and has a meticulous eye for historical detail and correct national tradition in dress or uniform. Some of her dolls have won awards in the Council of Industrial Design/British Travel Association competition for souvenir dolls [260].

For her 'Twosome' dolls Peggy Nisbet has borrowed an idea that was popular years ago for a novelty doll. The little topsy-turvey or two headed doll, the *Doppelbaby* of the nineteenth-century German factory, has a modern counterpart in Cinderella's rags to riches story as represented by a doll's head with a tattered brown dress and hands holding a twig broom, which can be reversed and transformed into a fairy tale princess in gleaming white satin. Another favourite character similarly treated is 'Mary Poppins', made popular by the film version of the book by P. L. Travers. The secret of such dolls lies in a very full skirt billowing from the waist.

The power of a film or television series in creating demand for a character doll is obvious and A. A. Milne's Christopher Robin with his Pooh Bear is another Nisbet creation. The process for the actual launching of such a doll is very expensive. When a suitable wax model has been prepared and approved and appropriate clothing chosen, it may cost as much as £2000 or $4800 to make the metal mould from which the doll may be manufactured in quantity; only a huge success

259 Doll dressed by Bernardine nuns who live under a perpetual vow of silence and brought back in the '80s by a tourist who visited their convent near Biarritz

260 Peggy Nisbet Historical Character dolls: Henry VIII and his wives

will justify the initial expense. Christopher Robin in vinyl may not present quite the image that his contemporaries remember – the nanny-tended child of the 'twenties, in loose tunic smock and shorts and floppy linen sun-hat, or wearing rubber mac, sou'wester hat and wellington boots – but he is more acceptable to the modern child who knows his Christopher Robin only through the eyes of Walt Disney rather than in the delicate pen-drawings of E. H. Shepard who, drawing from life, originally illustrated the books of A. A. Milne with pictures of his little son and his toys.

The invention of moving pictures, wireless and television have worked a revolution in the play and pastimes of children. Some educationists bemoan the fact; others welcome the new methods of teaching with the widening scope offered. Either way it is too late to halt the progress, just as we cannot return to horse-travel in place of motorways. The difference to children is not so much in the power of their imagination, but in the manner in which this is diverted and channelled by outside influences. Ideas and images are introduced into their brains and they are left to wait for the next instalment. City children especially are early mesmerized by the magic box of television and indoctrinated by the clever propaganda which prompts them all to want toys made in imitation of film heroes.

With an audience of such dimensions, the brilliant invention of 'Thunderbirds', animated dolls acting science fiction adventures, has earned vast sums of money for its creator, Mr Gerry Anderson, and his associates. The secret of their success, he believes, is the 'suspension of disbelief': 'You can put them in a situation that would raise a howl of mirth if you used live actors. You can make the incredible credible.' The same was, of course, true of fairy stories, where the hero could use a cloak of invisibility or winged shoes. Anderson and his wife have built up from very small beginnings a series of films which have held children and adults spellbound the world over. Commercial dolls in the image of the puppet actors have also caught on. Supercar, Fireball, XL 5 and Stingray have carried the firm from a private house to a large warehouse and finally to a studio specially built with many technicians who lavish meticulous care on the details of costume and sets. Each character has an expensive and beautifully made wig and about six different heads showing variations in expression from sadness to happiness, rage, surprise and anger. A simple code of morality is preached with recognizable heroes and villains, and there is a responsible awareness of the influence such a programme may have on a large, and international, audience. To children the adventures seem real; to adults part of the fascination lies in the technical perfection and mystery of a miniature art, but even adults have confessed to becoming involved with these super-modern Lilliputians and to identifying themselves with their successes or frustrations [261a].

Apart from their popularity as toys and educational media, puppets have taken the stage in the field of modern advertising and one enterprising firm has realized the potential of dolls for display purposes. Barway Display Services Ltd of London have invented an anonymous character marionette beautifully designed in fibre glass or polished

261 Barway display doll;
5 ft 9 inches

wood [261]. The head swivels and is completely featureless, so that wigs may be added or features applied to transform it into any character required. The limbs are completely free-moving and jointed in the old puppet technique with loose hook and eye and ball connection at ankle, knee and elbow. The body is loose-waisted and flat-chested and may assume a feminine shape by 'interchangeable bust units'. Such a phrase is enough to indicate how modern, how unromantic is the image of such figures compared with, say, the padded voluptuous curves of nineteenth-century fashion dummies.

The hands are stylized and slightly spoon-shaped like those of early wooden dolls, and the feet, in true puppet tradition, are merely flat wedges. But reminiscent as the shape may be of the early lay-figures, this is a child of its age, versatile in use and never detracting from the loose modern fashions it may model, virtually indestructible and capable of being used again and again. The dolls may be suspended by nylon string, by chain or ribbon, and can assume any position. They are sold or hired in three sizes, adult, child and infant.

Besides playing the lead in many children's stories and picture books, dolls have figured in modern times in art and literature and even films. For instance, the erotic symbolism of the limp and naked female figure has been seized upon by the Surrealist movement as a powerful prop. The German artist Hans Bellmer has used a strangely battered doll for enormous 'blown-up' photographs of suggestive poses, many of which were censored when exhibited in a London gallery in 1965. Ernest Trova used an armless dummy which he called the 'Falling Man' in extravaganzas where the doll appears as the victim: 'an anonymous diagrammatic human presence caught in an exquisite web of useless shiny machinery' – a comment on modern life. The distorted posturing, the sightless gaze of a doll flung down naked, can indeed arouse disturbing thoughts of helplessness, forlornness, neglect – the puppet robbed of a life which only kind hands can give to it. Rilke wrote: 'The doll-soul goes on living in the heart of man,' and found something essentially sinister in the utter silence and unresponsiveness of the plaything which he thought confronted a child for the first time in its life with the horror of empty space and loneliness.

Pablo Picasso, considered by many to be the most versatile genius of our age, has on occasion turned his attention to sculpting dolls. In 1907 he carved figures from wood and painted them white; they were straight one-piece creatures with boldly carved features like images from Easter Island in miniature, just over twelve inches in height. In 1952, when his little daughter Paloma (the 'dove') was three, he made ceramic dolls with squarish heads and long straight bodies, painted features and arms bound on to the body with cord. The dolls have faces very like Paloma herself as she appears in lithographs and oil paintings by her father from about the same period: large eyes, chubby cheeks and pronounced chin with full lips. They are not the sort of dolls that any father would, or could, make for his child, but are ceramic shapes no doubt inspired by the little girl he loved to play with. All examples remain in the possession of the family but as a genuine product of the master they would, if sold, probably be some of the most expensive dolls ever made.

Infatuation with dolls and the encouragement of the modern vogue for collecting has led to a new generation of doll-artists intent on producing, for their own satisfaction or commercially, models intended from the beginning as collectors' pieces – in much the same way that issues of postage stamps are now regularly produced and controlled in limited editions with an eye not to letter-writers but to philatelists. Among them must be sought the coveted treasures of tomorrow, the new antiques. Examples of the cloth sculptures of Dorothy Heyer, Bruyère portrait dolls [263], dolls made in wood by Ruth Williams (Darcy) and by Avis Lee of Chicago, bisque and parian dolls by Martha Thompson and reproductions by Emma Clear already figure in museums in the United States. A comprehensive catalogue and description of some of the modern doll-artists in the United States was published in 1965 by Helen Bullard, herself a creative artist. The craft has swung full circle and the fascination of the early toys has promoted a new creative following.

I have touched on modern dolls not merely as an end to the story but with the thought that they will one day be collected. What of the play-dolls of the future? It is difficult to imagine quite what mechanical gimmick might be introduced or how new materials could be developed for her construction. Perhaps a built-in computer could give the doll the illusion of thought and programmed action, or plastic perfection could provide her anatomically with parts on which a child surgeon could operate. My own children were invariably playing 'dentists' or 'doctors' and performing extractions of teeth and removal of tonsils on their dolls.

262 Rubber Ideal Baby with nursing bottle and round mouth; 14 inches

The play-doll is an adult luxury imposed on the relatively simple need of a child for a play companion or solace to loneliness. The traditional baby doll will no doubt continue to be in demand among those parents who prefer to give their children 'orthodox' toys and games, or who are limited to the simplest things because of expense. Psychologically, this has been thought to be an answer to the jealousy which appears when a little child has to receive a new baby sister or brother in the family. It accounts for the great success of the 'functional' baby doll like Michtom's 'Betsy Wetsy', who drank and wetted napkins, 'Tiny Tears' by Palitoy, which was the star of the 1966 Toy Fair at Brighton, and Mattel's 'Cheerful Tearful' whose expression changed by a mechanism encased in its face fabric and who could shed real tears [264].

The sequence of doll history is clearer to me now at the end of the book than before. The emergence of dolls as we know them seems to have run along two different lines of evolution in Europe: a religious spirit springing from the Catholic countries of southern Europe prompted the image of the baby doll and the sanctity of motherhood; the fashion doll was the other original line of descent which eventually lost its useful purpose and also became a plaything, with Paris the centre, not only as leader of fashion, but as fashioner of dolls. Spirituality in the German, prettiness and frivolity in the French and

commerce in the modern world seem to have promoted the dolls' progress.

Already, however, there seems to be a waning interest among young girls in the old-fashioned inanimate doll which has been supplanted by so many other interests. Manufacturers have been hard put to it to think up novelties that will make dolls attractive and desirable to modern children once they are past the nursery stage. But if children's interest needs stimulating by new materials and fresh inventions, the interest of the adult, both men and women, advances all the time, without any apparent stimulus. It can only be explained as part of the general reorientation of people living in affluent, materialistic societies towards the arts and towards the study and collection of objects which may have little intrinsic value in themselves but are markers of history. By an odd reversal of the trend in the nineteenth century, when the doll developed almost exclusively as a child's plaything, we are, though perhaps for different reasons, returning to the former situation, when dolls were primarily the concern of grown-ups. This growing interest is perfectly understandable. Dolls form an ideal subject for collection, combining all those features which are indispensable to a collector's pleasure: the fascination of a long history, the difficulty of the search, the unending variety and the facility and beauty of their display either privately or in competition.

Moreover, dolls are universally enjoyable and are welcomed, as children are, with affection: it is in this almost human quality that they differ from most other collectable objects. Of the play-dolls at least it can be said that they have been closest to the children of the past; most of them bear marks of it, and carry with them a reminder, experienced as something tangible of a former age – a past known to us from history books and pictures but only made real in small relics like children's toys and dolls, most intimate of bygones. It is this aspect that forms a link of friendliness and shared pleasure between all those, a growing band, who collect dolls, for many of these seem not to be simply collectors of dolls, but collectors of children too, represented by what the Japanese have aptly named 'Ambassadors of Good Will'.

263 Bruyère portrait doll of 1941; copy of a portrait of Amalia C. Baird when 2½ years old; 13 inches

264 'Cheerful Tearful' doll by Mattel Inc. 1965; the secret is in her arm which controls a variety of facial expressions

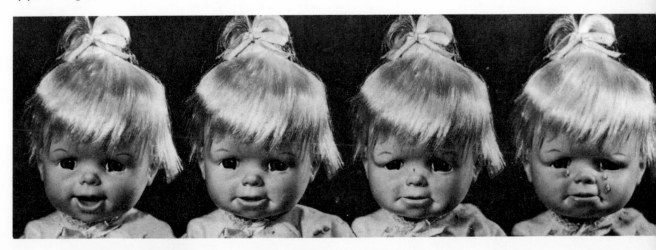

DOLLMAKERS
MARKS

Early dolls only rarely have any clue to their maker by name or trademark. With the increased competition in the second half of the nineteenth century, however, it became more usual to stamp or mark a doll with the name of the maker or patentee, either as an advertisement or as a protection against imitation. After the Tariff Act of 1890 it was enforced that a doll should be marked with the name of its country of origin. The list below is not intended to be a comprehensive list of marks, or a full index to the hundreds of makers, but is a guide to some of the more usual collectors' items. For a detailed list of makers, including those recorded in directories of the period but not specifically identified by doll examples, consult *Dolls: Makers and Marks* and for reproductions of official patents and trademarks the *Doll Directories* of Mrs Luella Hart (see BIBLIOGRAPHY).

Aetna Doll and Toy Co., USA *'Can't Break 'Em' dolls*

Alexander Doll Co., New York

H ⅄ A ....Alexandre, Henri, Paris 1880–90 *Bébé Phénix*

........Alt, Beck and Gottschalck, Nauendorf, Thuringia 1894–

Arnold Print Works, North Adams, Massachusetts, USA 1876–1900

Barrois, E., Paris 1860–79 *dolls and dolls' accessories*

B & D Bawo & Dotter, New York, early twentieth century

Berreux, Mlle J., Paris 1865–78

Blampoix, Maison, Paris 1842–81

Bru, Léon Casimir, Paris 1867–90

Borgfeldt & Co., George, New York 1881–1914

Chad Valley Co. Ltd (Johnson Brothers Ltd), Birmingham, England 1860–

Chase, Mrs Martha Jenks, Pawtucket, Rhode Island, USA 1889–

........Conta & Boehme, Pössneck, Saxony, founded 1790

........Copenhagen, (Royal Copenhagen Porcelain Factory), *dolls' heads and limbs* 1844–84

Crandall, Charles M & Co., Montrose, Pennsylvania 1876

Cremer, William Henry, London, toy seller, England 1860–

Darrow, Franklin Elijah, Bristol, Connecticut, USA 1865 *raw-hide dolls*

........Dean, H. S., London 1900– *rag dolls*

Decamps, Gaston, Paris 1908– *mechanical dolls and automata* (see Roullet-Decamps)

Dehais, Maison, Paris 1836–1914 (later run by his nephew L. Renou) *mechanical toys and automata*

D ....Derolland, Basile, Paris (Asnières-sur-Oise Factory) 1870 *rubber toys*

L. D. Deloac, L., Paris

J. D. Dorst, Julius, Sonneberg 1839– *wooden toys*

........Dressel, Cuno & Otto, Sonneberg, Thuringia (said to have been founded 1700)

Edison, Thomas, Alva, New Jersey, USA 1878 *phonograph doll*

Edward, Charles, London 1850–65 *wax dolls*

Ɛ ....Edwards, John, London *wax dolls* 1856–85

Ellis, Joel Addison, Hartley Springfield, Vermont, USA 1873 *patent wooden doll*

........Falck-Roussel (Adolphe Falck), Paris 1885 *Bébé Mignon*

Fleischmann, Adolf, Sonneberg 1844– *papier mâché dolls*

Fleischmann & Bloedel, Fürth, Bavaria 1873–1890 *Eden Bébé*
1898 *Bébé Triomphe*

F G ....Gaultier Frères (Gaultier et fils ainé founded 1860) St Maurice, Seine, Paris *porcelain doll heads*

Gesland, E., Paris 1860–1916

Giroux, Alphonse 1839–1873 *dolls and mechanical toys*

Goldsmith, Philip, Cincinnati, USA 1875–1894

Gottschalk & Co. (Paris agent for German dolls) 1863– *porcelain heads and dolls' eyes*

Goodyear, Charles *patent rubber dolls* made by Benjamin Lee and the New York Rubber co. 1851

Greiner, Ludwig Philadelphia, USA 1840–83 *papier mâché dolls*

G. D. Grandjean, ainé et cie., Paris late 19th century, *Bébé Bijou*
(Claimed to be inventor of jointed *bébé*: over one million dolls produced in 1888)

Handwerck, Heinrich, Waltershausen, Germany 1891 *Bébé Cosmopolite*
Handwerck, Max, Waltershausen, Germany, 1900 *Bébé Élite*
Hawkins, George, New York, USA 1868 *papier mâché heads*
Hertwig & Co., Katzhütte, Thuringia *china doll makers* (name heads)
Heubach, Gebrüder, Koppelsdorf, Thuringia 1820–
Horsman, Edward Imeson, New York, USA 1865–
Huret, Mlle Calixte, Paris 1851–73
Hyatt, John Wesley and Isaiah Celluloid Novelty Co., Newark,
  New Jersey, USA 1865–80
Ideal Toy Co., New York (*see* Michtom, Benjamin)
I. R. COMB CO. India Rubber Comb Co. Goodyear Patent 1851
Insam & Prinoth, Grodenthal 1820– *wooden dolls*
Ives, E. R., Plymouth, Connecticut, USA 1866 founded *mechanical toys*
Jaquet-Droz, Pierre and Henri Louis (his son), Neuchâtel, Switzerland 1721–91
  androides, automata
Jullien, A., Paris 1875 *Bébé L'Universel*
E. J. Jumeau, Pierre François 1843–78; Emile 1899
K. & R. Kammer & Reinhardt, Waltershausen, Germany late 19th century
Kaulitz, Marion, Munich, Germany 1908–
Kestner, J. D., Waltershausen, Germany early 19th century
Kestner, J. D. junior, Waltershausen, Germany late 19th century
Kling & Co., Ohrdruf, Thuringia 1836–
K. H. Kley & Hahn, Ohrdruf, Germany 1900–14, *Walkure doll*
Kruse, Käthe, Bad Kosen, Germany 1912– *patent fabric dolls*
Lacmann, Jacob 1860–83 *patent doll body* 1874
A. L. & Cie. Lang family of Oberammergau, Bavaria 1775– present-day *crèche dolls*
Limoges Lanternier, A. & Co., Limoges, France *porcelain*
BEBES A. L. Lefebvre, Alexandre, Paris 1863–
Lenci Dolls (Scavini) Turin, Italy 1914– present day
Lindner, Louis & Son, Sonneberg, Germany *Bébé Lindner*
Lowenthal & Co., Hamburg 1836– *papier mâché*
Limbach Porcelain factory, Thuringia, Germany
Maelzel, Johannes, Regensberg 1820 period *mechanical dolls and automata*
Marsh, Charles, London 1878–95 *wax dolls*
Marsh, Mary Ann 1895–1901 (wife of Charles) *wax dolls and dolls'
  hospital*
Marsh, William 1865 (father of Charles?) *wax dolls*
Martin Frank D., Springfield, Vermont, USA 1874– *wooden dolls*
Martin, Elie, inventor of ONDINE *swimming doll* 1876
F. M. Martin, Fernand *small mechanical figures worked by clockwork*
Mason, Henry Hubbard, Springfield, Vermont, USA 1880– *jointed wooden
  dolls*
Meech, H. J., H. G. (Meech Bros.), London 1865–87, (dollmaker to the Royal
  Family) *wax dolls*
Michtom, Benjamin, Ideal Toy Co., New York
Minerva Metal Heads, Buschow & Beck, Rossen, Saxony
Montanari, Madame Augusta, London 1850–65 *wax dolls*
Montanari, Richard *wax dolls and 'rag' dolls* 1855–86
C. P. Pannier, M., Paris 1870–90 *dolls and dolls' clothes*
Peacock, Thomas, London 1862– *used English wax dolls*
Peck, Mrs Lucy, London *wax dolls and models*
Petit, Jacob, Parisian porcelain factory, Fontainebleau *made some doll heads
  of hard paste*
Pierotti, Henry (Enrico), London 1847–71 *wax doll maker*
Pierotti, Charles William, traded under father's name –1892
Pierotti, Charles Ernest (son of C. W.) –1935
D. S. Potiers, G., Paris *dolls and mechanical toys* 1867–
R. D. Rabery-Delphieu (later Alexandre Rabery) 1873 *Bébé de Paris*
Rheinische Gummi- u. Celluloid-Fabrik, Mannheim, Neckarau
Rohmer, Marie Antoinette Léontine, Paris, 1857–80

ℛℙ ....Rookwood Pottery, Cincinnati, Ohio, established 1880

Roullet-Decamps, (R. D. mark on winding keys) founded 1865 by Jean Roullet. *Parisian makers of mechanical dolls* 1893 *L'intrépide Bébé*

Renou, L. M., Paris 1890s *Punch dolls and marottes, mechanical and musical* (Successor to the firm Dehais)

Steiff, Margarete, Würtemburg, Germany 1905– *soft toys and dolls*

.........Schilling, Ferdinand, Sonneberg, Germany 1880–

.....................Schmidt, Bruno, Waltershausen, Germany 1900

.........Schmitt & Sons, Paris 1863– *Bébé Schmitt*

Schoenhut, Albert, Philadelphia, Pennsylvania, USA 1872–

S.F.B.J. *Société Française de la Fabrication des Bébés Jouets*

S.G.D.G. *Sans Guarantie du Gouvernement:* French pending patent

S. H.   Simon & Halbig, Ohrdruf, Thuringia 1870–

Simonne, Paris 1863–78 *dolls and bébés*

.....................Steiner, Jules Nicholas, Paris 1855– (claimed to have invented *bébé* type doll) 1892 *Le Parisien*

Theroude, Alexandre Nicholas, Paris 1842– *mechanical toys*

.........Vichy, G., Paris 1862–90 *mechanical dolls*

Villard & Weill, Paris 1834–1906

Voit, Andreas, Hildbürghausen, Thuringia 1835– *papier mâché*

Wiegand, Carl, New York 1876–

BIBLIOGRAPHY

d'ALLEMAGNE, Henry René *Histoire des Jouets* Paris, 1903

BOHN, Max von *Puppen* Berlin, 1929

BULLARD, Helen *The American Doll Artist* Boston, 1965

BATEMAN, Thelma *Delightful Dolls* Washington, 1966

CALMETTES, Pierre *Les Joujoux* Paris, 1924

CHAPUIS, A. and DROZ, E. *Les Automates* Neuchâtel, 1949

CHAPUIS, A. and GELIS, E. *Le Monde des Automates* Paris, 1928

COLEMAN, Elizabeth A. *Dolls: Makers and Marks* Washington DC, 1963

Collector's Manual Doll Collectors of America Inc., Boston, 1956, 1964

CREMER, W. H. *Toys for Little Folks* London, 1875

DODERLEIN, Wilhelm *Alte Krippen* Munich, 1965

EARLY, A. K. *English Dolls, Effigies and Puppets* London, 1955

ELDERKIN, Kate 'Jointed dolls in Antiquity' *American Journal of Archaeology* XXXI, 1930

FAURHOLT, Estrid and JACOBS, Flora Gill, *Dolls and Doll Houses* Tokyo, 1967

GERKEN, Jo Elizabeth *Wonderful Dolls of Wax* Doll Research Associates, Lincoln, Nebraska, 1964

GROBER, Karl *Children's Toys* London, 1929

HERCIK, Emmanuel *Folk toys of Czechoslovakia* Prague, 1952

HART, Luella *Directory of British Dolls; Directory of French Dolls* 1964 *Directory of German Dolls*, Oakland, California, 1965

JOHL, Janet Pagter *The Fascinating Story of Dolls* New York, 1943 *More about Dolls* New York, 1946 *Still More about Dolls* New York, 1950

JOHNOVA, Helena *Lidove Hracky* Prague, 1965

KOENIG, Marie *Musée des Poupées* Paris, 1909

LOVETT, Dr E. *The Child's Doll: Origin, Legend, Folklore* 1915

McCLINTOCK, Inez and Marshall *Toys in America* Washington, 1961

MAINGOT, Eliane *Les Automates* Paris, 1959

MATHES, E. and R. C. 'Decline and Fall of the Wooden Doll' in *Doll Collectors Manual*, 1964

RUGGLES, Rowena Godding *The One Rose* Oakland, 1964

SAKAMOTO, Kazaya (trans. Charles Pomeroy) *Japanese Folk Toys* Tokyo, 1965

SCHOONMAKER, Patricia *Research on Kammer and Reinhardt Dolls* Hollywood, California, 1965

SINGLETON, Esther *Dolls* New York, 1927

YAMADA, Tokubei *Japanese Dolls* Japan Travel Bureau, 1955

INDEX